# P, NP, and NP-Completeness
*The Basics of Computational Complexity*

The focus of this book is the P versus NP Question and the theory of NP-completeness. It also provides adequate preliminaries regarding computational problems and computational models.

The P versus NP Question asks whether finding solutions is harder than checking the correctness of solutions. An alternative formulation asks whether discovering proofs is harder than verifying their correctness. It is widely believed that the answer to these equivalent formulations is positive, and this is captured by saying that P is different from NP.

Although the P versus NP Question remains unresolved, the theory of NP-completeness offers evidence for the intractability of specific problems in NP by showing that they are universal for the entire class. Amazingly enough, NP-complete problems exist, and hundreds of natural computational problems arising in many different areas of mathematics and science are NP-complete.

ODED GOLDREICH is a Professor of Computer Science at the Weizmann Institute of Science and an Incumbent of the Meyer W. Weisgal Professorial Chair. He is an editor for the *SIAM Journal on Computing*, the *Journal of Cryptology*, and *Computational Complexity* and previously authored the books *Modern Cryptography, Probabilistic Proofs and Pseudorandomness*, the two-volume work *Foundations of Cryptography*, and *Computational Complexity: A Conceptual Perspective*.

# P, NP, and NP-Completeness
## The Basics of Computational Complexity

ODED GOLDREICH

*Weizmann Institute of Science*

CAMBRIDGE
UNIVERSITY PRESS

# CAMBRIDGE
## UNIVERSITY PRESS

32 Avenue of the Americas, New York NY 10013-2473, USA

Cambridge University Press is part of the University of Cambridge.

It furthers the University's mission by disseminating knowledge in the pursuit of education, learning and research at the highest international levels of excellence.

www.cambridge.org
Information on this title: www.cambridge.org/9780521192484

First published 2010

*A catalogue record for this publication is available from the British Library*

*Library of Congress Cataloguing in Publication data*

Goldreich, Oded.
P, NP, and NP-completeness : the basics of computational complexity / Oded Goldreich.
p.   cm.
Includes bibliographical references and index.
ISBN 978-0-521-19248-4 (hardback) – ISBN 978-0-521-12254-2 (pbk.)
1. Computational complexity.   2. Computer algorithms.   3. Approximation theory.
4. Polynomials.   I. Title.
QA267.7.G652   2010
005.1–dc22        2010023587

ISBN  978-0-521-19248-4  Hardback
ISBN  978-0-521-12254-2  Paperback

to Dana

# Contents

*List of Figures*                                                    *page* xi
*Preface*                                                                  xiii
*Overview*                                                                 xvii
*To the Teacher*                                                            xxi
*Notations and Conventions*                                                 xxv
*Main Definitions and Results*                                            xxvii

**1     Computational Tasks and Models**                                      1
       Teaching Notes                                                         2
1.1    Representation                                                         3
1.2    Computational Tasks                                                    5
       1.2.1 Search Problems                                                  5
       1.2.2 Decision Problems                                                6
       1.2.3 Promise Problems (an Advanced Comment)                           8
1.3    Uniform Models (Algorithms)                                           8
       1.3.1 Overview and General Principles                                 9
       1.3.2 A Concrete Model: Turing Machines                              11
             1.3.2.1 The Actual Model                                       12
             1.3.2.2 The Church-Turing Thesis                               16
       1.3.3 Uncomputable Functions                                         18
             1.3.3.1 On the Existence of Uncomputable Functions            18
             1.3.3.2 The Halting Problem                                    19
             1.3.3.3 A Few More Undecidability Results                      21
       1.3.4 Universal Algorithms                                           22
             1.3.4.1 The Existence of Universal Algorithms                  23
             1.3.4.2 A Detour: Kolmogorov Complexity                        24
       1.3.5 Time (and Space) Complexity                                    26

|       | 1.3.6  Oracle Machines and Turing-Reductions | 29 |
|       | 1.3.7  Restricted Models | 31 |
| 1.4   | Non-Uniform Models (Circuits and Advice) | 31 |
|       | 1.4.1  Boolean Circuits | 32 |
|       |    1.4.1.1  The Basic Model | 32 |
|       |    1.4.1.2  Circuit Complexity | 35 |
|       | 1.4.2  Machines That Take Advice | 36 |
|       | 1.4.3  Restricted Models | 37 |
|       |    1.4.3.1  Boolean Formulae | 38 |
|       |    1.4.3.2  Other Restricted Classes of Circuits | 39 |
| 1.5   | Complexity Classes | 40 |
|       | Exercises | 41 |

**2  The P versus NP Question**  48

|       | Teaching Notes | 49 |
| 2.1   | Efficient Computation | 50 |
| 2.2   | The Search Version: Finding versus Checking | 53 |
|       | 2.2.1  The Class P as a Natural Class of Search Problems | 54 |
|       | 2.2.2  The Class NP as Another Natural Class of Search Problems | 56 |
|       | 2.2.3  The P versus NP Question in Terms of Search Problems | 57 |
| 2.3   | The Decision Version: Proving versus Verifying | 58 |
|       | 2.3.1  The Class P as a Natural Class of Decision Problems | 59 |
|       | 2.3.2  The Class NP and NP-Proof Systems | 59 |
|       | 2.3.3  The P versus NP Question in Terms of Decision Problems | 62 |
| 2.4   | Equivalence of the Two Formulations | 63 |
| 2.5   | Technical Comments Regarding NP | 65 |
| 2.6   | The Traditional Definition of NP | 66 |
| 2.7   | In Support of P Being Different from NP | 69 |
| 2.8   | Philosophical Meditations | 70 |
|       | Exercises | 71 |

**3  Polynomial-time Reductions**  74

|       | Teaching Notes | 75 |
| 3.1   | The General Notion of a Reduction | 75 |
|       | 3.1.1  The Actual Formulation | 76 |
|       | 3.1.2  Special Cases | 77 |
|       | 3.1.3  Terminology and a Brief Discussion | 79 |
| 3.2   | Reducing Optimization Problems to Search Problems | 81 |

3.3   Self-Reducibility of Search Problems                                    83
      3.3.1 Examples                                                          85
      3.3.2 Self-Reducibility of NP-Complete Problems                         87
3.4   Digest and General Perspective                                         88
      Exercises                                                              89

**4**   **NP-Completeness**                                                 96
      Teaching Notes                                                         97
4.1   Definitions                                                            98
4.2   The Existence of NP-Complete Problems                                  99
      Bounded Halting and Non-Halting                                       102
4.3   Some Natural NP-Complete Problems                                     103
      4.3.1 Circuit and Formula Satisfiability: CSAT and SAT                104
            4.3.1.1 The NP-Completeness of CSAT                             105
            4.3.1.2 The NP-Completeness of SAT                              109
      4.3.2 Combinatorics and Graph Theory                                  113
      4.3.3 Additional Properties of the Standard Reductions                120
      4.3.4 On the Negative Application of NP-Completeness                   121
      4.3.5 Positive Applications of NP-Completeness                        122
4.4   NP Sets That Are Neither in P nor NP-Complete                         126
4.5   Reflections on Complete Problems                                      130
      Exercises                                                             133

**5**   **Three Relatively Advanced Topics**                                142
      Teaching Notes                                                        142
5.1   Promise Problems                                                      142
      5.1.1 Definitions                                                     143
            5.1.1.1 Search Problems with a Promise                         143
            5.1.1.2 Decision Problems with a Promise                       144
            5.1.1.3 Reducibility Among Promise Problems                    145
      5.1.2 Applications and Limitations                                    146
            5.1.2.1 Formulating Natural Computational Problems             146
            5.1.2.2 Restricting a Computational Problem                    147
            5.1.2.3 Non-generic Applications                               147
            5.1.2.4 Limitations                                            148
      5.1.3 The Standard Convention of Avoiding Promise Problems           149
5.2   Optimal Search Algorithms for NP                                      151
5.3   The Class coNP and Its Intersection with NP                          154
      Exercises                                                            158

**Historical Notes**                                               165

**Epilogue: A Brief Overview of Complexity Theory**                169

**Appendix: Some Computational Problems**                          177
A.1   Graphs                                                       177
A.2   Boolean Formulae                                             179

*Bibliography*                                                     181
*Index*                                                            183

# List of Figures

0.1 Outline of the suggested course. *page* xxiv

1.1 A single step by a Turing machine. 12

1.2 Multiple steps of the machine depicted in Figure 1.1. 15

1.3 A circuit computing $f(x_1, x_2, x_3, x_4) = (x_1 \oplus x_2, x_1 \wedge \neg x_2 \wedge x_4)$. 34

1.4 Recursive construction of parity circuits and formulae. 38

1.5 A 3DNF formula computing $x_1 \oplus x_2 \oplus x_3$. 39

2.1 Solving $S$ by using a solver for $R$. 64

2.2 Solving $R$ by using a solver for $S'_R$. 65

3.1 The Cook-reduction that arises from a Karp-reduction. 78

3.2 The Cook-reduction that arises from a Levin-reduction. 80

3.3 The three proofs of Theorem 3.8. 95

4.1 Overview of the emulation of a computation by a circuit. 106

4.2 Consecutive computation steps of a Turing machine. 107

4.3 The idea underlying the reduction of CSAT to SAT. 111

4.4 The reduction to G3C – the clause gadget and its sub-gadget. 119

4.5 The reduction to G3C – connecting the gadgets. 120

4.6 The (non-generic) reductions presented in Section 4.3. 121

5.1 A schematic depiction of a promise problem. 145

5.2 The world view under $\mathcal{P} \neq \text{co}\mathcal{N}P \cap \mathcal{N}P \neq \mathcal{N}P$. 158

# Preface

The quest for efficiency is ancient and universal, as time and other resources are always in shortage. Thus, the question of which tasks can be performed efficiently is central to the human experience.

A key step toward the systematic study of the aforementioned question is a rigorous definition of the notion of a task and of procedures for solving tasks. These definitions were provided by computability theory, which emerged in the 1930s. This theory focuses on computational tasks, considers automated procedures (i.e., computing devices and algorithms) that may solve such tasks, and studies the class of solvable tasks.

In focusing attention on computational tasks and algorithms, computability theory has set the stage for the study of the computational resources (like time) that are required by such algorithms. When this study focuses on the resources that are necessary for *any* algorithm that solves a particular task (or a task of a particular type), it is viewed as belonging to the theory of Computational Complexity (also known as Complexity Theory). In contrast, when the focus is on the design and analysis of specific algorithms (rather than on the intrinsic complexity of the task), the study is viewed as belonging to a related area that may be called Algorithmic Design and Analysis. Furthermore, Algorithmic Design and Analysis tends to be sub-divided according to the domain of mathematics, science, and engineering in which the computational tasks arise. In contrast, Complexity Theory typically maintains a unity of the study of computational tasks that are solvable within certain resources (regardless of the origins of these tasks).

Complexity Theory is a central field of the theoretical foundations of computer science (CS). It is concerned with the study of the *intrinsic complexity of computational tasks*. That is, a typical Complexity theoretic study refers to the computational resources required to solve a computational task (or a class of such tasks), rather than referring to a specific algorithm or an algorithmic schema. Actually, research in Complexity Theory tends to *start with and focus on the computational resources themselves*, and addresses the effect of limiting these resources on the class of tasks that can be solved. Thus, Computational Complexity is the general study of what can be achieved within limited time (and/or other limitations on natural computational resources).

The most famous question of Complexity Theory is the P-vs-NP Question. This question can be phrased as asking whether *finding* solutions to certain problems is harder than *checking* the correctness of solutions to these problems. Indeed, this phrasing refers to so-called search problems (i.e., problems of searching for solutions). An alternative phrasing, which refers to so-called decision problems, asks whether or not deciding the validity of assertions can be facilitated by the presentation of adequate proofs. Equivalently, the question is whether discovering proofs (of the validity of assertions) is harder than verifying their correctness; that is, is proving harder than verifying?

The fundamental nature of the P-vs-NP Question is evident in each of the foregoing formulations, which are in fact equivalent. It is widely believed that the answer to these equivalent formulations is that finding (resp., proving) is harder than checking (resp., verifying); that is, *it is believed that P is different from NP*, where P corresponds to the class of efficiently solvable problems and NP corresponds to the seemingly wider class of problems allowing for efficient verification of potential solutions.

Indeed, the P-vs-NP Question has been unresolved since the early 1970s, and it is the author's guess that the question will remain unresolved for centuries, waiting for the development of a deeper understanding of the nature of efficient computation. However, life will continue in the meantime, and it will bring along a variety of NP-problems, where some of these problems will be placed in P (by presenting efficient algorithms solving them) and others will resist such attempts and will be conjectured to be too computationally hard to belong to P. Actually, the latter description is not a wild guess; this has been the state of affairs for several decades now.

At present, when faced with a seemingly hard problem in NP, we can only hope to prove that it is not in P by assuming that NP is different from P. Thus, we seek ways of proving that if the problem at hand is in P, then NP equals P, which means that all problems in NP are in P. This is where the theory of NP-completeness comes into the picture. Intuitively, a problem in NP is called NP-complete if any efficient algorithm for it can be converted into an efficient algorithm for any other problem in NP. It follows that if some NP-complete problem is in P, then all problems in NP are in P. Hence, if NP is different from P, then no NP-complete problem can be in P. Consequently, the P-vs-NP

Question is captured by the question of whether or not an individual (NP-complete) problem can be solved efficiently. Amazingly enough, NP-complete problems exist, and furthermore, hundreds of natural computational problems arising in many different areas of mathematics and science are NP-complete.

The aforementioned conversion of an efficient algorithm for one problem into efficient algorithms for other problems is actually performed by a translation of the latter problems' instances. Such a translation is called a reduction, and the theory of NP-completeness is based on the notion of efficient reductions. In general, one computational problem is (efficiently) reducible to another problem if it is possible to (efficiently) solve the former when provided access to an (efficient) algorithm for solving the latter. A problem (in NP) is NP-complete if any problem in NP is efficiently reducible to it, which means that *each individual NP-complete problem "encodes" all problems in NP*. The fact that NP-complete problems exist, let alone in such an abundance and variety, is indeed amazing.

Since its discovery, NP-completeness has been used as the main tool by which the intrinsic complexity of certain problems is demonstrated. A vast number of NP-completeness results have been discovered since the early 1970s. These discoveries have been guiding theoretical research as well as technological development by indicating when one needs to relax computational problems in order to obtain efficient procedures. This impact is neither confined to computer science nor to the need to solve some computational problems. It typically occurs when researchers or engineers seek a simple characterization of objects that satisfy some property, whereas it turns out that deciding whether a given object has this property is an NP-complete problem. Needless to say, in such a case, no *simple* characterization is likely to exist, and so one better abandon the search for it. Indeed, diverse scientific disciplines, which were unsuccessfully struggling with some of their internal questions, came to realize that these questions are inherently difficult since they are closely related to computational problems that are NP-complete.

**The Current Book.** The main focus of the current book is on the P-vs-NP Question and on the theory of NP-completeness. Indeed, a large portion of the book is devoted to presenting and studying the various formulations of the P-vs-NP Question. This portion may be viewed as a mathematical articulation of the intuitive gap between searching for solutions and checking their validity (or between proving theorems and verifying the correctness of proofs). Another large portion of the book is devoted to the presentation of the theory of NP-completeness, while providing a treatment of the general notion of efficient reductions between computational problems. This portion may be viewed as a mathematical articulation of the daily notion of a "reduction" (i.e., solving one problem by using a known procedure for another problem), augmented with the fundamental and surprising feature of "universality" (i.e., the existence of complete problems to which all problems can be reduced).

The book, which includes adequate preliminaries regarding computational problems and computational models, aims to provide a wide perspective on the issues in its core. For example, the treatment of efficient reductions goes beyond the minimum that suffices for a presentation of the theory of NP-completeness, and this feature supports the study of the relative complexity of search and decision problems. In general, the book is believed to present the very basics of Complexity Theory, while bearing in mind that most readers do not intend to specialize in Complexity Theory (and yet hoping that some will be motivated to do so).

**Relation to a Different Book by the Author.** The current book is a significant revision of Chapter 2 (and Section 1.2) of the author's book *Computational Complexity: A Conceptual Perspective* [13]. The revision was aimed at making the book more friendly to the novice. In particular, numerous technical expositions were further detailed and many exercises were added.

**Web Site for Notices Regarding This Book.** The author intends to maintain a Web site listing corrections of various types. The location of the site is

        http://www.wisdom.weizmann.ac.il/~oded/bc-book.html

**Acknowledgments.** The author is grateful to Asilata Bapat and Michael Forbes for their careful reading of a draft of this book and for the numerous corrections and suggestions that they provided.

# Overview

This book starts by providing the relevant background on *computability theory*, which is the setting in which Complexity theoretic questions are being studied. Most importantly, this preliminary chapter (i.e., Chapter 1) provides a treatment of central notions, such as search and decision problems, algorithms that solve such problems, and their complexity. Special attention is given to the notion of a universal algorithm.

The main part of this book (i.e., Chapters 2–5) focuses on the P-vs-NP Question and on the theory of NP-completeness. Additional topics covered in this part include the general notion of an efficient reduction (with a special emphasis on reductions of search problems to corresponding decision problems), the existence of problems in NP that are neither NP-complete nor in P, the class coNP, optimal search algorithms, and promise problems. A brief overview of this main part follows.

**The P-vs-NP Question.** Loosely speaking, the P-vs-NP Question refers to search problems for which the correctness of solutions can be efficiently checked (i.e., there is an efficient algorithm that given a solution to a given instance determines whether or not the solution is correct). Such search problems correspond to the class NP, and the P-vs-NP Question corresponds to whether or not all these search problems can be solved efficiently (i.e., is there an efficient algorithm that given an instance finds a correct solution). Thus, the P-vs-NP Question can be phrased as asking *whether finding solutions is harder than checking the correctness of solutions*.

An alternative formulation, in terms of decision problems, refers to assertions that have efficiently verifiable proofs (of relatively short length). Such sets of assertions also correspond to the class NP, and the P-vs-NP Question corresponds to whether or not proofs for such assertions can be found efficiently (i.e., is there an efficient algorithm that given an assertion determines its validity and/or finds a proof for its validity?). Thus, the P-vs-NP Question can also be phrased as asking *whether discovering proofs is harder than veri-fying their correctness*; that is, is proving harder than verifying (or are proofs valuable at all).

In these equivalent formulations of the P-vs-NP Question, P corresponds to the class of efficiently solvable problems, whereas NP corresponds to a natural class of problems for which it is reasonable to seek efficient solvability (i.e., NP corresponds to the seemingly wider class of problems allowing for efficient verification of potential solutions). We also note that in both cases, equality between P and NP contradicts our intuitions regarding the notions that underlie the formulation of NP (i.e., the notions of solving search problems and proving theorems).

Indeed, it is widely believed that the answer to these two equivalent for-mulations of the P-vs-NP Question is that *P is different from NP*; that is, finding (resp., discovering) is harder than checking (resp., verifying). The fact that this natural conjecture is unsettled seems to be one of the big sources of frustration of Complexity Theory. The author's opinion, however, is that this feeling of frustration is unjustified and is rooted in unrealistic expectations (i.e., naive underestimations of the difficulty of relating complexity classes of such a nature). In any case, at present, when faced with a seemingly hard problem in NP, we cannot expect to prove that the problem is not in P unconditionally. The best we can expect is a conditional proof that the said problem is not in P, based on the assumption that NP is different from P. The contrapositive is proving that if the said problem is in P, then so is any problem in NP (i.e., NP equals P). The theory of NP-completeness captures this idea.

**NP-Completeness.** The theory of NP-completeness is based on the notion of an efficient reduction, which is a relation between computational problems. Loosely speaking, one computational problem is efficiently reducible to another problem if it is possible to efficiently solve the former when provided with an (efficient) algorithm for solving the latter. Thus, the first problem is not harder to solve than the second one. A problem (in NP) is NP-complete if any problem in NP is efficiently reducible to it, which means that the first problem "encodes" all problems in NP (and so, in some sense, is the hardest among them). Indeed, the fate of the entire class NP (with respect to inclusion in P) rests with each individual NP-complete problem. In particular, showing that a problem is NP-complete implies that this problem is not in P unless NP equals P.

The fact that NP-complete problems can be defined does not mean that they exist. Indeed, the ability of an individual problem to encode all problems in a class as diverse as NP is unfamiliar in daily life, and a layperson is likely to guess that such a phenomenon is self-contradictory (especially when being told that the complete problem has to be in the same class). Nevertheless, NP-complete problems exist, and furthermore, hundreds of natural computational problems arising in many different areas of mathematics and science are NP-complete.

The list of known NP-complete problems includes finding a satisfiable assignment to a given Boolean formula (or deciding whether such an assignment exists), finding a 3-coloring of the vertices of a given graph (or deciding whether such a coloring exists), and so on. The core of establishing the NP-completeness of these problems is showing that each of them can encode any other problem in NP. Thus, these demonstrations provide a method of encoding instances of any NP problem as instances of the target NP-complete problem.

**The Actual Organization.** The foregoing paragraphs refer to material that is covered in Chapters 2–4. Specifically, Chapter 2 is devoted to the P-vs-NP Question per se, Chapter 3 is devoted to the notion of an efficient reduction, and Chapter 4 is devoted to the theory of NP-completeness. We mention that NP-complete problems *are not the only seemingly hard problems in NP*; that is, if P is different from NP, then NP contains problems that are neither NP-complete nor in P (see Section 4.4).

Additional related topics are discussed in Chapter 5. In particular, in Section 5.2, it is shown that the P-vs-NP Question is not about inventing sophisticated algorithms or ruling out their existence, but rather boils down to the analysis of a single known algorithm; that is, we will present an optimal search algorithm for any problem in NP, while having no clue about its time-complexity.

Each of the main chapters (i.e., Chapters 1–4) starts with a short overview, which sets the stage for the entire chapter. These overviews provide the basic motivation for the notions defined, as well as a high-level summary of the main results, and hence should not be skipped. The chapter's overview is followed by teaching notes, which assume familiarity with the material and thus are better skipped by the novice. Each chapter ends with exercises, which are designed to help verify the basic understanding of the main text (and not to test or inspire creativity). In a few cases, exercises (augmented by adequate guidelines) are used for presenting related advanced material.

The book also includes a short historical account (see Historical Notes), a brief overview of Complexity Theory at large (see Epilogue), and a laconic review of some popular computational problems (see Appendix).

# To the Teacher

According to a common opinion, the most important aspect of a scientific work is the technical result that it achieves, whereas explanations and motivations are merely redundancy introduced for the sake of "error correction" and/or comfort. It is further believed that, as with a work of art, the interpretation of the work should be left to the reader.

The author strongly disagrees with the aforementioned opinions, and argues that there is a fundamental difference between art and science, and that this difference refers exactly to the meaning of a piece of work. Science is concerned with meaning (and not with form), and in its quest for truth and/or understanding, science follows philosophy (and not art). The author holds the opinion that the most important aspects of a scientific work are the intuitive question that it addresses, the reason that it addresses this question, the way it phrases the question, the approach that underlies its answer, and the ideas that are embedded in the answer. Following this view, it is important to communicate these aspects of the work.

The foregoing issues are even more acute when it comes to Complexity Theory, firstly because conceptual considerations seem to play an even more central role in Complexity Theory than in other scientific fields. Secondly (and even more importantly), Complexity Theory is extremely rich in conceptual content. Thus, communicating this content is of primary importance, and failing to do so misses the most important aspects of Complexity Theory.

Unfortunately, the conceptual content of Complexity Theory is rarely communicated (explicitly) in books and/or surveys of the area. The annoying (and quite amazing) consequences are students who have only a vague understanding of the *meaning* and general relevance of the fundamental notions and results that they were taught. The author's view is that these consequences are easy to avoid by taking the time to explicitly discuss the *meaning* of definitions and results. A closely related issue is using the "right" definitions (i.e., those that

reflect better the fundamental nature of the notion being defined) and emphasizing the (conceptually) "right" results. The current book is written accordingly;
two concrete and central examples follow.

The first example refers to the presentation of the P-vs-NP Question, where
we avoid using (polynomial-time) non-deterministic machines. We believe that
these fictitious "machines" have a negative effect from both a conceptual and a
technical point of view. The conceptual damage caused by defining NP in terms
of (polynomial-time) non-deterministic machines is that it is unclear why one
should care about what such machines can do. Needless to say, the reason to
care is clear when noting that these fictitious "machines" offer a (convenient
but rather slothful) way of phrasing fundamental issues. The technical damage
caused by using non-deterministic machines is that they tend to confuse the
students.

In contrast to using a fictitious model as a pivot, we define NP in terms of
proof systems such that the fundamental nature of this class and the P-vs-NP
Question are apparent. We also push to the front a formulation of the P-vs-NP
Question in terms of search problems. We believe that this formulation may
appeal to non-experts even more than the formulation of the P-vs-NP Question
in terms of decision problems. The aforementioned formulation refers to classes
of search problems that are analogous to the decision problem classes P and NP.
Specifically, we consider the classes $\mathcal{PF}$ and $\mathcal{PC}$ (see Definitions 2.2 and 2.3),
where $\mathcal{PF}$ consists of search problems that are efficiently solvable and $\mathcal{PC}$
consists of search problems having efficiently checkable solutions.[1]

To summarize, we suggest presenting the P-vs-NP Question both in terms
of search problems and in terms of decision problems. Furthermore, when presenting the decision-problem version, we suggest introducing NP by explicitly
referring to the terminology of proof systems (rather than using the more standard formulation, which is based on non-deterministic machines). We mention
that the formulation of NP as proof systems is also a better starting point for the
study of more advanced issues (e.g., counting classes, let alone probabilistic
proof systems).

Turning to the second example, which refers to the theory of NP-
completeness, we highlight a central recommendation regarding the presentation of this theory. We believe that from a conceptual point of view, the
mere existence of NP-complete problems is an amazing fact. We thus suggest
emphasizing and discussing this fact per se. In particular, we recommend first
proving the mere existence of NP-complete problems, and only later establishing the fact that certain natural problems such as SAT are NP-complete. Also,
when establishing the NP-completeness of SAT, we recommend decoupling

---

[1] Indeed, these classes are often denoted $\mathcal{FP}$ and $\mathcal{FNP}$, respectively.

the emulation of Turing machines by circuits (used for establishing the NP-completeness of CSAT) from the emulation of circuits by formulae (used in the reduction of CSAT to SAT).

**Organization.** In Chapter 1, we present the basic framework of Computational Complexity, which serves as a stage for the rest of the book. In particular, we formalize the notions of search and decision problems (see Section 1.2), algorithms solving them (see Section 1.3), and their time complexity (see Section 1.3.5). In Chapter 2, we present the two formulations of the P-vs-NP Question. The general notion of a reduction is presented in Chapter 3, where we highlight its applicability outside the domain of NP-completeness. In particular, in Section 3.3 we treat reductions of search problems to corresponding decision problems. Chapter 4 is devoted to the theory of NP-completeness, whereas Chapter 5 treats three relatively advanced topics (i.e., the framework of promise problems, the existence of optimal search algorithms for NP, and the class coNP). The book ends with an Epilogue, which provides a brief overview of Complexity Theory, and an Appendix that reviews some popular computational problems (which are used as examples in the main text).

**The Chapters' Overviews.** Each of the main chapters (i.e., Chapters 1–4) starts with a short overview, which provides the basic motivation for the notions defined in that chapter as well as a high-level summary of the chapter's main results. We suggest using these overviews as a basis for motivational discussions preceding the actual technical presentation.

**Additional Teaching Notes.** Each chapter overview is followed by additional teaching notes. These notes articulate various choices made in the presentation of the material in the corresponding chapter.

**Basing a Course on the Current Book.** The book can serve as a basis for an undergraduate course, which may be called *Basics of Computational Complexity*. The core material for this course is provided by Chapters 1–4. Specifically, Sections 1.1–1.3 provide the required elements of computability theory, and Chapters 2–4 provide the basic elements of Complexity Theory. In addition, §1.4.1.1 and §1.4.3.1 (or, alternatively, Appendix A.2) provide preliminaries regarding Boolean circuits and formulae that are required in Section 4.3 (which refers to CSAT and SAT). For a schematic outline of the course, see Figure 0.1.

**On the Choice of Additional (Basic and Advanced) Topics.** As depicted in Figure 0.1, depending on time constraints, we suggest augmenting the core material with a selection of additional basic and advanced topics. As for

| TOPIC | SECTIONS |
|---|---|
| Elements of computability theory | 1.1–1.3 |
| The P-vs-NP Question | 2.1–2.4, 2.7 |
| Optional: definitional variations | 2.5, 2.6 |
| Polynomial-time reductions | 3.1–3.3 |
| The existence of NP-complete problems | 4.1–4.2 |
| Natural NP-complete problems (e.g., CSAT, SAT, VC) | 4.3 |
| Preliminaries on Boolean circuits and formulae | 1.4.1, 1.4.3, A.2 |
| Add'l basic topics: NPI, promise problems, optimal search | 4.4, 5.1, 5.2 |
| Advanced topics, if time permits | from [13, 1] |

Figure 0.1. Outline of the suggested course.

the basic topics, we recommend at least mentioning the class NPI, promise problems, and the optimal search algorithms for NP. Regarding the choice of advanced topics, we recommend an introduction to probabilistic proof systems. In our opinion, this choice is most appropriate because it provides natural extensions of the notion of an NP-proof system and offers very appealing positive applications of NP-completeness. Section 4.3.5 provides a brief overview of probabilistic proof systems, while [13, Chap. 9] provides an extensive overview (which transcends the needs of a basic complexity course). Alternative advanced topics can be found in [13, 1].

**A Revision of the CS Curriculum.** The best integration of the aforementioned course in undergraduate CS education calls for a revision of the standard CS curriculum. Indeed, we believe that there is no real need for a semester-long course in *Computability* (i.e., a course that focuses on what can be computed rather than on what can be computed efficiently). Instead, CS undergraduates should take a course in Computational Complexity, which should contain the computability aspects that serve as a basis for the study of efficient computation (i.e., the rest of this course). Specifically, the computability aspects should occupy at most one-third of the course, and the focus should be on basic complexity issues (captured by P, NP, and NP-completeness), which may be augmented by a selection of some more advanced material. Indeed, such a course can be based on the current book (possibly augmented by a selection of some additional topics from, say, [13, 1]).

# Notations and Conventions

Although we do try to avoid using various notations and conventions that may not be familiar to the reader, some exceptions exists – especially in advanced discussions. In order to be on the safe side, we list here some standard notations and conventions that are (lightly) used in the book.

**Standard Asymptotic Notation.** When referring to integral functions, we use the standard asymptotic notation; that is, for $f, g : \mathbb{N} \to \mathbb{N}$, we write $f = O(g)$ if there exists a constant $c > 0$ such that $f(n) \leq c \cdot g(n)$ holds for all sufficiently large $n \in \mathbb{N}$. We usually denote by "poly" an unspecified polynomial, and write $f(n) = \mathrm{poly}(n)$ instead of "there exists a polynomial $p$ such that $f(n) \leq p(n)$ for all $n \in \mathbb{N}$."

**Standard Combinatorial and Graph Theory Terms and Notation.** For a natural number $n \in \mathbb{N}$, we denote $[n] \stackrel{\text{def}}{=} \{1, \ldots, n\}$. Many of the computational problems that we mention refer to finite (undirected) graphs. Such a graph, denoted $G = (V, E)$, consists of a set of vertices, denoted $V$, and a set of edges, denoted $E$, which are unordered pairs of vertices. By default, graphs are undirected, whereas directed graphs consist of vertices and directed edges, where a directed edge is an order pair of vertices. For further background on graphs and computational problems regarding graphs, the reader is referred to Appendix A.1.

**Typographic Conventions.** We denote formally defined complexity classes by calligraphic letters (e.g., $\mathcal{NP}$), but we do so only after defining these classes. Furthermore, when we wish to maintain some ambiguity regarding the specific formulation of a class of problems, we use Roman font (e.g., NP may denote either a class of search problems or a class of decision problems). Likewise, we denote formally defined computational problems by typewriter font (e.g., SAT). In contrast, generic problems and algorithms will be denoted by italic font.

**Our Use of Footnotes.** In trying to accommodate a diverse spectrum of readers, we use footnotes for presentation of additional details that most readers may wish to skip but some readers may find useful. The most common usage of footnotes is for providing additional technical details that may seem obvious to most readers but be missed by some others. Occasionally, footnotes are also used for advanced comments.

# Main Definitions and Results

Following is a list of the main definitions and results presented in the book. The list only provides a laconic description of each of the items, while a full description can be found in the actual text (under the provided reference). The list is ordered approximately according to the order of appearance of the corresponding topics in the main text.

**Search and Decision Problems.** The former refer to finding solutions to given instances, whereas the latter refer to determining whether the given instance has a predetermined property. See Definitions 1.1 and 1.2, respectively.

**Turing Machines.** The model of Turing machines offers a relatively simple formulation of the notion of an algorithm. See Section 1.3.2.

**Theorem 1.4.** *The set of computable functions is countable, whereas the set of all functions (from strings to strings) is not countable.*

**Theorem 1.5.** *The Halting Problem is undecidable.*

**Universal Algorithms.** A universal machine computes the partial function $u$ that is defined on pairs $(\langle M \rangle, x)$ such that $M$ halts on input $x$, in which case it holds that $u(\langle M \rangle, x) = M(x)$. See Section 1.3.4.

**Efficient and Inefficient.** Efficiency is associated with polynomial-time computations, whereas computations requiring more time are considered inefficient or intractable (or infeasible). See Section 2.1.

**The Class $\mathcal{PF}$ (Polynomial-time Find).** The class of efficiently solvable search problems. See Definition 2.2.

**The Class $\mathcal{PC}$ (Polynomial-time Check).** The class of search problems having efficiently checkable solutions. See Definition 2.3.

**The Notations $S_R$ and $R(x)$ Associated with a Search Problem $R$.** For any search problem, $R$, we denote the set of solutions to the instance $x$ by $R(x)$ (i.e., $R(x) = \{y : (x, y) \in R\}$), and denote the set of instances having solutions by $S_R$ (i.e., $S_R = \{x : R(x) \neq \emptyset\}$).

**The Class $\mathcal{P}$.** The class of efficiently solvable decision problems. See Definition 2.4.

**The Class $\mathcal{NP}$.** The class of decision problems having efficiently verifiable proof systems. See Definition 2.5.

**Theorem 2.6.** $\mathcal{PC} \subseteq \mathcal{PF}$ *if and only if* $\mathcal{P} = \mathcal{NP}$.

**The P-vs-NP Question.** It is widely believed that P is different from NP. This belief is supported by both philosophical and empirical considerations. See Section 2.7.

**The Traditional Definition of $\mathcal{NP}$.** Traditionally, $\mathcal{NP}$ is defined as the class of sets that can be decided by a *fictitious* device called a non-deterministic polynomial-time machine (which explains the source of the notation NP). See Section 2.6.

**Cook-reductions.** A problem $\Pi$ is Cook-reducible to a problem $\Pi'$ if $\Pi$ can be solved efficiently when given access to any procedure (or oracle) that solves the problem $\Pi'$. See Definition 3.1.

**Karp-reductions.** A decision problem $S$ is Karp-reducible to a decision problem $S'$ if there exists a polynomial-time computable function $f$ such that, for every $x$, it holds that $x \in S$ if and only if $f(x) \in S'$. See Definition 3.3.

**Levin-reductions.** A search problem $R$ is Levin-reducible to a search problem $R'$ if there exists polynomial-time computable functions $f$ and $g$ such that (1) $f$ is a Karp-reduction of $S_R$ to $S_{R'}$, and (2) for every $x \in S_R$ and $y' \in R'(f(x))$ it holds that $(x, g(x, y')) \in R$. See Definition 3.4.

**Theorem 3.2.** *Every search problem in $\mathcal{PC}$ is Cook-reducible to some decision problem in $\mathcal{NP}$.*

**Self-reducibility of Search Problems.** The decision implicit in a search problem $R$ is deciding membership in the set $S_R$, and $R$ is called self-reducible if it is Cook-reducible to $S_R$. See Section 3.3.

**NP-Completeness (of Decision Problems).** A decision problem $S$ is $\mathcal{NP}$-complete if (1) $S$ is in $\mathcal{NP}$, and (2) every decision problem in $\mathcal{NP}$ is Karp-reducible to $S$. See Definition 4.1.

**NP-Completeness of Search Problems.** A search problem $R$ is $\mathcal{PC}$-complete (or NP-complete) if (1) $R$ is in $\mathcal{PC}$, and (2) every search problem in $\mathcal{PC}$ is Levin-reducible to $R$. See Definition 4.2.

**Theorem 4.3.** *There exist NP-complete search and decision problems.*

**Theorems 4.5 and 4.6 (Also Known as Cook–Levin Theorem).** Circuit satisfiability (CSAT) and formula satisfiability (SAT) are NP-complete.

**Proposition 4.4.** *If an $\mathcal{NP}$-complete decision problem $S$ is Karp-reducible to a decision problem $S' \in \mathcal{NP}$ (resp., a $\mathcal{PC}$-complete search problem $R$ is Levin-reducible to a search problem $R' \in \mathcal{PC}$), then $S'$ is $\mathcal{NP}$-complete (resp., $R'$ is $\mathcal{PC}$-complete).*

**Theorem 4.12.** *Assuming $\mathcal{NP} \neq \mathcal{P}$, there exist decision problems in $\mathcal{NP} \setminus \mathcal{P}$ that are not NP-complete* (even when allowing Cook-reductions).

**Promise Problems.** Promise problems are natural generalizations of search and decision problems that are obtained by explicitly specifying a set of legitimate instances (rather than considering any string as a legitimate instance). See Section 5.1.

**Theorem 5.5.** *There exists an optimal algorithm for any candid search problem in NP*, where the candid search problem of the binary relation $R$ consists of finding solutions whenever they exist (and behaving arbitrarily otherwise; see Definition 5.2).

**Theorem 5.7.** *If every set in $\mathcal{NP}$ can be Cook-reduced to some set in $\mathcal{NP} \cap$ co$\mathcal{NP}$, then $\mathcal{NP} =$ co$\mathcal{NP}$*, where co$\mathcal{NP} = \{\{0, 1\}^* \setminus S : S \in \mathcal{NP}\}$.

# 1

# Computational Tasks and Models

**Overview:** We assume that the reader is familiar with computing devices but may associate the notion of computation with specific incarnations of it. Our first goal is to promote viewing computation as a general phenomenon, which may capture both artificial and natural processes. Loosely speaking, a computation is a process that modifies a relatively large environment via repeated applications of a simple and predetermined rule. Although each application of the rule has a very limited effect, the effect of many applications of the rule may be very complex.

We are interested in the transformation of the environment effected by the computational process (or computation), where the computation rule is designed to achieve a desired effect. Typically, the initial environment to which the computation is applied encodes an input string, and the end environment (i.e., at termination of the computation) encodes an output string. Thus, the computation defines a mapping from inputs to outputs, and such a mapping can be viewed as solving a search problem (i.e., given an instance $x$ find a solution $y$ that relates to $x$ in some predetermined way) or a decision problem (i.e., given an instance $x$ determine whether or not $x$ has some predetermined property).

Indeed, our focus will be on solving computational tasks (mostly search and decision problems), where a computational task refers to an infinite set of instances such that each instance is associated with a set of valid solutions. In the case of search problem this set may contain several different solutions (per each instance), but in the case of a decision problem the set of solutions is a singleton that consists of a binary value (per each instance).

In order to provide a basis for a rigorous study of the complexity of computational tasks, we need to define computation (and its complexity) rigorously. This, in turn, requires specifying a concrete model of computation, which corresponds to an abstraction of a real computer (be it a PC, mainframe, or network of computers) and yet is simpler (and thus facilitates further study). We will refer to the model of Turing machines, but any reasonable alternative model will do.

We also discuss two fundamental features of any reasonable model of computation: the existence of problems that cannot be solved by any computing device (in this model) and the existence of universal computing devices (in this model).

**Organization.** We start by introducing the general framework for our discussion of computational tasks (or problems). This framework refers to the *representation of instances* as binary sequences (see Section 1.1) and focuses on *two types of tasks*: searching for solutions and making decisions (see Section 1.2). Once computational tasks are defined, we turn to methods for solving such tasks, which are described in terms of some *model of computation*. The description of such models is the main contents of this chapter.

Specifically, we consider two types of models of computation: uniform models and non-uniform models (see Sections 1.3 and 1.4, respectively). The *uniform models correspond to the intuitive notion of an algorithm*, and will provide the stage for the rest of the book (which focuses on efficient algorithms). In contrast, non-uniform models (e.g., Boolean circuits) facilitate a closer look at the way a computation progresses, and will be used only sporadically in this book. Thus, *whereas Sections 1.1–1.3 are absolute prerequisites for the rest of this book, Section 1.4 is not.*

## Teaching Notes

This chapter provides the necessary preliminaries for the rest of the book; that is, we discuss the notion of a computational task and present computational models for describing methods for solving such tasks.

Sections 1.1–1.3 correspond to the contents of a traditional *Computability* course, except that our presentation emphasizes some aspects and deemphasizes others. In particular, the presentation highlights the notion of a universal machine (see Section 1.3.4), explicitly discusses the complexity of computation

(Section 1.3.5), and provides a definition of oracle machines (Section 1.3.6). This material (with the exception of Kolmogorov Complexity) is taken for granted in the rest of the current book. In contrast, Section 1.4 presents basic preliminaries regarding non-uniform models of computation (e.g., various types of Boolean circuits), and these are used only lightly in the rest of the book.

We strongly recommend avoiding the standard practice of teaching the student to program with Turing machines. These exercises seem very painful and pointless. Instead, one should prove that the Turing machine model is exactly as powerful as a model that is closer to a real-life computer (see the "sanity check" in §1.3.2.2); that is, a function can be computed by a Turing machine if and only if it is computable by a machine of the latter model. For starters, one may prove that a function can be computed by a single-tape Turing machine if and only if it is computable by a multi-tape (e.g., two-tape) Turing machine.

As noted in Section 1.3.7, we reject the common coupling of computability theory with the theory of automata and formal languages. Although the historical links between these two theories (at least in the West) cannot be denied, this fact cannot justify coupling two fundamentally different theories (especially when such a coupling promotes a wrong perspective on computability theory). Thus, in our opinion, the study of any of the lower levels of Chomsky's Hierarchy [16, Chap. 9] should be decoupled from the study of computability theory (let alone the study of Complexity Theory). Indeed, this is related to the discussion of the "revision of the CS curriculum" in the preliminary section "To the Teacher."

The perspective on non-uniform models of computation provided by Section 1.4 is more than the very minimum that is required for the rest of this book. If pressed for time, then the teacher may want to skip all of Section 1.4.2 as well as some of the material in Section 1.4.1 and Section 1.4.3 (i.e., avoid §1.4.1.2 as well as §1.4.3.2). Furthermore, for a minimal presentation of Boolean formulae, one may use Appendix A.2 instead of §1.4.3.1.

## 1.1 Representation

In mathematics and most other sciences, it is customary to discuss objects without specifying their representation. This is not possible in the theory of computation, where the representation of objects plays a central role. In a sense, a computation merely transforms one representation of an object to another representation of the same object. In particular, a computation designed to solve some problem merely transforms the problem instance to its solution, where the latter can be thought of as a (possibly partial) representation of the instance. Indeed, the answer to any fully specified question is implicit in the question itself, and computation is employed to make this answer explicit.

Computational tasks refer to objects that are represented in some canonical way, where such canonical representation provides an "explicit" and "full" (but not "overly redundant") description of the corresponding object. Furthermore, when we discuss natural computational problems, we always use a natural representation of the corresponding objects. We will only consider *finite* objects like numbers, sets, graphs, and functions (and keep distinguishing these types of objects although, actually, they are all equivalent). While the representation of numbers, sets, and functions is quite straightforward (see the following), we refer the reader to Appendix A.1 for a discussion of the representation of graphs.

In order to facilitate a study of methods for solving computational tasks, these tasks are defined with respect to infinitely many possible instances (each being a finite object). Indeed, the comparison of different methods seems to require the consideration of infinitely many possible instances; otherwise, the choice of the language in which the methods are described may totally dominate and even distort the discussion (cf., e.g., the discussion of Kolmogorov Complexity in §1.3.4.2).

**Strings.** We consider finite objects, each represented by a finite binary sequence called a string. For a natural number $n$, we denote by $\{0, 1\}^n$ the set of all strings of length $n$, hereafter referred to as $n$-bit (long) strings. The set of all strings is denoted $\{0, 1\}^*$; that is, $\{0, 1\}^* = \cup_{n \in \mathbb{N}} \{0, 1\}^n$, where $0 \in \mathbb{N}$. For $x \in \{0, 1\}^*$, we denote by $|x|$ the length of $x$ (i.e., $x \in \{0, 1\}^{|x|}$), and often denote by $x_i$ the $i^{\text{th}}$ bit of $x$ (i.e., $x = x_1 x_2 \cdots x_{|x|}$). For $x, y \in \{0, 1\}^*$, we denote by $xy$ the string resulting from concatenation of the strings $x$ and $y$.

At times, we associate $\{0, 1\}^* \times \{0, 1\}^*$ with $\{0, 1\}^*$; the reader should merely consider an adequate encoding (e.g., the pair $(x_1 \cdots x_m, y_1 \cdots y_n) \in \{0, 1\}^* \times \{0, 1\}^*$ may be encoded by the string $x_1 x_1 \cdots x_m x_m 01 y_1 \cdots y_n \in \{0, 1\}^*$). Likewise, we may represent sequences of strings (of fixed or varying length) as single strings. When we wish to emphasize that such a sequence (or some other object) is to be considered as a single object, we use the notation $\langle \cdot \rangle$ (e.g., "the pair $(x, y)$ is encoded as the string $\langle x, y \rangle$").

**Numbers.** Unless stated differently, natural numbers will be encoded by their binary expansion; that is, the string $b_{n-1} \cdots b_1 b_0 \in \{0, 1\}^n$ encodes the number $\sum_{i=0}^{n-1} b_i \cdot 2^i$, where typically we assume that this representation has no leading zeros (i.e., $b_{n-1} = 1$), except when the number itself is zero. Rational numbers will be represented as pairs of natural numbers. In the rare cases in which one considers real numbers as part of the input to a computational problem, one actually means rational approximations of these real numbers.

Sets are usually represented as lists, which means that the representation introduces an order that is not specified by the set itself. Indeed, in general, the representation may have features that are not present in the represented object. Functions are usually represented as sets of argument–value pairs (i.e., functions are represented as binary relations, which in turn are sets of ordered pairs).

**Special Symbols.** We denote the empty string by $\lambda$ (i.e., $\lambda \in \{0, 1\}^*$ and $|\lambda| = 0$), and the empty set by $\emptyset$. It will be convenient to use some special symbols that are not in $\{0, 1\}^*$. One such symbol is $\perp$, which typically denotes an indication (e.g., produced by some algorithm) that something is wrong.

## 1.2 Computational Tasks

Two fundamental types of computational tasks are the so-called search problems and decision problems. In both cases, the key notions are the problem's *instances* and the problem's *specification*.

### 1.2.1 Search Problems

A search problem consists of a specification of a (possibly empty) set of valid solutions for each possible instance. Given an instance, one is required to find a corresponding solution (or to determine that no such solution exists). For example, consider the problem in which one is given a system of equations and is asked to find a valid solution. Needless to say, much of computer science is concerned with solving various search problems (e.g., finding shortest paths in a graph, finding an occurrence of a given pattern in a given string, finding the median value in a given list of numbers, etc). Furthermore, search problems correspond to the daily notion of "solving a problem" (e.g., finding one's way between two locations), and thus a discussion of the possibility and complexity of solving search problems corresponds to the natural concerns of most people.

In the following definition of solving search problems, the potential solver is a function (which may be thought of as a solving strategy), and the sets of possible solutions associated with each of the various instances are "packed" into a single binary relation.

**Definition 1.1** (solving a search problem): *Let* $R \subseteq \{0, 1\}^* \times \{0, 1\}^*$ *and* $R(x) \stackrel{\text{def}}{=} \{y : (x, y) \in R\}$ *denote the set of solutions for the instance* $x$. *A function* $f : \{0, 1\}^* \to \{0, 1\}^* \cup \{\perp\}$ solves the search problem of $R$ *if for every* $x$ *the following holds: if* $R(x) \neq \emptyset$ *then* $f(x) \in R(x)$ *and otherwise* $f(x) = \perp$.

Indeed, $R = \{(x, y) \in \{0, 1\}^* \times \{0, 1\}^* : y \in R(x)\}$. The solver $f$ is required to find a solution to the given instance $x$ whenever such a solution exists; that is, given $x$, the solver is required to output some $y \in R(x)$ whenever the set $R(x)$ is not empty. It is also required that the solver $f$ never outputs a wrong solution; that is, if $R(x) \neq \emptyset$ then $f(x) \in R(x)$, and if $R(x) = \emptyset$ then $f(x) = \perp$. This means that $f$ indicates whether or not $x$ has any solution (since $f(x) \in \{0, 1\}^*$ if $x$ has a solution, whereas $f(x) = \perp \notin \{0, 1\}^*$ otherwise). Note that the solver is not necessarily determined by the search problem (i.e., the solver is uniquely determined if and only if $|R(x)| \leq 1$ holds for every $x$).

Of special interest is the case of search problems having a unique solution (for each possible instance); that is, the case that $|R(x)| = 1$ for every $x$. In this case, $R$ is essentially a (total) function, and solving the search problem of $R$ means computing (or evaluating) the function $R$ (or rather the function $R'$ defined by $R'(x) \stackrel{\text{def}}{=} y$ if and only if $R(x) = \{y\}$). Popular examples include sorting a sequence of numbers, multiplying integers, finding the prime factorization of a composite number, and so on.[1]

### 1.2.2 Decision Problems

A decision problem consists of a specification of a subset of the possible instances. Given an instance, one is required to determine whether the instance is in the specified set. For example, consider the problem where one is given a natural number and is asked to determine whether or not the number is a prime (i.e., whether or not the given number is in the set of prime numbers). Note that one typically presents decision problems in terms of deciding whether a given object has some predetermined property, but this can always be viewed as deciding membership in some predetermined set (i.e., the set of objects having this property). For example, when talking about determining whether or not a given graph is connected, we refer to deciding membership in the set of connected graphs.

---

[1] For example, sorting is represented as a binary relation that contains all pairs of sequences such that the second sequence is a sorted version of the first sequence. That is, the pair $((x_1, \ldots, x_n),$ $(y_1, \ldots, y_n))$ is in the relation if and only if there exists a permutation $\pi$ over $[n]$ such that $y_i = x_{\pi(i)}$ and $y_i < y_{i+1}$ for every relevant $i$.

One important type of decision problems concerns those derived from search problems by considering the set of instances having a solution (with respect to some fixed search problem); that is, for any binary relation $R \subseteq \{0, 1\}^* \times \{0, 1\}^*$ we consider the set $\{x : R(x) \neq \emptyset\}$. Indeed, being able to determine whether or not a solution exists is a prerequisite to being able to solve the corresponding search problem (as per Definition 1.1).

In general, decision problems refer to the natural task of making binary decisions, a task that is not uncommon in daily life (e.g., determining whether a traffic light is red). In any case, in the following definition of solving decision problems, the potential solver is again a function; specifically, in this case the solver is a Boolean function, which is supposed to indicate membership in a predetermined set.

**Definition 1.2** (solving a decision problem): *Let $S \subseteq \{0, 1\}^*$. A function $f$ : $\{0, 1\}^* \to \{0, 1\}$ solves the decision problem of $S$ (or decides membership in $S$) if for every $x$ it holds that $f(x) = 1$ if and only if $x \in S$.*

That is, the solver $f$ is required to indicate whether or not the instance $x$ resides in the predetermined set $S$. This indication is modeled by a binary value, where 1 corresponds to a positive answer and 0 corresponds to a negative answer. Thus, given $x$, the solver is required to output 1 if $x \in S$, and output 0 otherwise (i.e., if $x \notin S$).

Note that the function that solves a decision problem is uniquely determined by the decision problem; that is, if $f$ solves (the decision problem of) $S$, then $f$ equals the characteristic function of $S$ (i.e., the function $\chi_S : \{0, 1\}^* \to \{0, 1\}$ defined such that $\chi_S(x) = 1$ if and only if $x \in S$).

As hinted already in Section 1.2.1, the solver of a search problem implicitly determines membership in the set of instances that have solutions. That is, *if $f$ solves the search problem of $R$, then the Boolean function $f' : \{0, 1\}^* \to \{0, 1\}$ defined by $f'(x) \stackrel{\text{def}}{=} 1$ if and only if $f(x) \neq \bot$ solves the decision problem of $\{x : R(x) \neq \emptyset\}$.*

**Terminology.** We often identify the decision problem of a set $S$ with $S$ itself, and also identify $S$ with its characteristic function. Likewise, we often identify the search problem of a relation $R$ with $R$ itself.

**Reflection.** Most people would consider search problems to be more natural than decision problems: Typically, people seeks solutions more often than they stop to wonder whether or not solutions exist. Definitely, search problems are not less important than decision problems; it is merely that their study tends to require more cumbersome formulations. This is the main reason that most expositions choose to focus on decision problems. The current book attempts to devote at least a significant amount of attention to search problems, too.

### 1.2.3 Promise Problems (an Advanced Comment)

Many natural search and decision problems are captured more naturally by the terminology of promise problems, in which the domain of possible instances is a subset of $\{0, 1\}^*$ rather than $\{0, 1\}^*$ itself. In particular, note that the natural formulation of many search and decision problems refers to instances of a certain type (e.g., a system of equations, a pair of numbers, a graph), whereas the natural representation of these objects uses only a strict subset of $\{0, 1\}^*$. For the time being, we ignore this issue, but we shall revisit it in Section 5.1. Here we just note that in typical cases, the issue can be ignored by postulating that every string represents some legitimate object; for example, each string that is not used in the natural representation of these objects is postulated to be a representation of some fixed object (e.g., when representing graphs, we may postulate that each string that is not used in the natural representation of graphs is in fact a representation of the 1-vertex graph).

## 1.3 Uniform Models (Algorithms)

We finally reach the heart of the current chapter, which is the definition of (uniform) models of computation. Before presenting these models, let us briefly explain the need for their formal definitions.

Indeed, we are all familiar with computers and with the ability of computer programs to manipulate data. But this familiarity is rooted in positive experience; that is, we have some experience regarding some things that computers can do. In contrast, Complexity Theory is focused at what computers cannot do, or rather with drawing the line between what can be done and what cannot be done. Drawing such a line requires a precise formulation of *all* possible computational processes; that is, we should have a clear definition of *all* possible computational processes (rather than some familiarity with some computational processes).

We note that while our main motivation for defining formal models of computation is to capture the intuitive notion of an algorithm, such models also provide a useful perspective on a wide variety of processes that take place in the world.

**Organization of Section 1.3.** We start, in Section 1.3.1, with a general and abstract discussion of the notion of computation. Next, in Section 1.3.2, we provide a high-level description of the model of Turing machines. This is done merely for the sake of providing a concrete model that supports the study of computation and its complexity, whereas the material in this book will not depend on the specifics of this model. In Section 1.3.3 and Section 1.3.4 we discuss two fundamental properties of any reasonable model of computation: the existence of uncomputable functions and the existence of universal computations. The time (and space) complexity of computation is defined in Section 1.3.5. We also discuss oracle machines and restricted models of computation (in Section 1.3.6 and Section 1.3.7, respectively).

## 1.3.1 Overview and General Principles

Before being formal, let us offer a general and abstract description of the notion of computation. This description applies both to artificial processes (taking place in computers) and to processes that are aimed at modeling the evolution of the natural reality (be it physical, biological, or even social).

A computation is a process that modifies an environment via repeated applications of a predetermined rule. The key restriction is that this rule is *simple*: In each application it depends and affects only a (small) portion of the environment, called the active zone. We contrast the *a priori bounded* size of the active zone (and of the modification rule) with the *a priori unbounded* size of the entire environment. We note that although each application of the rule has a very limited effect, the effect of many applications of the rule may be very complex. Put in other words, a computation may modify the relevant environment in a very complex way, although it is merely a process of repeatedly applying a simple rule.

As hinted, the notion of computation can be used to model the "mechanical" aspects of the natural reality, that is, the rules that determine the evolution of the reality (rather than the specific state of the reality at a specific time). In this case, the starting point of the study is the actual evolution process that takes place in the natural reality, and the goal of the study is finding the (computation) rule that underlies this natural process. In a sense, the goal of science at large can be phrased as finding (simple) rules that govern various aspects of reality (or rather one's abstraction of these aspects of reality).

Our focus, however, is on artificial computation rules designed by humans in order to achieve specific desired effects on a corresponding artificial environment. Thus, our starting point is a desired functionality, and our aim is to design computation rules that effect it. Such a computation rule is referred to as an algorithm. Loosely speaking, an algorithm corresponds to a computer program written in a high-level (abstract) programming language. Let us elaborate.

We are interested in the transformation of the environment as effected by the computational process (or the algorithm). Throughout (almost all of) this book, we will assume that, *when invoked on any finite initial environment, the computation halts after a finite number of steps.* Typically, the initial environment to which the computation is applied encodes an input string, and the end environment (i.e., at termination of the computation) encodes an output string. We consider the mapping from inputs to outputs induced by the computation; that is, for each possible input $x$, we consider the output $y$ obtained at the end of a computation initiated with input $x$, and say that the computation maps input $x$ to output $y$. Thus, a computation rule (or an algorithm) determines a function (computed by it): This function is exactly the aforementioned mapping of inputs to outputs.

In the rest of this book (i.e., outside the current chapter), we will also consider the number of steps (i.e., applications of the rule) taken by the computation on each possible input. The latter function is called the time complexity of the computational process (or algorithm). While time complexity is defined per input, we will often considers it per input length, taking the maximum over all inputs of the same length.

In order to define computation (and computation time) rigorously, one needs to specify some model of computation, that is, provide a concrete definition of environments and a class of rules that may be applied to them. Such a model corresponds to an abstraction of a real computer (be it a PC, mainframe, or network of computers). One simple abstract model that is commonly used is that of *Turing machines* (see Section 1.3.2). Thus, specific algorithms are typically formalized by corresponding Turing machines (and their time complexity is represented by the time complexity of the corresponding Turing machines). We stress, however, that almost all results in the theory of computation hold regardless of the specific computational model used, as long as it is "reasonable" (i.e., satisfies the aforementioned simplicity condition and can perform some apparently simple computations).

**What is being Computed?** The foregoing discussion has implicitly referred to algorithms (i.e., computational processes) as means of computing functions. Specifically, an algorithm $A$ computes the function $f_A : \{0, 1\}^* \to \{0, 1\}^* \cup \{\bot\}$ defined by $f_A(x) = y$ if, when invoked on input $x$, algorithm $A$ halts with output $y$. However, algorithms can also serve as means of "solving search problems" or "making decisions" (as in Definitions 1.1 and 1.2). Specifically, we will say that algorithm $A$ solves the search problem of $R$ (resp., decides membership in $S$) if $f_A$ solves the search problem of $R$ (resp., decides membership in $S$). In the rest of this exposition we associate the algorithm $A$ with the function $f_A$ computed by it; that is, we write $A(x)$ instead of $f_A(x)$. For the sake of future reference, we summarize the foregoing discussion in a definition.

**Definition 1.3** (algorithms as problem solvers): *We denote by $A(x)$ the output of algorithm $A$ on input $x$. Algorithm $A$ solves the search problem $R$ (resp., the decision problem $S$) if $A$, viewed as a function, solves $R$ (resp., $S$).*

### 1.3.2 A Concrete Model: Turing Machines

The model of Turing machines offers a relatively simple formulation of the notion of an algorithm. The fact that the model is very simple complicates the design of machines that solve problems of interest, but makes the analysis of such machines simpler. Since the focus of Complexity Theory is on the analysis of machines and not on their design, the trade-off offered by this model is suitable for our purposes. We stress again that the model is merely used as a concrete formulation of the intuitive notion of an algorithm, whereas we actually care about the intuitive notion and not about its formulation. In particular, all results mentioned in this book hold for any other "reasonable" formulation of the notion of an algorithm.

The model of Turing machines provides only an extremely coarse description of real-life computers. Indeed, Turing machines are not meant to provide an accurate portrayal of real-life computers, but rather to capture their inherent limitations and abilities (i.e., a computational task can be solved by a real-life computer if and only if it can be solved by a Turing machine). In comparison to real-life computers, the model of Turing machines is extremely oversimplified and abstracts away many issues that are of great concern to computer practice. However, these issues are irrelevant to the higher-level questions addressed by Complexity Theory. Indeed, as usual, good practice requires more refined understanding than the one provided by a good theory, but one should first provide the latter.

Historically, the model of Turing machines was invented before modern computers were even built, and was meant to provide a concrete model of computation and a definition of computable functions.[2] Indeed, this concrete

---

[2] In contrast, the abstract definition of "recursive functions" yields a class of "computable" functions without referring to any model of computation (but rather based on the intuition that any such model should support recursive functional composition).

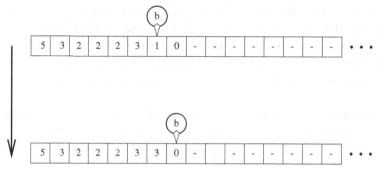

Figure 1.1. A single step by a Turing machine.

model clarified fundamental properties of computable functions and plays a key role in defining the complexity of computable functions.

The model of Turing machines was envisioned as an abstraction of the process of an algebraic computation carried out by a human using a sheet of paper. In such a process, at each time, the human looks at some location on the paper, and depending on what he/she sees and what he/she has in mind (which is little . . . ), he/she modifies the contents of this location and shifts his/her look to an adjacent location.

### 1.3.2.1 The Actual Model

Following is a high-level description of the model of Turing machines. While this description should suffice for our purposes, more detailed (low-level) descriptions can be found in numerous textbooks (e.g., [30]). Recall that, in order to describe a computational model, we need to specify the set of possible environments, the set of machines (or computation rules), and the effect of applying such a rule on an environment.

**The Environment.** The main component in the *environment* of a Turing machine is an infinite sequence of cells, each capable of holding a single symbol (i.e., member of a finite set $\Sigma \supset \{0, 1\}$). This sequence is envisioned as starting at a leftmost cell, and extending infinitely to the right (cf. Figure 1.1). In addition, the environment contains the current location of the machine on this sequence, and the internal state of the machine (which is a member of a finite set $Q$). The aforementioned sequence of cells is called the tape, and its contents combined with the machine's location and its internal state is called the instantaneous configuration of the machine.

**The Machine Itself (i.e., the Computation Rule).** The main component in the *Turing machine itself* is a finite rule (i.e., a finite function) called the transition function, which is defined over the set of all possible symbol-state pairs. Specifically, the transition function is a mapping from $\Sigma \times Q$ to $\Sigma \times Q \times \{-1, 0, +1\}$, where $\{-1, +1, 0\}$ correspond to a movement instruction (which is either "left" or "right" or "stay," respectively). In addition, the machine's description specifies an initial state and a halting state, and the computation of the machine halts when the machine enters its halting state. (Envisioning the tape as in Figure 1.1, we use the convention by which if the machine ever tries to move left of the end of the tape, then it is considered to have halted.)

We stress that in contrast to the finite description of the machine, the tape has an a priori unbounded length (and is considered, for simplicity, as being infinite).

**A Single Application of the Computation Rule.** A single *computation step* of such a Turing machine depends on its current location on the tape, on the contents of the corresponding cell, and on the internal state of the machine. Based on the latter two elements, the transition function determines a new symbol-state pair as well as a movement instruction (i.e., "left" or "right" or "stay"). The machine modifies the contents of the said cell and its internal state accordingly, and moves as directed. That is, suppose that the machine is in state $q$ and resides in a cell containing the symbol $\sigma$, and suppose that the transition function maps $(\sigma, q)$ to $(\sigma', q', D)$. Then, the machine modifies the contents of the said cell to $\sigma'$, modifies its internal state to $q'$, and moves one cell in direction $D$. Figure 1.1 shows a single step of a Turing machine that, when in state "b" and seeing a binary symbol $\sigma \in \{0, 1\}$, replaces $\sigma$ with the symbol $\sigma + 2$, maintains its internal state, and moves one position to the right.[3]

Formally, we define the successive configuration function that maps each instantaneous configuration to the one resulting by letting the machine take a single step. This function modifies its argument in a very minor manner, as described in the foregoing paragraph; that is, the contents of at most one cell (i.e., at which the machine currently resides) is changed, and in addition the internal state of the machine and its location may change, too.

---

[3] Figure 1.1 corresponds to a machine that, when in the initial state (i.e., "a"), replaces the symbol $\sigma \in \{0, 1\}$ by $\sigma + 4$, modifies its internal state to "b," and moves one position to the right. (See also Figure 1.2, which depicts multiple steps of this machine.) Indeed, "marking" the leftmost cell (in order to allow for recognizing it in the future) is a common practice in the design of Turing machines.

Providing a concrete representation of the successive configuration function requires providing a concrete representation of instantaneous configurations. For example, we may represent each instantaneous configuration of a machine with symbol set $\Sigma$ and state set $Q$ as a triple $(\alpha, q, i)$, where $\alpha \in \Sigma^*, q \in Q$ and $i \in \{1, 2, \ldots, |\alpha|\}$. Let $T : \Sigma \times Q \to \Sigma \times Q \times \{-1, 0, +1\}$ be the transition function of the machine. Then, the successive configuration function maps $(\alpha, q, i)$ to $(\alpha', q', i + d)$ such that $\alpha'$ differs from $\alpha$ only in the $i^{\text{th}}$ location, which is determined according to the first element in $T(\alpha_i, q)$. The new state (i.e., $q'$) and the movement (i.e., $d$) are determined by the other two elements of $T(\alpha_i, q)$. Specifically, except for some pathological cases, the successive configuration function maps $(\alpha, q, i)$ to $(\alpha', q', i + d)$ if and only if $T(\alpha_i, q) = (\alpha'_i, q', d)$ and $\alpha'_j = \alpha_j$ for every $j \neq i$, where $\alpha_j$ (resp., $\alpha'_j$) denotes the $j^{\text{th}}$ symbol of $\alpha$ (resp., $\alpha'$). The aforementioned pathological cases refer to cases in which the machine resides in one of the "boundary locations" and needs to move farther in that direction. One such case is the case that $i = 1$ and $d = -1$, which causes the machine to halt (rather than move left of the left boundary of the tape). The opposite case refers to $i = |\alpha|$ and $d = +1$, where the machine moves to the right of the rightmost non-blank symbol, which is represented by extending $\alpha'$ with a blank symbol "-" (i.e., $|\alpha'| = |\alpha| + 1$ and $\alpha'_{|\alpha|+1} = $ -).

**Initial and Final Environments.** The initial environment (or configuration) of a Turing machine consists of the machine residing in the first (i.e., leftmost) cell and being in its initial state. Typically, one also mandates that in the initial configuration, a prefix of the tape's cells holds bit values, which concatenated together are considered the input, and the rest of the tape's cells hold a special ("blank") symbol (which in Figures 1.1 and 1.2 is denoted by "-"). Thus, the initial configuration of a Turing machine has a finite (explicit) description. Once the machine halts, the output is defined as the contents of the cells that are to the left of its location (at termination time).[4] Note, however, that the machine need not halt at all (when invoked on some initial environment).[5] Thus, each machine defines a (possibly partial) function mapping inputs to outputs, called the function computed by the machine. That is, *the function computed by machine M maps x to y if, when invoked on input x, machine M halts with output y, and is undefined on x if machine M does halt on input x.*

---

[4] By an alternative convention, the machine must halt when residing in the leftmost cell, and the output is defined as the maximal prefix of the tape contents that contains only bit values. In such a case, the special non-Boolean output $\bot$ is indicated by the machine's state (and indeed in this case the set of states, $Q$, contains several halting states).

[5] A simple example is a machine that "loops forever" (i.e., it remains in the same state and the same location regardless of what it reads). Recall, however, that we shall be mainly interested in machines that do halt after a finite number of steps (when invoked on any initial environment).

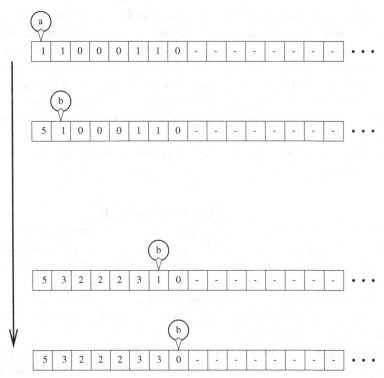

Figure 1.2. Multiple steps of the machine depicted in Figure 1.1.

As stated up front, the Turing machine model is only meant to provide an extremely coarse portrayal of real-life computers. However, the model is intended to reflect the inherent limitations and abilities of real-life computers. Thus, it is important to verify that the Turing machine model is exactly as powerful as a model that provides a more faithful portrayal of real-life computers (see the "sanity check" in §1.3.2.2); that is, a function can be computed by a Turing machine if and only if it is computable by a machine of the latter model. For starters, one may prove that a function can be computed by a single-tape Turing machine if and only if it is computable by a multi-tape (e.g., two-tape) Turing machine (as defined next); see Exercise 1.3.

**Multi-tape Turing Machines.** We comment that in most expositions, one refers to the location of the "head of the machine" on the tape (rather than to the "location of the machine on the tape"). The standard terminology is more intuitive when extending the basic model, which refers to a single tape, to a model that supports a constant number of tapes. In the corresponding model of so-called multi-tape machines, the machine maintains a single head on each such tape, and each step of the machine depends on and effects the cells that are at the machine's head location on each tape. The input is given on one designated tape, and the output is required to appear on some other designated tape. As we shall see in Section 1.3.5, the extension of the model to multi-tape Turing machines is crucial to the definition of space complexity. A less fundamental advantage of the model of multi-tape Turing machines is that it is easier to design multi-tape Turing machines that compute functions of interest (see, e.g., Exercise 1.4).

### 1.3.2.2 The Church-Turing Thesis

The entire point of the model of Turing machines is its simplicity. That is, in comparison to more "realistic" models of computation, it is simpler to formulate the model of Turing machines and to analyze machines in this model. The Church-Turing Thesis asserts that nothing is lost by considering the Turing machine model: *A function can be computed by some Turing machine if and only if it can be computed by some machine of any other* "reasonable and general" *model of computation.*

This is a thesis, rather than a theorem, because it refers to an intuitive notion (i.e., the notion of a *reasonable and general model of computation*) that is left undefined on purpose. The model should be reasonable in the sense that it should allow only computation rules that are "simple" in some intuitive sense. For example, we should be able to envision a mechanical implementation of these computation rules. On the other hand, the model should allow the computation of "simple" functions that are definitely computable according to our intuition. At the very least, the model should allow the emulatation of Turing machines (i.e., computation of the function that, given a description of a Turing machine and an instantaneous configuration, returns the successive configuration).

**A Philosophical Comment.** The fact that a thesis is used to link an intuitive concept to a formal definition is common practice in any science (or, more broadly, in any attempt to reason rigorously about intuitive concepts). Any attempt to rigorously define an intuitive concept yields a formal definition that necessarily differs from the original intuition, and the question of correspondence between these two objects arises. This question can never be rigorously treated because one of the objects that it relates to is undefined. That is, the question of correspondence between the intuition and the definition always transcends a rigorous treatment (i.e., it always belongs to the domain of the intuition).

**A Sanity Check: Turing Machines can Emulate an Abstract RAM.** To gain confidence in the Church-Turing Thesis, one may attempt to define an abstract Random-Access Machine (RAM), and verify that it can be emulated by a Turing machine. An abstract RAM consists of an infinite number of memory cells, each capable of holding an integer, a finite number of similar registers, one designated as program counter, and a program consisting of instructions selected from a finite set. The set of possible instructions includes the following instructions:

- reset($r$), where $r$ is an index of a register, results in setting the value of register $r$ to zero.
- inc($r$), where $r$ is an index of a register, results in incrementing the content of register $r$. Similarly dec($r$) causes a decrement.
- load($r_1, r_2$), where $r_1$ and $r_2$ are indices of registers, results in loading to register $r_1$ the contents of the memory location $m$, where $m$ is the current contents of register $r_2$.
- store($r_1, r_2$), stores the contents of register $r_1$ in the memory, analogously to load.
- cond-goto($r, \ell$), where $r$ is an index of a register and $\ell$ does not exceed the program length, results in setting the program counter to $\ell - 1$ if the content of register $r$ is non-negative.

The program counter is incremented after the execution of each instruction, and the next instruction to be executed by the machine is the one to which the program counter points (and the machine halts if the program counter exceeds the program's length). The input to the machine may be defined as the contents of the first $n$ memory cells, where $n$ is placed in a special input register, and all other memory cells are assumed to be empty (i.e., contain blanks).

We note that the abstract RAM model (as defined) is as powerful as the Turing machine model (see the following details). However, in order to make the RAM model closer to real-life computers, we may augment it with additional instructions that are available on real-life computers like the instruction add($r_1, r_2$) (resp., mult($r_1, r_2$)) that results in adding (resp., multiplying) the contents of registers $r_1$ and $r_2$ (and placing the result in register $r_1$). Likewise, we may augment the model with explicit loop-constructs (although such constructs are easily implementable using the cond-goto instruction).

We suggest proving that *this abstract RAM can be emulated by a Turing machine*, see Exercise 1.5. We emphasize this direction of the equivalence of the two models, because the RAM model is introduced in order to convince the reader that Turing machines are not too weak (as a model of general computation). The fact that they are not too strong seems self-evident. Thus, it seems pointless to prove that the RAM model can emulate Turing machines. (Still, note that this is indeed the case, by using the RAM's memory cells to store the contents of the cells of the Turing machine's tape, and holding its head location in a special register.)

**Reflections.** Observe that the abstract RAM model is significantly more cumbersome than the Turing machine model. Furthermore, seeking a sound choice of the instruction set (i.e., the instructions to be allowed in the model) creates a vicious cycle (because the sound guideline for such a choice should have been allowing only instructions that correspond to "simple" operations, whereas the latter correspond to easily computable functions ... ). This vicious cycle was avoided in the foregoing paragraph by trusting the reader to include only instructions that are available in some real-life computer. (We comment that this empirical consideration is justifiable in the current context because our current goal is merely linking the Turing machine model with the reader's experience of real-life computers.)

### 1.3.3 Uncomputable Functions

Strictly speaking, the current subsection is not necessary for the rest of this book, but we feel that it provides a useful perspective.

#### 1.3.3.1 On the Existence of Uncomputable Functions

In contrast to what every layman would think, *not all functions are computable*. Indeed, an important message to be communicated to the world is that *not every well-defined task can be solved* by applying a "reasonable" automated procedure (i.e., a procedure that has a simple description that can be applied to any instance of the problem at hand). Furthermore, not only is it the case that there exist uncomputable functions, but it is rather the case that most functions are uncomputable. In fact, only relatively few functions are computable.

**Theorem 1.4** (on the scarcity of computable functions): *The set of computable functions is countable, whereas the set of all functions* (from strings to strings) *is not countable. Furthermore, the latter set has the same cardinality as the power set of the natural numbers, which in turn has the same cardinality as the set of real numbers.*

We stress that the theorem holds for any reasonable model of computation. In fact, it relies only on the postulate that each machine in the model has a finite description (i.e., can be described by a string).

**Proof:** Since each computable function is computable by a machine that has a finite description, there is an injection of the set of computable functions to the set of strings (whereas the set of all strings is in 1-1 correspondence to the natural numbers). On the other hand, there is a 1-1 correspondence between the set of Boolean functions (i.e., functions from strings to a single bit) and the power set of the natural numbers. This correspondence associates each subset $S \in \mathbb{N}$ to the function $f : \mathbb{N} \to \{0, 1\}$ such that $f(i) = 1$ if and only if $i \in S$. Establishing the remaining set theoretic facts is not really in the scope of the current book. Specifically, we refer to the following facts:

1. The set of all Boolean functions has the same cardinality as the set of all functions (from strings to strings).
2. The power set of the natural numbers has the same cardinality as the set of real numbers.
3. Each of the foregoing sets (e.g., the real numbers) is not countable.[6]

The theorem follows.  ∎

### 1.3.3.2 The Halting Problem

In contrast to the discussion in Section 1.3.1, at this point we also consider machines that may not halt on some inputs. The functions computed by such machines are partial functions that are defined only on inputs on which the machine halts. Again, we rely on the postulate that each machine in the model has a finite description, and denote the description of machine $M$ by $\langle M \rangle \in \{0, 1\}^*$. The halting function, $h : \{0, 1\}^* \times \{0, 1\}^* \to \{0, 1\}$, is defined such that $h(\langle M \rangle, x) \stackrel{\text{def}}{=} 1$ if and only if $M$ halts on input $x$. The following result goes beyond Theorem 1.4 by pointing to an explicit function (of natural interest) that is not computable.

**Theorem 1.5** (undecidability of the halting problem): *The halting function is not computable.*

The term undecidability means that the corresponding decision problem cannot be solved by an automated procedure. That is, Theorem 1.5 asserts that the

---

[6] **Advanced comment:** This fact is usually established by a "diagonalization" argument, which is actually the core of the proof of Theorem 1.5. For further discussion, the interested reader is referred to [3, Chap. 2].

decision problem associated with the set $h^{-1}(1) = \{(\langle M \rangle, x) : h(\langle M \rangle, x) = 1\}$ is not solvable by an algorithm (i.e., there exists no algorithm that, given a pair $(\langle M \rangle, x)$, decides whether or not $M$ halts on input $x$). Actually, the following proof shows that there exists no algorithm that, given $\langle M \rangle$, decides whether or not $M$ halts on input $\langle M \rangle$. The conceptual significance of Theorem 1.5 is discussed in §1.3.3.3 (following Theorem 1.6).

**Proof:** We will show that even the restriction of h to its "diagonal" (i.e., the function $d(\langle M \rangle) \stackrel{\text{def}}{=} h(\langle M \rangle, \langle M \rangle)$) is not computable. Note that the value of $d(\langle M \rangle)$ refers to the question of what happens when we feed $M$ with its own description, which is indeed a "nasty" (but legitimate) thing to do. We will actually do something "worse": toward the contradiction, we will consider the value of d when evaluated at a (machine that is related to a) hypothetical machine that supposedly computes d.

We start by considering a related function, $d'$, and showing that this function is uncomputable. The function $d'$ is defined on purpose so as to foil any attempt to compute it; that is, for every machine $M$, the value $d'(\langle M \rangle)$ is defined to differ from $M(\langle M \rangle)$. Specifically, the function $d' : \{0, 1\}^* \to \{0, 1\}$ is defined such that $d'(\langle M \rangle) \stackrel{\text{def}}{=} 1$ *if and only if M halts on input* $\langle M \rangle$ *with output 0*. That is, $d'(\langle M \rangle) = 0$ if either $M$ does not halt on input $\langle M \rangle$ or its output does not equal the value 0. Now, suppose, toward the contradiction, that $d'$ is computable by some machine, denoted $M_{d'}$. Note that machine $M_{d'}$ is supposed to halt on every input, and so $M_{d'}$ halts on input $\langle M_{d'} \rangle$. But, by definition of $d'$, it holds that $d'(\langle M_{d'} \rangle) = 1$ if and only if $M_{d'}$ halts on input $\langle M_{d'} \rangle$ with output 0 (i.e., if and only if $M_{d'}(\langle M_{d'} \rangle) = 0$). Thus, $M_{d'}(\langle M_{d'} \rangle) \neq d'(\langle M_{d'} \rangle)$ in contradiction to the hypothesis that $M_{d'}$ computes $d'$.

We next prove that d is uncomputable, and thus h is uncomputable (because $d(z) = h(z, z)$ for every $z$). To prove that d is uncomputable, we show that if d is computable then so is $d'$ (which we already know not to be the case). Indeed, suppose toward the contradiction that $A$ is an algorithm for computing d (i.e., $A(\langle M \rangle) = d(\langle M \rangle)$ for every machine $M$). Then, we construct an algorithm for computing $d'$, which given $\langle M' \rangle$, invokes $A$ on $\langle M'' \rangle$, where $M''$ is defined to operate as follows:

1. On input $x$, machine $M''$ emulates $M'$ on input $x$.
2. If $M'$ halts on input $x$ with output 0 then $M''$ halts.
3. If $M'$ halts on input $x$ with an output different from 0 then $M''$ enters an infinite loop (and thus does not halt).
   Otherwise (i.e., $M'$ does not halt on input $x$), then machine $M''$ does not halt (because it just stays stuck in Step 1 forever).

Note that the mapping from $\langle M' \rangle$ to $\langle M'' \rangle$ is easily computable (by augmenting $M'$ with instructions to test its output and enter an infinite loop if necessary), and that $d(\langle M'' \rangle) = d'(\langle M' \rangle)$, because $M''$ halts on $x$ if and only if $M'$ halts on $x$ with output 0. We thus derived an algorithm for computing $d'$ (i.e., transform the input $\langle M' \rangle$ into $\langle M'' \rangle$ and output $A(\langle M'' \rangle)$), which contradicts the already established fact by which $d'$ is uncomputable. Thus, our contradiction hypothesis that there exists an algorithm (i.e., $A$) that computes $d$ is proved false, and the theorem follows (because if the restriction of $h$ to its diagonal (i.e., $d$) is not computable, then $h$ itself is surely not computable). ∎

**Digest.** The core of the second part of the proof of Theorem 1.5 is an algorithm that solves one problem (i.e., computes $d'$) by using as a subroutine an algorithm that solves another problem (i.e., computes $d$ (or $h$)).[7] In fact, the first algorithm is actually an algorithmic scheme that refers to a "functionally specified" subroutine rather than to an actual (implementation of such a) subroutine, which may not exist. Such an algorithmic scheme is called a Turing-reduction (see formulation in Section 1.3.6). Hence, we have Turing-reduced the computation of $d'$ to the computation of $d$, which in turn Turing-reduces to $h$. The "natural" ("positive") meaning of a Turing-reduction of $f'$ to $f$ is that, when given an algorithm for computing $f$, we obtain an algorithm for computing $f'$. In contrast, the proof of Theorem 1.5 uses the "unnatural" ("negative") counter-positive: If (as we know) there exists no algorithm for computing $f' = d'$ then there exists no algorithm for computing $f = d$ (which is what we wanted to prove). Jumping ahead, we mention that resource-bounded Turing-reductions (e.g., polynomial-time reductions) play a central role in Complexity Theory itself, and again they are used mostly in a "negative" way. We will define such reductions and extensively use them in subsequent chapters.

### 1.3.3.3 A Few More Undecidability Results
We briefly review a few appealing results regarding undecidable problems.

**Rice's Theorem.** The undecidability of the Halting Problem (or rather the fact that the function $h$ is uncomputable) is a special case of a more general phenomenon: Every non-trivial decision problem *regarding the function computed by a given Turing machine* has no algorithmic solution. We state this fact next, clarifying the definition of the aforementioned class of problems. (Again, we refer to Turing machines that may not halt on all inputs.)

---

[7] The same holds also with respect to the first part of the proof, which uses the fact that the ability to compute $h$ yields the ability to compute $d$. However, in this case the underlying algorithmic scheme is so obvious that we chose not to state it explicitly.

**Theorem 1.6** (Rice's Theorem): *Let $\mathcal{F}$ be any non-trivial subset[8] of the set of all computable partial functions, and let $S_{\mathcal{F}}$ be the set of strings that describe machines that compute functions in $\mathcal{F}$. Then deciding membership in $S_{\mathcal{F}}$ cannot be solved by an algorithm.*

Theorem 1.6 can be proved by a Turing-reduction from d. We do not provide a proof because this is too remote from the main subject matter of the book. (Still, the interested reader is referred to Exercise 1.6.)

We stress that Theorems 1.5 and 1.6 hold for any reasonable model of computation (referring both to the potential solvers and to the machines the description of which is given as input to these solvers). Thus, Theorem 1.6 means that *no algorithm can determine any non-trivial property of the function computed by a given computer program* (written in any programming language). For example, *no algorithm can determine whether or not a given computer program halts on each possible input*. The relevance of this assertion to the project of program verification is obvious. See further discussion of this issue at the end of Section 4.2.

**The Post Correspondence Problem.** We mention that undecidability also arises outside of the domain of questions regarding computing devices (given as input). Specifically, we consider the Post Correspondence Problem in which the input consists of two sequences of (non-empty) strings, $(\alpha_1, \ldots, \alpha_k)$ and $(\beta_1, \ldots, \beta_k)$, and the question is whether or not there exists a sequence of indices $i_1, \ldots, i_\ell \in \{1, \ldots, k\}$ such that $\alpha_{i_1} \cdots \alpha_{i_\ell} = \beta_{i_1} \cdots \beta_{i_\ell}$. (We stress that the length of this sequence is *not a priori bounded*.)[9]

**Theorem 1.7:** *The Post Correspondence Problem is undecidable.*

Again, the omitted proof is by a Turing-reduction from d (or h), and the interested reader is referred to Exercise 1.8.

### 1.3.4 Universal Algorithms

So far we have used the postulate that in any reasonable model of computation, each machine (or computation rule) has a finite description. Furthermore, in the proof of Theorem 1.5, we also used the postulate that such a model allows for

---

[8] The set $S$ is called a non-trivial subset of $U$ if both $S$ and $U \setminus S$ are non-empty. Clearly, if $\mathcal{F}$ is a trivial set of computable functions then the corresponding decision problem can be solved by a "trivial" algorithm that outputs the corresponding constant bit.

[9] In contrast, the existence of an adequate sequence of a specified length can be determined in time that is exponential in this length.

easy modification of a description of a machine that computes a function into a description of a machine that computes a closely related function. Here, we go one step further and postulate that the description of machines (in this model) is "effective" in the following natural sense: *There exists an algorithm that, given a description of a machine* (resp., computation rule) *and a corresponding environment, determines the environment that results from performing a single step of this machine on this environment* (resp., the effect of a single application of the computation rule).[10] This algorithm can, in turn, be implemented in the said model of computation (assuming this model is general; see the Church-Turing Thesis). Successive applications of this algorithm lead to the notion of a universal machine, which (for concreteness) is formulated next in terms of Turing machines.

**Definition 1.8** (universal machines): *A universal Turing machine is a Turing machine that when given a description of a machine M and a corresponding input x returns the value of M(x) if M halts on x and otherwise does not halt.*

That is, a universal Turing machine computes the partial function $u$ that is defined on pairs $(\langle M \rangle, x)$ such that $M$ halts on input $x$, in which case it holds that $u(\langle M \rangle, x) = M(x)$. That is, $u(\langle M \rangle, x) = M(x)$ if $M$ halts on input $x$, and $u$ is undefined on $(\langle M \rangle, x)$ otherwise. We note that if $M$ halts on all possible inputs then $u(\langle M \rangle, x)$ is defined for every $x$.

### 1.3.4.1 The Existence of Universal Algorithms

We stress that the mere fact that we have defined something (i.e., a universal Turing machine) does not mean that it exists. Yet, as hinted in the foregoing discussion and obvious to anyone who has written a computer program (and thought about what he/she was doing), universal Turing machines do exist.

**Theorem 1.9:** *There exists a universal Turing machine.*

Theorem 1.9 asserts that the partial function $u$ is computable. In contrast, it can be shown that any extension of $u$ to a total function is uncomputable. That is, for any total function $\hat{u}$ that agrees with the partial function $u$ on all the inputs on which the latter is defined, it holds that $\hat{u}$ is uncomputable (see Exercise 1.10).

**Proof:** Given a pair $(\langle M \rangle, x)$, we just emulate the computation of machine $M$ on input $x$. This emulation is straightforward because (by the effectiveness of the description of $M$) we can iteratively determine the next instantaneous configuration of the computation of $M$ on input $x$. If the said computation

---

[10] For details, see Exercise 1.9.

halts, then we will obtain its output and can output it (and so, on input $(\langle M \rangle, x)$, our algorithm returns $M(x)$). Otherwise, we turn out emulating an infinite computation, which means that our algorithm does not halt on input $(\langle M \rangle, x)$. Thus, the foregoing emulation procedure constitutes a universal machine (i.e., yields an algorithm for computing u).  ∎

As hinted already, the existence of universal machines is the fundamental fact underlying the paradigm of general-purpose computers. Indeed, a specific Turing machine (or algorithm) is a device that solves a specific problem. A priori, solving each problem would have required building a new physical device that allows for this problem to be solved in the physical world (rather than as a thought experiment). The existence of a universal machine asserts that it is enough to build one physical device, that is, a general purpose computer. Any specific problem can then be solved by writing a corresponding program to be executed (or emulated) by the general-purpose computer. Thus, universal machines correspond to general-purpose computers, and provide the philosophical basis for separating hardware from software. Furthermore, the existence of universal machines says that software can be viewed as (part of the) input.

In addition to their practical importance, the existence of universal machines (and their variants) has important consequences in the theories of computing and Computational Complexity. To demonstrate the point, we note that Theorem 1.6 implies that many questions about the behavior of a fixed (universal) machine on certain input types are undecidable. For example, it follows that for some fixed machines (i.e., universal ones), there is no algorithm that determines whether or not the (fixed) machine halts on a given input (see Exercise 1.7). Also, revisiting the proof of Theorem 1.7 (see Exercise 1.8), it follows that the Post Correspondence Problem remains undecidable even if the input sequences are restricted to having a specific length (i.e., $k$ is fixed). A more important application of universal machines to the theory of computing is presented next (i.e., in §1.3.4.2).

### 1.3.4.2  A Detour: Kolmogorov Complexity

The existence of universal machines, which may be viewed as universal languages for writing effective and succinct descriptions of objects, plays a central role in Kolmogorov Complexity. Loosely speaking, the latter theory is concerned with the length of (effective) descriptions of objects, and views the minimum such length as the inherent "complexity" of the object; that is, "simple" objects (or phenomena) are those having a short description (resp., short explanation), whereas "complex" objects have no short description. Needless to say, these (effective) descriptions have to refer to some fixed "language" (i.e., to a fixed machine that, given a succinct description of an object, produces its explicit description). Fixing any machine $M$, a string $x$ is called a description of $s$ with respect to $M$ if $M(x) = s$. The complexity of $s$ with respect to $M$, denoted $K_M(s)$, is the length of the shortest description of $s$ with respect to $M$. Certainly, we want to fix $M$ such that every string has a description with respect to $M$, and furthermore such that this description is not "significantly" longer than the description with respect to a different machine $M'$. This desire is fulfilled by the following theorem, which makes it natural to use a universal machine as the "point of reference" (i.e., as the aforementioned $M$).

**Theorem 1.10** (complexity wrt a universal machine): *Let $U$ be a universal machine. Then, for every machine $M'$, there exists a constant $c$ such that $K_U(s) \le K_{M'}(s) + c$ for every string $s$.*

The theorem follows by (setting $c = O(|\langle M' \rangle|)$ and) observing that if $x$ is a description of $s$ with respect to $M'$ then $(\langle M' \rangle, x)$ is a description of $s$ with respect to $U$. Here it is important to use an adequate encoding of pairs of strings (e.g., the pair $(\sigma_1 \cdots \sigma_k, \tau_1 \cdots \tau_\ell)$ is encoded by the string $\sigma_1 \sigma_1 \cdots \sigma_k \sigma_k 01 \tau_1 \cdots \tau_\ell$). Fixing any universal machine $U$, we define the Kolmogorov Complexity of a string $s$ as $K(s) \overset{\text{def}}{=} K_U(s)$. The reader may easily verify the following facts:

1. $K(s) \le |s| + O(1)$, for every $s$.

   (Hint: Apply Theorem 1.10 to a machine that computes the identity mapping.)

2. There exist infinitely many strings $s$ such that $K(s) \ll |s|$.

   (Hint: Consider $s = 1^n$. Alternatively, consider any machine $M$ such that $|M(x)| \gg |x|$ for every $x$.)

3. Some strings of length $n$ have complexity at least $n$. Furthermore, for every $n$ and $i$,

$$|\{s \in \{0, 1\}^n : K(s) \le n - i\}| < 2^{n-i+1}$$

   (Hint: Different strings must have different descriptions with respect to $U$.)

It can be shown that *the function $K$ is uncomputable*; see Exercise 1.11. The proof is related to the paradox captured by the following "description" of a natural number: the smallest natural number that cannot be described by an English sentence of up to a thousand letters. (The paradox amounts to observing that if the foregoing number is well defined, then we reach contradiction by noting that the foregoing sentence uses fewer than one thousand letters.) Needless to say, the foregoing sentence presupposes that any English sentence is a legitimate description in some adequate sense (e.g., in the sense captured by Kolmogorov Complexity). Specifically, the foregoing sentence presupposes that we can determine the Kolmogorov Complexity of each natural number, and thus that we can effectively produce the smallest number that has Kolmogorov Complexity exceeding some threshold (by relying on the fact that natural numbers have arbitrarily large Kolmogorov Complexity). Indeed, the paradox suggests a proof to the fact that the latter task cannot be performed; that is, *there exists no algorithm that given t produces the lexicographically first string s such that $K(s) > t$*, because if such an algorithm $A$ would have existed then $K(s) \le O(|\langle A \rangle|) + \log t$ in contradiction to the definition of $s$.

### 1.3.5 Time (and Space) Complexity

Fixing a model of computation (e.g., Turing machines) and *focusing on algorithms that halt on each input*, we consider the number of steps (i.e., applications of the computation rule) taken by the algorithm on each possible input. The latter function is called the time complexity of the algorithm (or machine); that is, $t_A : \{0, 1\}^* \to \mathbb{N}$ is called the time complexity of algorithm $A$ if, for every $x$, on input $x$ algorithm $A$ halts after exactly $t_A(x)$ steps.

We will be mostly interested in the dependence of the time complexity on the input length when taking the maximum over all inputs of the relevant length. That is, for $t_A$ as in the foregoing paragraph, we will consider $T_A : \mathbb{N} \to \mathbb{N}$ defined by $T_A(n) \stackrel{\text{def}}{=} \max_{x \in \{0,1\}^n} \{t_A(x)\}$. Abusing terminology, we sometimes refer to $T_A$ as the time complexity of $A$.

**A Small Detour: Linear Speedup and the O-Notation.** Many models of computation allow for speed-up computation by any constant factor; see Exercise 1.14, which refers to the Turing machine model. This motivates the ignoring of constant factors in stating (time) complexity upper bounds, and leads to an extensive usage of the corresponding O-notation in computer science. Recall that we say that $f : \mathbb{N} \to \mathbb{N}$ is $O(g)$, where $g : \mathbb{N} \to \mathbb{N}$, if there exists a (positive) constant $c$ such that for every (sufficiently large) $n \in \mathbb{N}$ it holds that $f(n) \le c \cdot g(n)$. (The parenthetical augmentations are intended to overcome some pathological cases, where one wishes to use natural bounding functions that "misbehave" on finitely many inputs; e.g., $g(n) = n$ evaluates to zero on 0, and $g(n) = n \log_2 n$ evaluates to zero on 1).

**The Time Complexity of a Problem.** As stated in the Preface, typically Complexity Theory is not concerned with the (time) complexity of a specific algorithm. It is rather concerned with the (time) complexity of a problem, assuming that this problem is solvable at all (by some algorithm). Intuitively, the time complexity of such a problem is defined as the time complexity of the fastest algorithm that solves this problem (assuming that the latter term is well defined).[11] Actually, we shall be interested in upper and lower bounds on the (time) complexity of algorithms that solve the problem. Thus, when we say that a certain problem $\Pi$ has complexity $T$, we actually mean that $\Pi$ has complexity at most $T$. Likewise, when we say that $\Pi$ requires time $T$, we actually mean that $\Pi$ has time complexity at least $T$.

Recall that the foregoing discussion refers to some fixed model of computation. Indeed, the complexity of a problem $\Pi$ may depend on the specific model of computation in which algorithms that solve $\Pi$ are implemented. The following Cobham-Edmonds Thesis asserts that the variation (in the time complexity) is not too big, and in particular is irrelevant to the P-vs-NP Question (as well as to almost all of the current focus of Complexity Theory).

**The Cobham-Edmonds Thesis.** As just stated, the time complexity of a problem may depend on the model of computation. For example, deciding membership in the set $\{xx : x \in \{0, 1\}^*\}$ can be done in linear time on a two-tape Turing machine, but requires quadratic time on a single-tape Turing machine (see Exercise 1.13). On the other hand, any problem that has time complexity $t$ in the model of multi-tape Turing machines has complexity $O(t^2)$ in the model of single-tape Turing machines (see Exercise 1.12). The Cobham-Edmonds Thesis asserts that the time complexities in any two "reasonable and general" models of computation are polynomially related. That is, *a problem has time complexity $t$ in some* "reasonable and general" *model of computation if and only if it has time complexity* poly($t$) *in the model of* (single-tape) *Turing machines*.

Indeed, the Cobham-Edmonds Thesis strengthens the Church-Turing Thesis. It asserts not only that the class of solvable problems is invariant as far as "reasonable and general" models of computation are concerned, but also that the time complexity (of the solvable problems) in such models is polynomially related.

We note that when compared to the Church-Turing Thesis, the Cobham-Edmonds Thesis relies on a more refined perception of what constitutes a reasonable model of computation. Specifically, we should not allow unit-cost operations (i.e., computational steps) that effect an unbounded amount of data,

---

[11] **Advanced comment:** We note that the naive assumption that a "fastest algorithm" (for solving a problem) exists is not always justified (even when ignoring constant factors; see [13, Sec. 4.2.2]). On the other hand, the assumption is essentially justified in some important cases (see, e.g., Theorem 5.5). But even in these cases the said algorithm is "fastest" (or "optimal") only up to a constant factor.

or alternatively we should charge each operation proportionally to the amount of data being effected by it. A typical example arises in the abstract RAM model rediscussed next.

Referring to the abstract RAM model (as defined in §1.3.2.2), we note that a problem has time complexity $t$ in the abstract RAM model if and only if it has time complexity poly($t$) in the model of (single-tape) Turing machines. While this assertion requires no qualification when referring to the bare model (which only includes the operation reset($\cdot$), inc($\cdot$), dec($\cdot$), load($\cdot$, $\cdot$), store($\cdot$, $\cdot$), and cond-goto($\cdot$, $\cdot$)), we need to be careful with respect to augmenting this instruction set with additional (abstract) instructions that (correspond to instructions that) are available on real-life computers. Consider, for example, augmenting the instruction set with add($r_1$, $r_2$) (resp., mult($r_1$, $r_2$)) that represents adding (resp., multiplying) the contents of registers $r_1$ and $r_2$ (and placing the result in register $r_1$). Note that using the addition instruction $t$ times may increase the length (of the bit representation) of the numbers stored in these registers by at most $t$ units,[12] but $t$ applications of the multiplication instruction may increase this length by a factor of $2^t$ (via repeated squaring). Thus, we should either restrict these operations to fixed-length integers (as done in real-life computers) or charge each of these operations in proportion to the length of the actual contents of the relevant (abstract) registers.

**Efficient Algorithms.** As hinted in the foregoing discussions, much of Complexity Theory is concerned with efficient algorithms. The latter are defined as polynomial-time algorithms (i.e., algorithms that have time complexity that is upper-bounded by a polynomial in the length of the input). By the Cobham-Edmonds Thesis, the definition of this class is invariant under the choice of a "reasonable and general" model of computation. For further discussion of the association of efficient algorithms with polynomial-time computation see Section 2.1.

**Universal Machines, Revisited.** The notion of time complexity gives rise to a time-bounded version of the universal function u (presented in Section 1.3.4). Specifically, we define $u'(\langle M \rangle, x, t) \stackrel{\text{def}}{=} y$ if on input $x$ machine $M$ halts within $t$ steps and outputs the string $y$, and $u'(\langle M \rangle, x, t) \stackrel{\text{def}}{=} \perp$ if on input $x$ machine $M$ makes more than $t$ steps. Unlike u, the function $u'$ is a total function. Furthermore, unlike any extension of u to a total function, the function $u'$

---

[12] The same consideration applies also to the other basic instructions (e.g., inc($\cdot$)), which justifies our ignoring the issue when discussing the basic instruction set. In fact, using only the basic instructions yields an even slower increase in the length of the stored numbers.

is computable. Moreover, $u'$ is computable by a machine $U'$ that, on input $X = (\langle M \rangle, x, t)$, halts after $\text{poly}(|\langle M \rangle| + |x| + t)$ steps. Indeed, machine $U'$ is a variant of a universal machine (i.e., on input $X$, machine $U'$ merely emulates $M$ for $t$ steps rather than emulating $M$ till it halts (and potentially indefinitely)). Note that the number of steps taken by $U'$ depends on the specific model of computation (and that some overhead is unavoidable because emulating each step of $M$ requires reading the relevant portion of the description of $M$).

**Space Complexity.** Another natural measure of the "complexity" of an algorithm (or a task) is the amount of memory consumed by the computation. We refer to the memory used for storing some intermediate results of the computation. Since computations that utilize memory that is sub-linear in their input length are of natural interest, it is important to use a model in which one can differentiate memory used for computation from memory used for storing the initial input or the final output. In the context of Turing machines, this is done by considering multi-tape Turing machines such that the input is presented on a special read-only tape (called the input tape), the output is written on a special write-only tape (called the output tape), and intermediate results are stored on a work-tape. Thus, the input and output tapes cannot be used for storing intermediate results. The space complexity of such a machine $M$ is defined as a function $s_M$ such that $s_M(x)$ is the number of cells of the work-tape that are scanned by $M$ on input $x$. As in the case of time complexity, we will usually refer to $S_A(n) \stackrel{\text{def}}{=} \max_{x \in \{0,1\}^n} \{s_A(x)\}$. In this book we do not discuss space complexity any further, but rather refer the interested reader to [13, Chap. 5].

### 1.3.6 Oracle Machines and Turing-Reductions

The notion of Turing-reductions, which was discussed in Section 1.3.3, is captured by the following definition of so-called *oracle machines*. Loosely speaking, an oracle machine is a machine that is augmented such that it may pose questions to the outside. We consider the case in which these questions, called queries, are answered consistently by some function $f : \{0, 1\}^* \to \{0, 1\}^*$, called the oracle. That is, if the machine makes a query $q$, then the answer it obtains is $f(q)$. In such a case, we say that the oracle machine is given access to the oracle $f$. For an oracle machine $M$, a string $x$ and a function $f$, we denote by $M^f(x)$ the output of $M$ on input $x$ when given access to the oracle $f$. (Reexamining the second part of the proof of Theorem 1.5, observe that we have actually described an oracle machine that computes $d'$ when given access to the oracle $d$.)

Oracle machines provide a formulation of procedures that use "functionally specified" subroutines. That is, the functionality of the subroutine is specified (by the aforementioned function $f$), but its operation remains unspecified. In contrast, the oracle machine (i.e., $M$) provides a full specification of how the subroutine (represented by $f$) is used. Such procedures (or rather such efficient procedures) are the subject of Chapter 3, and further discussion will appear there. Our aim in the current section is merely introducing the basic framework, which is analogous to our introducing the notion of algorithms in the current chapter, whereas the entire book focuses on efficient algorithms.

The notion of an oracle machine extends the notion of a standard computing device (machine), and thus a rigorous formulation of the former extends a formal model of the latter. Specifically, extending the model of Turing machines, we derive the following model of oracle Turing machines.

**Definition 1.11** (using an oracle):

- *An* oracle machine *is a Turing machine with a special additional tape, called the* oracle tape, *and two special states, called* oracle invocation *and* oracle spoke.
- *The* computation of the oracle machine $M$ on input $x$ and access to the oracle $f$ : $\{0, 1\}^* \to \{0, 1\}^*$ *is defined based on the successive configuration function. For configurations with a state different from* oracle invocation *the next configuration is defined as usual. Let $\gamma$ be a configuration in which the machine's state is* oracle invocation *and suppose that the actual contents of the oracle tape is $q$ (i.e., $q$ is the contents of the maximal prefix of the tape that holds bit values).*[13] *Then, the configuration following $\gamma$ is identical to $\gamma$, except that the state is* oracle spoke, *and the actual contents of the oracle tape is $f(q)$. The string $q$ is called $M$'s* query *and $f(q)$ is called the* oracle's reply.
- *The output of the oracle machine $M$ on input $x$ when given oracle access to $f$ is denoted $M^f(x)$.*

We stress that the running time of an oracle machine is the number of steps made during its (own) computation, and that the oracle's reply on each query is obtained in a single step. Combining Definition 1.11 with the notion of solving a problem (see Definitions 1.1 and 1.2), we obtain the definition of a Turing-reduction.

---

[13] This fits the definition of the *actual initial contents of a tape of a Turing machine* (cf. Section 1.3.2). A common convention is that the oracle can be invoked only when the machine's head resides at the leftmost cell of the oracle tape.

**Definition 1.12** (Turing reduction): *A problem* Π *is* Turing-reducible *to a problem* Π' *if there exists an oracle machine M such that for every function f that solves* Π' *it holds that M^f solves* Π.

It follows that if there exists an algorithm for solving Π', then there exists an algorithm for solving Π. Indeed, in the proof of Theorem 1.5 we used the contrapositive of the foregoing (i.e., if no algorithm can solve Π, then no algorithm can solve Π'). Recall that (efficient) reductions are the subject matter of Chapter 3, and so we shall return to them at greater length at that point.

### 1.3.7 Restricted Models

We mention that restricted models of computation are often mentioned in the context of a course on computability, but they will play no role in the current book. One such model is the model of finite automata, which in some variant coincides with Turing machines that have space complexity zero (equiv., constant).

In our opinion, the most important motivation for the study of these restricted models of computation is that they provide simple models for some natural (or artificial) phenomena. This motivation, however, seems only remotely related to the study of the complexity of various computational tasks, which calls for the consideration of general models of computation and the evaluation of the complexity of computation with respect to such models.

## 1.4 Non-Uniform Models (Circuits and Advice)

In the current book, we only use non-uniform models of computation as a source of some natural computational problems (cf. Section 4.3.1). Specifically, we will refer to the satisfiability of Boolean circuits (defined in §1.4.1.1) and formulae (defined in §1.4.3.1). We mention, however, that these models are typically considered for other purposes (see a brief discussion that follows).

By a non-uniform model of computation we mean a model in which for each possible input length a different computing device is considered, while there is no "uniformity" requirement relating devices that correspond to different input lengths. Furthermore, this collection of devices is infinite by nature, and (in the absence of a uniformity requirement) this collection may not even have a finite description. Nevertheless, each device in the collection has a finite description. In fact, the relationship between the size of the device (resp., the length of its description) and the length of the input that it handles will be of major concern. Specifically, the size of these devices gives rise to a complexity measure that can be used to upper-bound the time complexity of corresponding algorithms.

Non-uniform models of computation are considered either toward the development of techniques for proving complexity lower bounds or as providing simplified upper bounds on the ability of efficient algorithms.[14] In both cases, the uniformity condition is eliminated in the interest of simplicity and with the hope (and belief) that nothing substantial is lost as far as the issues at hand are concerned. In the context of developing lower bounds, the hope is that the finiteness of all parameters (i.e., the input length and the device's description) will allow for the application of combinatorial techniques to analyze the limitations of certain settings of parameters. We mention that this hope has materialized in some restricted cases (see Section 1.4.3).

We will focus on two related models of non-uniform computing devices: Boolean circuits (Section 1.4.1) and "machines that take advice" (Section 1.4.2). The former model is more adequate for the study of the evolution of computation (i.e., development of "lower bound techniques"), whereas the latter is more adequate for modeling purposes (e.g., limiting the ability of efficient algorithms).

## 1.4.1  Boolean Circuits

The most popular model of non-uniform computation is the one of Boolean circuits. Historically, this model was introduced for the purpose of describing the "logic operation" of real-life electronic circuits. Ironically, nowadays this model provides the stage for some of the most practically removed studies in Complexity Theory (which aim at developing methods that may eventually lead to an understanding of the inherent limitations of efficient algorithms).

### 1.4.1.1  The Basic Model

A Boolean circuit is a directed acyclic graph[15] *with labels on the vertices,* to be discussed shortly. For the sake of simplicity, we disallow isolated vertices (i.e., vertices with no incoming or outgoing edges), and thus the graph's vertices are of three types: *sources, sinks,* and *internal vertices.*

---

[14] **Advanced comment:** The second case refers mainly to efficient algorithms that are given a pair of inputs (of (polynomially) related length) such that these algorithms are analyzed with respect to fixing one input (arbitrarily) and varying the other input (typically, at random). Typical examples include the context of de-randomization (cf. [13, Sec. 8.3]) and the setting of zero-knowledge (cf. [13, Sec. 9.2]).

[15] See Appendix A.1.

1. Internal vertices are vertices having incoming and outgoing edges (i.e., they have in-degree and out-degree at least 1). In the context of Boolean circuits, internal vertices are called gates. Each gate is labeled by a Boolean operation, where the operations that are typically considered are $\wedge$, $\vee$ and $\neg$ (corresponding to and, or and neg). In addition, we require that gates labeled $\neg$ have in-degree 1. The in-degree of $\wedge$-gates and $\vee$-gates may be any number greater than zero, and the same holds for the out-degree of any gate.

2. The graph sources (i.e., vertices with no incoming edges) are called input terminals. Each input terminal is labeled by a natural number (which is to be thought of as the index of an input variable). (For the sake of defining formulae (see §1.4.3.1), we allow different input terminals to be labeled by the same number.)[16]

3. The graph sinks (i.e., vertices with no outgoing edges) are called output terminals, and we require that they have in-degree 1. Each output terminal is labeled by a natural number such that if the circuit has $m$ output terminals then they are labeled $1, 2, \ldots, m$. That is, we disallow different output terminals to be labeled by the same number, and insist that the labels of the output terminals are consecutive numbers. (Indeed, the labels of the output terminals will correspond to the indices of locations in the circuit's output.)

See the example in Figure 1.3. For the sake of simplicity, we also mandate that the labels of the input terminals are consecutive numbers.[17]

A Boolean circuit with $n$ different input labels and $m$ output terminals induces (and indeed computes) a function from $\{0, 1\}^n$ to $\{0, 1\}^m$ defined as follows. For any fixed string $x \in \{0, 1\}^n$, we iteratively define the value of vertices in the circuit such that the input terminals are assigned the corresponding bits in $x = x_1 \cdots x_n$ and the values of other vertices are determined in the natural manner. That is:

- An input terminal with label $i \in \{1, \ldots, n\}$ is assigned the $i^{\text{th}}$ bit of $x$ (i.e., the value $x_i$).

---

[16] This is not needed in the case of general circuits, because we can just feed outgoing edges of the same input terminal to many gates. Note, however, that this is not allowed in the case of formulae, where all non-sinks are required to have out-degree exactly 1.

[17] This convention slightly complicates the construction of circuits that ignore some of the input values. Specifically, we use artificial gadgets that have incoming edges from the corresponding input terminals, and compute an adequate constant. To avoid having this constant as an output terminal, we feed it into an auxiliary gate such that the value of the latter is determined by the other incoming edge (e.g., a constant 0 fed into an $\vee$-gate). See an example of dealing with $x_3$ in Figure 1.3.

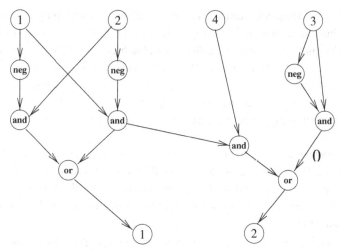

Figure 1.3. A circuit computing $f(x_1, x_2, x_3, x_4) = (x_1 \oplus x_2, x_1 \wedge \neg x_2 \wedge x_4)$.

- If the children of a gate (of in-degree $d$) that is labeled $\wedge$ have values $v_1, v_2, \ldots, v_d$, then the gate is assigned the value $\wedge_{i=1}^{d} v_i$. The value of a gate labeled $\vee$ (or $\neg$) is determined analogously.

  Indeed, the hypothesis that the circuit is acyclic implies that the following natural process of determining values for the circuit's vertices is well defined: As long as the value of some vertex is undetermined, there exists a vertex such that its value is undetermined but the values of all its children are determined. Thus, the process can make progress, and terminates when the values of all vertices (including the output terminals) are determined.

The value of the circuit on input $x$ (i.e., the output computed by the circuit on input $x$) is $y = y_1 \cdots y_m$, where $y_i$ is the value assigned by the foregoing process to the output terminal labeled $i$. We note that *there exists a polynomial-time algorithm that, given a circuit $C$ and a corresponding input $x$, outputs the value of $C$ on input $x$.* This algorithm determines the values of the circuit's vertices, going from the circuit's input terminals to its output terminals.

We say that a family of circuits $(C_n)_{n \in \mathbb{N}}$ computes a function $f : \{0, 1\}^* \to \{0, 1\}^*$ if for every $n$ the circuit $C_n$ computes the restriction of $f$ to strings of length $n$. In other words, for every $x \in \{0, 1\}^*$, it must hold that $C_{|x|}(x) = f(x)$.

**Bounded and Unbounded Fan-in.** It is often natural to consider circuits in which each gate has at most two incoming edges.[18] In this case, the types of

---

[18] Indeed, the term bounded fan-in suggests that the upper bound on the number of incoming edges may be any fixed constant, but such circuits can be emulated by circuits with two-argument operations while incurring only a constant factor blowup in their size. The same reason justifies the assertion that the choice of a full basis is immaterial, because each such

(two-argument) Boolean operations that we allow is immaterial (as long as we consider a "full basis" of such operations, i.e., a set of operations that can implement any other two-argument Boolean operation). Such circuits are called circuits of bounded fan-in. In contrast, other studies are concerned with circuits of unbounded fan-in, where each gate may have an arbitrary number of incoming edges. Needless to say, in the case of circuits of unbounded fan-in, the choice of allowed Boolean operations is important and one focuses on operations that are "uniform" (across the number of operands, e.g., $\wedge$ and $\vee$). Unless specified differently, we shall refer to circuits of unbounded fan-in; however, in many of the cases that we consider, the choice is immaterial.

### 1.4.1.2 Circuit Complexity

As stated earlier, the Boolean circuit model is used in Complexity Theory mainly as a basis for defining a (non-uniform) complexity measure. Specifically, the complexity of circuits is defined as their size.

**Circuit Size as a Complexity Measure.** The size of a circuit is the number of its edges. When considering a family of circuits $(C_n)_{n \in \mathbb{N}}$ that computes a function $f : \{0, 1\}^* \rightarrow \{0, 1\}^*$, we are interested in the size of $C_n$ as a function of $n$. Specifically, we say that this family has size complexity $s : \mathbb{N} \rightarrow \mathbb{N}$ if for every $n$ the size of $C_n$ is $s(n)$. The circuit complexity of a function $f$, denoted $s_f$, is the infimum of the size complexity of all families of circuits that compute $f$. Alternatively, for each $n$ we may consider the size of the smallest circuit that computes the restriction of $f$ to $n$-bit strings (denoted $f_n$), and set $s_f(n)$ accordingly. We stress that non-uniformity is implicit in this definition, because no conditions are made regarding the relation between the various circuits used to compute the function on different input lengths.[19]

**On the Circuit Complexity of Functions.** We highlight some simple facts regarding the circuit complexity of functions. These facts are in clear correspondence to facts regarding Kolmogorov Complexity mentioned in §1.3.4.2, and establishing them is left as an exercise (see Exercise 1.15).

1. Most importantly, any Boolean function can be computed by some family of circuits, and thus the circuit complexity of any function is well

---

basis allows for emulating any two-argument operation by a constant size circuit. Indeed, in both cases, we disregard constant factor changes in the circuit size.

[19] **Advanced comment:** We also note that, in contrast to footnote 11, the circuit model and the corresponding (circuit size) complexity measure support the notion of an optimal computing device: Each function $f$ has a unique size complexity $s_f$ (and not merely upper and lower bounds on its complexity).

defined. Furthermore, each function has at most exponential circuit complexity.

2. Some functions have polynomial circuit complexity. In particular, any function that has time complexity $t$ (i.e., is computed by an algorithm of time complexity $t$) has circuit complexity at most $\text{poly}(t)$. Furthermore, the corresponding circuit family is uniform (in a natural sense to be discussed in the next paragraph).

3. Almost all Boolean functions require exponential circuit complexity. Specifically, the number of functions mapping $\{0, 1\}^n$ to $\{0, 1\}$ that can be computed by some circuit of size $s$ is smaller than $s^{2s}$.

Note that the first fact implies that families of circuits can compute functions that are uncomputable by algorithms. Furthermore, this phenomenon occurs also when restricting attention to families of polynomial-size circuits. See further discussion in Section 1.4.2 (and specifically Theorem 1.14).

**Uniform Families.** A family of polynomial-size circuits $(C_n)_{n\in\mathbb{N}}$ is called uniform if given $n$ one can construct the circuit $C_n$ in $\text{poly}(n)$-time. Note that *if a function is computable by a uniform family of polynomial-size circuits then it is computable by a polynomial-time algorithm.* This algorithm first constructs the adequate circuit (which can be done in polynomial time by the uniformity hypothesis), and then evaluates this circuit on the given input (which can be done in time that is polynomial in the size of the circuit).

Note that limitations on the computing power of arbitrary families of polynomial-size circuits certainly hold for uniform families (of polynomial-size circuits), which in turn yield limitations on the computing power of polynomial-time algorithms. Thus, lower bounds on the circuit complexity of functions yield analogous lower bounds on their time complexity. Furthermore, as is often the case in mathematics and science, disposing of an auxiliary condition that is not well understood (i.e., uniformity) may turn out to be fruitful. Indeed, this has occured in the study of classes of restricted circuits, which is reviewed in Section 1.4.3.

### 1.4.2 Machines That Take Advice

General (non-uniform) circuit families and uniform circuit families are two extremes with respect to the "amounts of non-uniformity" in the computing device. Intuitively, in the former, non-uniformity is only bounded by the size of the device, whereas in the latter, the amount of non-uniformity is zero. Here we consider a model that allows for decoupling the size of the computing device from the amount of non-uniformity, which may range from zero to the device's size. Specifically, we consider algorithms that "take a non-uniform advice" that depends only on the input length. The amount of non-uniformity will be defined to equal the length of the corresponding advice (as a function of the input length).

**Definition 1.13** (taking advice): *We say that* algorithm $A$ computes the function $f$ using advice of length $\ell : \mathbb{N} \to \mathbb{N}$ *if there exists an infinite sequence* $(a_n)_{n \in \mathbb{N}}$ *such that*

1. *For every* $x \in \{0, 1\}^*$, *it holds that* $A(a_{|x|}, x) = f(x)$.
2. *For every* $n \in \mathbb{N}$, *it holds that* $|a_n| = \ell(n)$.

*The sequence* $(a_n)_{n \in \mathbb{N}}$ *is called the* advice sequence.

Note that any function having circuit complexity $s$ can be computed using advice of length $O(s \log s)$, where the length upper bound is due to the fact that a graph with $v$ vertices and $e$ edges can be described by a string of length $2e \log_2 v$. Note that the model of machines that use advice allows for some sharper bounds than the ones stated in §1.4.1.2: Every function can be computed using advice of length $\ell$ such that $\ell(n) = 2^n$, and some uncomputable functions can be computed using advice of length 1.

**Theorem 1.14** (the power of advice): *There exist functions that can be computed using one-bit advice but cannot be computed without advice.*

**Proof:** Starting with any uncomputable Boolean function $f : \mathbb{N} \to \{0, 1\}$, consider the function $f'$ defined as $f'(x) = f(|x|)$; that is, the value of $f'(x)$ only depends on the length of $x$ (and, specifically, equals $f(|x|)$). Note that $f$ is Turing-reducible to $f'$ (e.g., on input $n$ make any $n$-bit query to $f'$, and return the answer).[20] Thus, $f'$ cannot be computed without advice. On the other hand, $f'$ can be easily computed by using the advice sequence $(a_n)_{n \in \mathbb{N}}$ such that $a_n = f(n)$; that is, the algorithm merely outputs the advice bit (and indeed $a_{|x|} = f(|x|) = f'(x)$, for every $x \in \{0, 1\}^*$). ∎

### 1.4.3 Restricted Models

The model of Boolean circuits (cf. §1.4.1.1) allows for the introduction of many natural subclasses of computing devices. Following is a laconic review of a few

---

[20] Indeed, this Turing-reduction is not efficient (i.e., it runs in exponential time in $|n| = \log_2 n$), but this is immaterial in the current context.

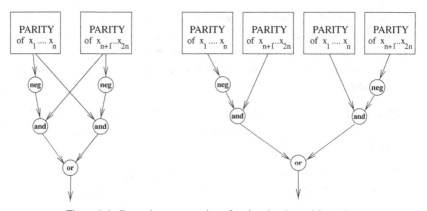

Figure 1.4. Recursive construction of parity circuits and formulae.

of these subclasses. (For further detail regarding the study of these subclasses, the interested reader is referred to [1].)

### 1.4.3.1 Boolean Formulae

In (general) Boolean circuits the non-sink vertices are allowed arbitrary out-degree. This means that the same intermediate value can be reused without being recomputed (and while increasing the size complexity by only one unit). Such "free" reusage of intermediate values is disallowed in Boolean formulae, which are formally defined as Boolean circuits in which all non-sink vertices have out-degree 1. This means that the underlying graph of a Boolean formula is a tree (see Appendix A.2), and it can be written as a Boolean expression over Boolean variables by traversing this tree (and registering the vertices' labels in the order traversed). Indeed, we have allowed different input terminals to be assigned the same label in order to allow formulae in which the same variable occurs multiple times.

As in the case of general circuits, one is interested in the size of these restricted circuits (i.e., the size of families of formulae computing various functions). We mention that quadratic lower bounds are known for the formula size of simple functions (e.g., `parity`), whereas these functions have linear circuit complexity. This discrepancy is depicted in Figure 1.4.

**Formulae in CNF and DNF.** A restricted type of Boolean formulae consists of formulae that are in conjunctive normal form (CNF). Such a formula consists of a conjunction of clauses, where each clause is a disjunction of literals, each being either a variable or its negation. That is, such formulae are represented by layered circuits of unbounded fan-in in which the first layer consists of

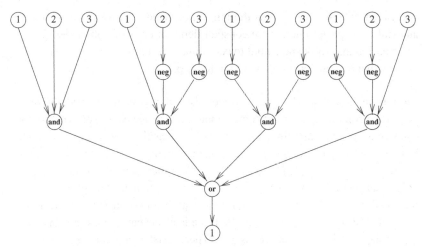

Figure 1.5. A 3DNF formula computing $x_1 \oplus x_2 \oplus x_3$ as $(x_1 \wedge x_2 \wedge x_3) \vee (x_1 \wedge \neg x_2 \wedge \neg x_3) \vee (\neg x_1 \wedge x_2 \wedge \neg x_3) \vee (\neg x_1 \wedge \neg x_2 \wedge x_3)$.

neg-gates that compute the negation of input variables, the second layer consists of or-gates that compute the logical-or of subsets of inputs and negated inputs, and the third layer consists of a single and-gate that computes the logical-and of the values computed in the second layer. Note that each Boolean function can be computed by a family of CNF formulae of exponential size (see Exercise 1.17), and that the size of CNF formulae may be exponentially larger than the size of ordinary formulae computing the same function (e.g., parity).[21] For a constant $k$ (e.g., $k = 2, 3$), a formula is said to be in $k$CNF if its CNF has disjunctions of size at most $k$. An analogous restricted type of Boolean formulae refers to formulae that are in disjunctive normal form (DNF). Such a formula consists of a disjunction of a conjunction of literals, and when each conjunction has at most $k$ literals we say that the formula is in $k$DNF. (Figure 1.5 depicts a 3DNF formula that computes the parity of three variables.)

### 1.4.3.2 Other Restricted Classes of Circuits

Two other restricted classes of circuits, which have received a lot of attention in Complexity Theory (but are not used in this book), are the classes of constant-depth circuits and monotone circuits.

**Constant-depth Circuits.** Circuits have a "natural structure" (i.e., their structure as graphs). One natural parameter regarding this structure is the depth

---

[21] See Exercise 1.18.

of a circuit, which is defined as the longest directed path from any source to any sink. Of special interest are constant-depth circuits of unbounded fan-in. We mention that sub-exponential lower bounds are known for the size of such circuits that compute a simple function (e.g., `parity`).

**Monotone Circuits.** The circuit model also allows for the consideration of monotone computing devices: A monotone circuit is one having only monotone gates (e.g., gates computing $\wedge$ and $\vee$, but no negation gates (i.e., $\neg$-gates)). Needless to say, monotone circuits can only compute monotone functions, where a function $f : \{0, 1\}^n \rightarrow \{0, 1\}$ is called monotone if for any $x \preceq y$ it holds that $f(x) \leq f(y)$ (where $x_1 \cdots x_n \preceq y_1 \cdots y_n$ if and only if for every bit position $i$ it holds that $x_i \leq y_i$). One natural question is whether, as far as monotone functions are concerned, there is a substantial loss in using only monotone circuits. The answer is *yes*: There exist monotone functions that have polynomial circuit complexity but require sub-exponential-size monotone circuits.

## 1.5 Complexity Classes

Complexity classes are sets of computational problems. Typically, such classes are defined by fixing three parameters:

1. A *type of computational problems* (see Section 1.2). Indeed, the most standard complexity classes refer to decision problems, but classes of search problems, promise problems, and other types of problems are also considered.
2. A *model of computation*, which may be either uniform (see Section 1.3) or non-uniform (see Section 1.4).
3. A *complexity measure* and a *limiting function* (or a set of functions), which when put together limit the class of computations of the previous item; that is, we refer to the class of computations that have complexity not exceeding the specified function (or set of functions).

   For example, in Section 1.3.5, we mentioned time complexity and space complexity, which apply to any uniform model of computation. We also mentioned polynomial-time computations, which are computations in which the time complexity (as a function) does not exceed some polynomial (i.e., is a member of the set of polynomial functions).

The most common complexity classes refer to decision problems, and are sometimes defined as classes of sets rather than classes of the corresponding decision problems. That is, one often says that a set $S \subseteq \{0, 1\}^*$ is in the class $\mathcal{C}$, rather than saying that *the problem of deciding membership in $S$* is in the class $\mathcal{C}$. Likewise, one talks of classes of relations rather than classes of the corresponding search problems (i.e., saying that $R \subseteq \{0, 1\}^* \times \{0, 1\}^*$ is in the class $\mathcal{C}$ means that *the search problem of $R$* is in the class $\mathcal{C}$).

# Exercises

*Exercise 1.1 (a quiz)*

1. What is the default representation of integers (in Complexity Theory)?
2. What are search and decision problems?
3. What is the motivation for considering the model of Turing machines?
4. What does the Church-Turing Thesis assert?
5. What is a universal algorithm?
6. What does undecidability mean?
7. What is the time complexity of an algorithm?
8. What does the Cobham-Edmonds Thesis assert?
9. What are Boolean circuits and formulae?

*Exercise 1.2* Prove that any function that can be computed by a Turing machine can be computed by a machine that never moves left of the end of the tape.

*Guideline:* Modify the original machine by "marking" the leftmost cell of the tape (by using special symbols such that the original contents is maintained). Needless to say, this marking corresponds to an extension of the tape's symbols.

*Exercise 1.3 (single-tape versus multi-tape Turing machines)* Prove that a function can be computed by a single-tape Turing machine if and only if it is computable by a multi-tape (e.g., two-tape) Turing machine.

*Guideline:* The emulation of the multi-tape Turing machine on a single-tape machine is based on storing all the original tapes on a single tape such that the $i^{\text{th}}$ cell of the single tape records the contents of the $i^{\text{th}}$ cell of each of the original tapes. In addition, the $i^{\text{th}}$ cell of the single tape records an indication as to which of the original heads reside in the $i^{\text{th}}$ cell of the corresponding original tapes. To emulate a single step of the original machine, the new machine scans its tape, finds all original head locations, and retrieves the corresponding cell contents. Based on this information, the emulating machine effects the corresponding step (according to the original transition function) by modifying its (single) tape's contents in an analogous manner.

***Exercise 1.4 (computing the sum of natural numbers)*** Prove that a Turing machine can add natural numbers; that is, outline a (multi-tape) Turing machine that on input a pair of integers (in binary representation) outputs their sum. Specifically, show that the straightforward addition algorithm can be implemented in linear time by a multi-tape Turing machine.

*Guideline:* A straightforward implementation of addition on a two-tape Turing machine starts by copying the two (input) integers (from the input tape) to the second tape such that the $i^{th}$ least significant bits of both integers reside in the $i^{th}$ cell (of the second tape).

***Exercise 1.5 (Turing machines vs abstract RAM)*** Prove that an abstract RAM can be emulated by a Turing machine.

*Guideline:* Recall that by our conventions, the abstract RAM computation is initialized such that only a prefix of the memory cells contains meaningful data, and (the length of) this prefix is specified in a special register. Thus, during the emulation (of the abstract RAM), we only need to keep track of the contents of these memory cells as well as the contents of any other memory cells that were accessed during the computation (and the contents of all registers). Consequently, during the emulation, the Turing machine's tape will contain a list of the RAM's memory cells that were accessed so far as well as their current contents. When we emulate a RAM instruction that refers to some memory location (which is specified in the contents of a fixed register), we first check whether the relevant RAM cell appears on our list, and accordingly either augment the list by a corresponding entry or modify this entry as required.

***Exercise 1.6 (Rice's Theorem (Theorem 1.6))*** Let $\mathcal{F}$ and $S_\mathcal{F}$ be as in Theorem 1.6. Present a Turing-reduction of d to $S_\mathcal{F}$.

*Guideline:* Let $f_\perp$ denote the function that is undefined on all inputs. Assume, without loss of generality, that $f_\perp \notin \mathcal{F}$, let $f_1$ denote an arbitrary function in $\mathcal{F}$, and let $M_1$ be an arbitrary fixed machine that computes $f_1$. Then, the reduction maps an input $\langle M \rangle$ for d to the input $\langle M' \rangle$ for $S_\mathcal{F}$ such that machine $M'$ operates as follows on input $x$:

1. First, machine $M'$ emulates $M$ on input $\langle M \rangle$.
2. If $M$ halts (in Step 1), then $M'$ emulates $M_1(x)$, and outputs whatever it does.

Note that the mapping from $\langle M \rangle$ to $\langle M' \rangle$ is easily computable (by augmenting $M$ with the fixed machine $M_1$). Now, if $d(\langle M \rangle) = 1$, then machine $M'$ reaches Step 2, and thus $M'(x) = f_1(x)$ for every $x$, which in turn implies $\langle M' \rangle \in S_\mathcal{F}$

(because $M'$ computes $f_1 \in \mathcal{F}$). On the other hand, if $d(\langle M \rangle) = 0$, then machine $M'$ remains stuck in Step 1, and thus $M'$ does not halt on any $x$, which in turn implies $\langle M' \rangle \notin S_{\mathcal{F}}$ (because $M'$ computes $f_\perp \notin \mathcal{F}$).

**Exercise 1.7** Prove that there exists a Turing machine $M$ such that there is no algorithm that determines whether or not $M$ halts on a given input.

*Guideline:* Let $M$ be a universal machine, and present a Turing-reduction from h to $h_M$, where $h_M(x) = h(\langle M \rangle, x)$.

**Exercise 1.8 (Post Correspondence Problem (Theorem 1.7))** The following exercise is significantly more difficult than the norm. Present a Turing-reduction of h to the Post Correspondence Problem, denoted PCP. Furthermore, use a reduction that maps an instance $(\langle M \rangle, x)$ of h to a pair of sequences $((\alpha_1, \ldots, \alpha_k), (\beta_1, \ldots, \beta_k))$ such that only $\alpha_1$ and $\beta_1$ depend on $x$, whereas $k$ as well as the other strings depend only on $M$.

*Guideline:* Consider a modified version of the Post Correspondence Problem, denoted MPCP, in which the first index in the solution sequence must equal 1 (i.e., $i_1 = 1$). Reduce h to MPCP, and next reduce MPCP to PCP. The main reduction (i.e., of h to MPCP) maps $(\langle M \rangle, x)$ to $((\alpha_1, \ldots, \alpha_k), (\beta_1, \ldots, \beta_k))$ such that a solution sequence (i.e., $i_1, \ldots, i_\ell$ s.t. $\alpha_{i_1} \cdots \alpha_{i_\ell} = \beta_1 \cdots \beta_{i_\ell}$) yields a full description of the computation of $M$ on input $x$ (i.e., the sequence of all instantaneous configurations in this computation). Specifically, $\alpha_1$ will describe the initial configuration of $M$ on input $x$, whereas $\beta_1$ will be essentially empty (except for a delimiter, denoted #, which is also used at the beginning and at the end of $\alpha_1$). Assuming that the set of tape-symbols and the set of states of $M$ are disjoint (i.e., $\Sigma \cap Q = \emptyset$), configurations will be described as sequences over their union (i.e., sequences over $\Sigma \cap Q$, where $\# \notin \Sigma \cup Q$). Other pairs $(\alpha_i, \beta_i)$ include

- For every tape-symbol $\sigma$, we shall have $\alpha_i = \beta_i = \sigma$ (for some $i$). We shall also have $\alpha_i = \beta_i = \#$ (for some $i$). Such pairs reflect the preservation of the tape's contents (whenever the head location is not present at the current cell).
- For every non-halting state $q$ and every transition regarding $q$, we shall have a pair reflecting this transition. For example, if the transition function maps $(q, \sigma)$ to $(q', \sigma', +1)$, then we have $\beta_i = q\sigma$ and $\alpha_i = \sigma'q'$ (for some $i$). For left movement (i.e., if the transition function maps $(q, \sigma)$ to $(q', \sigma', -1)$) we have $\beta_i = \tau q \sigma$ and $\alpha_i = q'\tau\sigma'$. Assuming that blank symbols (i.e., _) are only written to the left of other blank symbols (and when moving left), if the transition function maps $(q, \sigma)$ to $(q', \_, -1)$, then we have $\beta_i = \tau q \sigma$ and $\alpha_i = q'\tau$ (rather than $\alpha_i = q'\tau\_$).

- Assuming that the machine halts in state $p$ only when it resides in the leftmost cell (and after writing blanks in all cells), we have $\beta_i = p_-\#\#$ and $\alpha_i = \#$ (for some $i$).

Note that in a solution sequence $i_1, \ldots, i_\ell$ such that $\alpha_{i_1} \cdots \alpha_{i_\ell} = \beta_1 \cdots \beta_{i_\ell}$, for every $t < \ell$ it holds that $\beta_{i_1} \cdots \beta_{i_t}$ is a prefix of $\alpha_{i_1} \cdots \alpha_{i_t}$ such that the latter contains exactly one configuration less than the former. The relations between the pairs $(\alpha_i, \beta_i)$ guarantee that these prefixes are prefixes of the sequence of all instantaneous configurations in the computation of $M$ on input $x$, and a solution can be completed only if this computation halts. For details see [16, Sec. 8.5] or [30, Sec. 5.2].

**Exercise 1.9 (total functions extending the universal function)** Present an algorithm that, given a description of a Turing machine and a corresponding instantaneous configuration, determines the instantaneous configuration that results by performing a single step of the given machine on the given instantaneous configuration. Note that this exercise requires fixing a concrete representation of Turing machines and corresponding configurations.

*Guideline:* Use the representation of configurations provided in §1.3.2.1.

**Exercise 1.10 (total functions extending the universal function)** Let $u$ be the function computed by any universal machine (for a fixed reasonable model of computation). Prove that any extension of $u$ to a total function (i.e., any total function $\hat{u}$ that agrees with the partial function $u$ on all the inputs on which the latter is defined) is uncomputable.

*Guideline:* The claim is easy to prove for the special case of the total function $\hat{u}$ that extends $u$ such that the special symbol $\perp$ is assigned to inputs on which $u$ is undefined (i.e., $\hat{u}(\langle M \rangle, x) \overset{\text{def}}{=} \perp$ if $u$ is not defined on $(\langle M \rangle, x)$ and $\hat{u}(\langle M \rangle, x) \overset{\text{def}}{=} u(\langle M \rangle, x)$ otherwise). In this case $h(\langle M \rangle, x) = 1$ if and only if $\hat{u}(\langle M \rangle, x) \neq \perp$, and so the halting function $h$ is Turing-reducible to $\hat{u}$. In the general case, we may adapt the proof of Theorem 1.5 by using the fact that for any machine $M$ that halts on every input, it holds that $\hat{u}(\langle M \rangle, x) = u(\langle M \rangle, x)$ for every $x$ (and in particular for $x = \langle M \rangle$).

**Exercise 1.11 (uncomputability of Kolmogorov Complexity)** Prove that the Kolmogorov Complexity function, denoted $K$, is uncomputable.

*Guideline:* Consider, for every integer $t$, the string $s_t$ that is defined as the lexicographically first string of Kolmogorov Complexity exceeding $t$ (i.e., $s_t \overset{\text{def}}{=} \min_{s \in \{0,1\}^*} \{K(s) > t\}$). Note that $s_t$ is well defined and has length at most $t$ (see

Fact 3 in §1.3.4.2). Assuming that $K$ is computable, we reach a contradiction by noting that $s_t$ has description length $O(1) + \log_2 t$ (because it may be described by combining a fixed machine that computes $K$ with the integer $t$).

***Exercise 1.12 (single-tape versus multi-tape Turing machines, refined)*** In continuation of Exercise 1.3, show that any function that can be computed by a multi-tape Turing machine in time complexity $t$ can be computed by a single-tape Turing machine in time complexity $O(t^2)$.

***Exercise 1.13 (single-tape vs two-tape Turing machines, a complexity gap)*** The following exercise is significantly more difficult than the norm. Show that the emulation upper bound stated in Exercise 1.12 is optimal. Specifically, prove that deciding membership in the set $\{xx : x \in \{0, 1\}^*\}$ requires quadratic time on a single-tape Turing machine, and note that this decision problem can be solved in linear time on a two-tape Turing machine.

*Guideline:* Proving the quadratic time lower bound is quite non-trivial. One proof is by a "reduction" from a communication complexity problem [19, Sec. 12.2]. Intuitively, a *single-tape* Turing machine that decides membership in the aforementioned set can be viewed as a channel of communication between the two parts of the input. Specifically, focusing our attention on inputs of the form $y0^n z0^n$, for $y, z \in \{0, 1\}^n$, note that each time that the machine passes from the one part to the other part it carries $O(1)$ bits of information (in its internal state) while making at least $n$ steps. The proof is completed by invoking the linear lower bound on the communication complexity of the (two-argument) identity function (i.e, $\mathrm{id}(y, z) = 1$ if $y = z$ and $\mathrm{id}(y, z) = 0$ otherwise); cf. [19, Chap. 1].

***Exercise 1.14 (linear speedup of Turing machine)*** Prove that any problem that can be solved by a two-tape Turing machine that has time complexity $t$ can be solved by another two-tape Turing machine having time complexity $t'$, where $t'(n) = O(n) + (t(n)/2)$. Prove an analogous result for one-tape Turing machines, where $t'(n) = O(n^2) + (t(n)/2)$.

*Guideline:* Consider a machine that uses a larger alphabet, capable of encoding a constant (denoted $c$) number of symbols of the original machine, and thus capable of emulating $c$ steps of the original machine in $O(1)$ steps, where the constant in the O-notation is a universal constant (independent of $c$). Note that the $O(n)$ term accounts for a preprocessing that converts the binary input to work-alphabet of the new machine (which encodes $c$ input bits in one alphabet symbol). Thus, a similar result for one-tape Turing machines seems to require an additive $O(n^2)$ term.

**Exercise 1.15 (on the circuit complexity of functions)** Prove the following facts:

1. The circuit complexity of any Boolean function is at most exponential.

    *Guideline:* $f_n : \{0, 1\}^n \rightarrow \{0, 1\}$ can be computed by a circuit of size $O(n2^n)$ that implements a look-up table. See also Exercise 1.17.

2. Some functions have polynomial circuit complexity. In particular, any function that has time complexity $t$ (i.e., is computed by an algorithm of time complexity $t$), has circuit complexity poly($t$). Furthermore, the corresponding circuit family is uniform.

    *Guideline:* Consider a Turing machine that computes the function, and consider its computation on a generic $n$-bit long input. The corresponding computation can be emulated by a circuit that consists of $t(n)$ layers such that each layer represents an instantaneous configuration of the machine, and the relation between consecutive configurations is captured by ("uniform") local gadgets in the circuit. For further details see the proof of Theorem 4.5, which presents a similar emulation.

3. Almost all Boolean functions require exponential circuit complexity. Specifically, show that the number of functions mapping $\{0, 1\}^n$ to $\{0, 1\}$ that can be computed by some circuit of size $s$ is smaller than $s^{2s}$, which is smaller than $2^{2^n}$ unless $2s \log_2 s \geq 2^n$. Note that the total number of functions mapping $\{0, 1\}^n$ to $\{0, 1\}$ is $2^{2^n}$.

    *Guideline:* Show that, without loss of generality, we may consider circuits of bounded fan-in. The number of such circuits having $v$ vertices is at most $\left(2 \cdot \binom{v}{2} + v\right)^v$, where for each gate we either have a choice of binary operation (i.e., $\wedge$ or $\vee$) and two feeding vertices or a choice of a single feeding vertex (for a $\neg$-gate). Note that the input terminals each have a choice of an index of an input variable in $[n]$, and by our conventions $v \geq n$.

**Exercise 1.16 (the class $\mathcal{P}$/poly)** We denote by $\mathcal{P}/\ell$ the class of decision problems that can be solved in polynomial time with advice of length $\ell$, and by $\mathcal{P}$/poly the union of $\mathcal{P}/p$ taken over all polynomials $p$. Prove that a decision problem is in $\mathcal{P}$/poly if and only if it has polynomial circuit complexity.

*Guideline:* Suppose that a problem can be solved by a polynomial-time algorithm $A$ using the polynomially bounded advice sequence $(a_n)_{n \in \mathbb{N}}$. We obtain a family of polynomial-size circuits that solves the same problem by observing that the computation of $A(a_{|x|}, x)$ can be emulated by a circuit of poly($|x|$)-size, *which incorporates $a_{|x|}$ and is given $x$ as input*. That is, we construct a circuit $C_n$ such that $C_n(x) = A(a_n, x)$ holds for every $x \in \{0, 1\}^n$ (analogously to the way $C_x$ is constructed in the proof of Theorem 4.5, where it holds that $C_x(y) = M_R(x, y)$ for every $y$ of adequate length). On the other hand, given a family of polynomial-size circuits, we obtain a polynomial-time advice-taking machine that emulates this family when *using advice that provides the description of the relevant circuits*. (Indeed, we use the fact that a circuit of size $s$ can be described by a string of length $O(s \log s)$.)

**Exercise 1.17 (generic DNF and CNF formulae)** Prove that every Boolean function can be computed by a family of DNF (resp., CNF) formula of exponential size.

*Guideline:* For any $a \in \{0, 1\}^n$, consider the function $\delta_a : \{0, 1\}^n \rightarrow \{0, 1\}$ such that $\delta_a(x) = 1$ if $x = a$ and $\delta_a(x) = 0$ otherwise. Note that any function $\delta_a$ can be computed by a single conjunction of $n$ literals, and that any Boolean function $f : \{0, 1\}^n \rightarrow \{0, 1\}$ can be written as $\bigvee_{a:f(a)=1} \delta_a$. A corresponding CNF formula can be obtained by applying de-Morgan's Law to the DNF obtained for $\neg f$.

**Exercise 1.18 (on the size of general vs DNF formulae)** Prove that every DNF (resp., CNF) formula for computing parity must have exponential size. On the other hand, show that parity has quadratic-size formulae (and linear-size circuits).

*Guideline:* For the lower bound, observe that each conjunction in the candidate DNF must contain a literal for each variable. The upper bound follows by Figure 1.4.

# 2

# The P versus NP Question

**Overview:** Our daily experience is that it is harder to solve problems than it is to check the correctness of solutions to these problems. Is this experience merely a coincidence or does it represent a fundamental fact of life (or a property of the world)? This is the essence of the P versus NP Question, where *P represents search problems that are efficiently solvable and NP represents search problems for which solutions can be efficiently checked.*

Another natural question captured by the P versus NP Question is whether proving theorems is harder that verifying the validity of these proofs. In other words, the question is whether deciding membership in a set is harder than being convinced of this membership by an adequate proof. In this case, *P represents decision problems that are efficiently solvable, whereas NP represents sets that have efficiently verifiable proofs of membership.*

These two formulations of the P versus NP Question are indeed equivalent, and the common belief is that P is different from NP. That is, we believe that solving search problems is harder than checking the correctness of solutions for them and that finding proofs is harder than verifying their validity.

**Organization.** The two formulations of the P versus NP Question are rigorously presented and discussed in Sections 2.2 and 2.3, respectively. The equivalence of these formulations is shown in Section 2.4, and the common belief that P is different from NP is further discussed in Section 2.7. We start by discussing the notion of efficient computation (see Section 2.1).

# Teaching Notes

Most students have heard of P and NP before, but we suspect that many of them have not obtained a good explanation of what the P-vs-NP Question actually represents. This unfortunate situation is due to the use of the standard technical definition of NP (which refers to the fictitious and confusing device called a non-deterministic polynomial-time machine). Instead, we advocate the use of slightly more cumbersome definitions, sketched in the foregoing paragraphs (and elaborated in Sections 2.2 and 2.3), which clearly capture the fundamental nature of NP. Indeed, we advocate communicating the fundamental nature of the P-vs-NP Question by using two equivalent formulations, which refer to search problems (Section 2.2) and decision problems (Section 2.3), respectively.

**On the Search Problems' Formulation.** Complexity theorists are so accustomed to focusing on decision problems that they seem to forget that search problems are at least as natural as decision problems. Furthermore, to many non-experts, search problems may seem even more natural than decision problems: Typically, people seek solutions more often than they pause to wonder whether or not solutions exist. Thus, we recommend starting with a formulation of the P-vs-NP Question in terms of search problems. Admittedly, the cost is more cumbersome formulations, but it is more than worthwhile.

In order to reflect the importance of the search version, as well as to facilitate less cumbersome formulations, we chose to introduce concise notations for the two classes of search problems that correspond to P and NP: These classes are denoted PF and PC (standing for Polynomial-time Find and Polynomial-time Check, respectively). The teacher may prefer using notations and terms that are more evocative of P and NP (such as P-search and NP-search), and actually we also do so in some motivational discussions. (Still, in our opinion, in the long run, the students and the field may be served better by using standard-looking notations.)[1]

**On the Decision Problems' Formulation.** When presenting the P-vs-NP Question in terms of decision problems, we define NP as a class of sets having efficiently verifiable proofs of membership (see Definition 2.5). This definition clarifies the fundamental nature of the class NP, but is admittingly more

---

[1] Indeed, these classes are often denoted $\mathcal{FP}$ and $\mathcal{FNP}$, respectively. (We mention that "F" stands for function(s), although the definitions actually refer to binary relations.) However, since these notations are not widely used (and since they are somewhat misleading), we preferred to introduce new notations (which we consider better).

cumbersome than the more traditional definition of NP in terms of fictitious "non-deterministic machines" (see Definition 2.7).

Although Definitions 2.5 and 2.7 are equivalent (see Theorem 2.8), we believe that it is important to present NP as in Definition 2.5. Conceptually, this is the right choice because Definition 2.5 clarifies the fundamental nature of the class NP, whereas Definition 2.7 fails to do it. Indeed, a fictitious model can provide a basis for a sound definition, but it typically fails to provide motivation for its study (which may be provided by an equivalence to a natural definition). Furthermore, not all sound definitions are equally accessible. Specifically, many students find Definition 2.7 quite confusing, because they assume that it represents some natural model of computation, and consequently they allow themselves to be fooled by their intuition regarding such models. (Needless to say, the students' intuition regarding computation is irrelevant when applied to a fictitious model.) Thus, Definition 2.5 is also preferable to Definition 2.7 from a technical point of view.

## 2.1 Efficient Computation

As hinted in the foregoing discussions, much of Complexity Theory is concerned with efficient algorithms. The latter are defined as polynomial-time algorithms (i.e., algorithms that have time complexity that is upper-bounded by a polynomial in the length of the input). By the Cobham-Edmonds Thesis (see Section 1.3.5), the definition of this class is invariant under the choice of a "reasonable and general" model of computation. The association of efficient algorithms with polynomial-time computation is grounded in the following two considerations:

- *Philosophical consideration*: Intuitively, efficient algorithms are those that can be implemented within a number of steps that is a moderately growing function of the input length. To allow for reading the entire input, at least linear time should be allowed. On the other hand, apparently slow algorithms and in particular "exhaustive search" algorithms, which take exponential time, must be avoided. Furthermore, a good definition of the class of efficient algorithms should be closed under natural composition of algorithms (as well as be robust with respect to reasonable models of computation and with respect to simple changes in the encoding of problems' instances). Choosing polynomials as the set of time bounds for efficient algorithms satisfies all the foregoing requirements: Polynomials constitute a "closed" set of moderately growing functions, where "closure" means closure under addition, multiplication, and functional composition. These closure properties guarantee the closure of the class of efficient algorithms under natural composition of algorithms (as well as its robustness with respect to any reasonable and general model of computation). Furthermore, polynomial-time algorithms can conduct computations that are apparently simple (although not necessarily trivial), and on the other hand they do not include algorithms that are apparently inefficient (like exhaustive search).

• *Empirical consideration*: It is clear that algorithms that are considered efficient in practice have running time that is bounded by a small polynomial (at least on the inputs that occur in practice). The question is whether any polynomial-time algorithm can be considered efficient in an intuitive sense. The belief, which is supported by past experience, is that every *natural* problem that can be solved in polynomial time also has a "reasonably efficient" algorithm.

Although the association of efficient algorithms with polynomial-time computation is central to our exposition, we wish to highlight the fact that this association is not the source of any of the phenomena discussed in this book. That is, the same phenomena also occur when using other reasonable interpretations of the concept of efficient algorithms. A related comment applies to the formulation of computational problems that refer only to instances of a certain predetermined type. Both issues are discussed further in the following *advanced comments*.

**On Other Notions of Efficient Algorithms.** We stress that the association of efficient algorithms with polynomial-time computation is not essential to most of the notions, results, and questions of Complexity Theory. Any other class of algorithms that supports the aforementioned closure properties and allows for conducting some simple computations but not overly complex ones gives rise to a similar theory, albeit the formulation of such a theory may be more complicated. Specifically, all results and questions treated in this book are concerned with the relation among the complexities of different computational tasks (rather than with providing absolute assertions about the complexity of some computational tasks). These relations can be stated explicitly, by stating how any upper bound on the time complexity of one task gets translated to an upper bound on the time complexity of another task.[2] Such cumbersome

---

[2] For example, the NP-completeness of SAT (cf. Theorem 4.6) implies that any algorithm solving SAT in time $T$ yields an algorithm that factors composite numbers in time $T'$ such that $T'(n) = \text{poly}(n) \cdot (1 + T(\text{poly}(n)))$. More generally, if the correctness of solutions for $n$-bit instances of some search problem $R$ can be verified in time $t(n)$ then the hypothesis regarding

statements will maintain the contents of the standard statements; they will merely be much more complicated. Thus, we follow the tradition of focusing on polynomial-time computations, while stressing that this focus both is natural and provides the simplest way of addressing the fundamental issues underlying the nature of efficient computation.

**On the Representation of Problem Instances.** As noted in Section 1.2.3, many natural (search and decision) problems are captured more naturally by the terminology of promise problems (cf. Section 5.1), where the domain of possible instances is a subset of $\{0, 1\}^*$ rather than $\{0, 1\}^*$ itself. For example, computational problems in graph theory presume some simple encoding of graphs as strings, but this encoding is typically not onto (i.e., not all strings encode graphs), and thus not all strings are legitimate instances. However, in these cases, the set of legitimate instances (e.g., encodings of graphs) is efficiently recognizable (i.e., membership in it can be decided in polynomial time). Thus, artificially extending the set of instances to the set of all possible strings (and allowing trivial solutions for the corresponding dummy instances) does not change the complexity of the original problem. We discuss this issue further in Section 5.1.

**Summary.** We associate efficient computation with polynomial-time algorithms.[3] Recall that this association is justified by the fact that polynomials are moderately growing functions and the set of polynomials is closed under operations that correspond to the natural composition of algorithms. Furthermore, the class of polynomial-time algorithms is independent of the specific model of computation, as long as the latter is "reasonable" (cf. the Cobham-Edmonds Thesis).

**A Word About Inefficient Computations and Intractability.** Computations requiring more that polynomial time are considered inefficient or intractable. We typically refer to these terms only in motivational discussions, when discussing tasks that cannot be performed by efficient algorithms. Our focus is on efficient computations, and the technical presentation refers only to them.

---

SAT implies that solutions (for $n$-bit instances of $R$) can be found in time $T'$ such that $T'(n) = t(n) \cdot (1 + T(O(t(n))^2))$.

[3] **Advanced comment:** In this book, we consider *deterministic* (polynomial-time) algorithms as the basic model of efficient computation. A more liberal view includes also *probabilistic* (polynomial-time) algorithms (see [25] or [13, Chap. 6]). We stress that the most important facts and questions that are addressed in the current book have parallels with respect to probabilistic polynomial-time algorithms.

## 2.2 The Search Version: Finding versus Checking

Much of computer science is concerned with solving various search problems (as in Definition 1.1). A few examples, which will serve us throughout the book, are presented next.[4] In each of these examples, if no solution exists, then the solver should indicate that this is the case.

- Solving linear (or polynomial) systems of equations: Given a system of linear (or polynomial) equations, find an assignment to the variables that satisfies all equations.
  Formulae satisfiability is a related problem in which one is given a Boolean formula and is required to find an assignment that satisfies it. (When the formula is in CNF, this can be viewed as finding an assignment that satisfies a system of Boolean equations (which arise from the individual clauses).)
- Integer factorization: Given a natural number, find a non-trivial factor of this number.
- Finding a spanning tree: Given a (connected) graph, find a spanning tree in it (i.e., a connected subgraph that contains all vertices of the original graph but contains no simple cycles).
- Finding a Hamiltonian path (or cycle): Given a (connected) graph, find a simple path (cycle) that traverses all the vertices of the graph. Indeed, a Hamiltonian path is a spanning tree in which each intermediate vertex has degree 2.
- The traveling salesman problem (TSP): Given a matrix of distances between cities and a threshold, find a tour that passes all cities and covers a total distance that does not exceed the threshold. Indeed, the Hamiltonian cycle problem is a special case of TSP, where the distances are in $\{0, 1\}$ and represent the existence of the various edges in the graph.[5]
- Job scheduling: This term actually refers to a variety of problems, in which one is given a set of scheduling constraints and is required to find a scheduling of jobs to machines such that the given constraints are all satisfied.

In addition to the dominant role of search problems in computer science, solving search problems corresponds to the daily notion of "solving problems." Thus, search problems are of natural general interest. In the current section, we will consider the question of *which search problems can be solved efficiently*.

Indeed, efficiently solvable search problems are the subject matter of most basic courses on algorithmic design. Examples include sorting, finding patterns in strings, finding (rational) solutions to linear systems of (rational) equations,

---

[4] See Appendix for further details.

[5] That is, in the TSP instance, the distance between $i$ and $j$ equals 1 if $\{i, j\}$ is an edge in the graph, and equals 0 otherwise.

finding shortest paths in graphs, and many other graph-theoretic search problems. In contrast to these courses, our focus will be on search problems that cannot be solved efficiently.

**A Necessary Condition for Efficient Solvability.** One type of search problems that cannot be solved efficiently consists of those for which the solutions are too long in terms of the length of the problem's instances. In such a case, merely typing the solution amounts to an activity that is deemed inefficient, and so this case is not really interesting (from a computational point of view). Thus, we consider only search problems in which the length of the solution is bounded by a polynomial in the length of the instance. Recalling that search problems are associated with binary relations (see Definition 1.1), we focus our attention on polynomially bounded relations.

**Definition 2.1** (polynomially bounded relations): *We say that $R \subseteq \{0, 1\}^* \times \{0, 1\}^*$ is* polynomially bounded *if there exists a polynomial $p$ such that for every $(x, y) \in R$ it holds that $|y| \leq p(|x|)$.*

Recall that $(x, y) \in R$ means that $y$ is a solution to the problem instance $x$, where $R$ represents the problem itself. For example, in the case of finding a prime factor of a given integer, we refer to a relation $R$ such that $(x, y) \in R$ if the integer $y$ is a prime factor of the integer $x$. Likewise, in the case of finding a spanning tree in a given graph, we refer to a relation $R$ such that $(x, y) \in R$ if $y$ is a spanning tree of the graph $x$.

For a polynomially bounded relation $R$ it makes sense to ask whether or not, given a problem instance $x$, one can efficiently find an adequate solution $y$ (i.e., find $y$ such that $(x, y) \in R$). The polynomial bound on the length of the solution (i.e., $y$) guarantees that a negative answer is not merely due to the length of the required solution.

### 2.2.1 The Class P as a Natural Class of Search Problems

Recall that we are interested in the class of search problems that can be solved efficiently, that is, problems for which solutions (whenever they exist) can be found efficiently. Restricting our attention to polynomially bounded relations, we identify the corresponding fundamental class of search problems (or binary relations), denoted $\mathcal{PF}$ (standing for "Polynomial-time Find"). (The relationship between $\mathcal{PF}$ and the standard definition of P will be discussed in Sections 2.4 and 3.3.) The following definition refers to the formulation of solving search problems provided in Definition 1.1.

**Definition 2.2** (efficiently solvable search problems):

- *The search problem of a polynomially bounded relation* $R \subseteq \{0, 1\}^* \times \{0, 1\}^*$ *is* efficiently solvable *if there exists a polynomial-time algorithm A such that, for every x, it holds that if* $R(x) \stackrel{\text{def}}{=} \{y : (x, y) \in R\}$ *is not empty, then* $A(x) \in R(x)$, *and otherwise* $A(x) = \bot$ *(indicating that x has no solution).*[6]
- *We denote by* $\mathcal{PF}$ *the class of* (polynomially bounded) *search problems that are efficiently solvable. That is,* $R \in \mathcal{PF}$ *if R is polynomially bounded and there exists a polynomial-time algorithm that solves R.*

Note that $R(x)$ denotes the set of valid solutions for the problem instance $x$. Thus, the solver $A$ is required to find a valid solution (i.e., satisfy $A(x) \in R(x)$) whenever such a solution exists (i.e., $R(x)$ is not empty). On the other hand, if the instance $x$ has no solution (i.e., $R(x) = \emptyset$) then clearly $A(x) \notin R(x)$. The extra condition (also made in Definition 1.1) requires that in this case $A(x) = \bot$. Thus, algorithm $A$ always outputs a correct answer, which is a valid solution in the case that such a solution exists (and provides an indication that no solution exists otherwise).

We have defined a fundamental class of problems, and we do know of many natural problems in this class (e.g., solving linear equations over the rationals, finding shortest paths in graphs, finding patterns in strings, finding a perfect matching in a graph, and a variety of other search problems that are the focus of various courses on algorithms). However, these facts per se do not mean that we are able to characterize natural problems with respect to membership in this class. For example, we do not know whether or not the problem of finding the prime factors of a given integer is in this class (i.e., in $\mathcal{PF}$).

In fact, currently, we do not have a good understanding regarding the actual contents of the class $\mathcal{PF}$; that is, we are unable to characterize many natural problems with respect to membership in this class. This situation is quite common in Complexity Theory, and seems to be a consequence of the fact that complexity classes are defined in terms of the "external behavior" (of potential algorithms), rather than in terms of the "internal structure" (of the problem).

Turning back to $\mathcal{PF}$, we note that while it contains many natural search problems, there are also many natural search problems that are not known to be in $\mathcal{PF}$. A natural class containing a host of such problems is presented next.

---

[6] Recall that by Definition 1.1 this means that $A$ solves $R$.

### 2.2.2 The Class NP as Another Natural Class of Search Problems

Natural search problems have the property that valid solutions (for them) can be efficiently recognized. That is, given an instance $x$ of the problem $R$ and a candidate solution $y$, one can efficiently determine whether or not $y$ is a valid solution for $x$ (with respect to the problem $R$, i.e., whether or not $y \in R(x)$). For example, candidate solutions for a system of linear (or polynomial) equations can be easily verified for validity by instantiation and arithmetic manipulation. Likewise, it is easy to verify whether a given sequence of vertices constitutes a Hamiltonian path in a given graph.

The class of all search problems allowing for efficient recognizable (valid) solutions is a natural class per se, because it is not clear why one should care about a solution unless one can recognize a valid solution once given. Furthermore, this class is a natural domain of candidates for $\mathcal{PF}$, because the ability to efficiently recognize a valid solution seems to be a natural (albeit not absolutely necessary) prerequisite for a discussion regarding the complexity of finding such solutions.

We restrict our attention again to polynomially bounded relations, and consider the class of relations for which membership of pairs in the relation can be decided efficiently. We stress that we consider deciding membership of given pairs of the form $(x, y)$ in a fixed relation $R$, and not deciding membership of $x$ in the set $S_R \overset{\text{def}}{=} \{x : R(x) \neq \emptyset\}$. (The relationship between the following definition and the standard definition of NP will be discussed in Sections 2.4–2.6 and 3.3.)

**Definition 2.3** (search problems with efficiently checkable solutions):

- *The search problem of a polynomially bounded relation $R \subseteq \{0, 1\}^* \times \{0, 1\}^*$ has* efficiently checkable solutions *if there exists a polynomial-time algorithm $A$ such that, for every $x$ and $y$, it holds that $A(x, y) = 1$ if and only if $(x, y) \in R$.*

- *We denote by $\mathcal{PC}$ (standing for "Polynomial-time Check") the class of search problems that correspond to polynomially bounded binary relations that have efficiently checkable solutions. That is, $R \in \mathcal{PC}$ if the following two conditions hold:*

  1. *For some polynomial $p$, if $(x, y) \in R$ then $|y| \leq p(|x|)$.*
  2. *There exists a polynomial-time algorithm that given $(x, y)$ determines whether or not $(x, y) \in R$.*

Note that the algorithm postulated in Item 2 must also handle inputs of the form $(x, y)$ such that $|y| > p(|x|)$. Such inputs, which are evidently not in $R$ (by Item 1), are easy to handle by merely determining $|x|$, $|y|$ and $p(|x|)$.

Thus, the crux of Item 2 is typically in the case that the input $(x, y)$ satisfies $|y| \leq p(|x|)$.

The class $\mathcal{PC}$ contains thousands of natural problems (e.g., finding a traveling salesman tour of length that does not exceed a given threshold, finding the prime factorization of a given composite, finding a truth assignment that satisfies a given Boolean formula, etc). In each of these natural problems, the correctness of solutions can be checked efficiently (e.g., given a traveling salesman tour it is easy to compute its length and check whether or not it exceeds the given threshold); see Exercise 2.4.

The class $\mathcal{PC}$ is the natural domain for the study of which problems are in $\mathcal{PF}$, because the ability to efficiently recognize a valid solution is a *natural* prerequisite for a discussion regarding the complexity of finding such solutions. We warn, however, that $\mathcal{PF}$ contains (unnatural) problems that are not in $\mathcal{PC}$ (see Exercise 2.2).

### 2.2.3 The P versus NP Question in Terms of Search Problems

*Is it the case that every search problem in $\mathcal{PC}$ is in $\mathcal{PF}$?* That is, is it the case that the ability to efficiently check the correctness of solutions, with respect to some (polynomially bounded) relation $R$, implies the ability to find solutions with respect to $R$? In other words, if it is *easy to check* whether or not a given solution for a given instance is correct, then is it also *easy to find* a solution to a given instance?

If $\mathcal{PC} \subseteq \mathcal{PF}$ then this would mean that whenever solutions to given instances can be efficiently checked (for correctness), it is also the case that such solutions can be efficiently found (when given only the instance). This would mean that all reasonable search problems (i.e., all problems in $\mathcal{PC}$) are easy to solve. Needless to say, such a situation would contradict the intuitive feeling (and the daily experience) that some reasonable search problems are hard to solve. Furthermore, in such a case, the notion of "solving a problem" would lose its meaning (because finding a solution will not be significantly more difficult than checking its validity).

On the other hand, if $\mathcal{PC} \setminus \mathcal{PF} \neq \emptyset$ then there exist reasonable search problems (i.e., some problems in $\mathcal{PC}$) that are hard to solve. This conforms with our basic intuition by which some reasonable problems are easy to solve whereas others are hard to solve. Furthermore, it reconfirms the intuitive gap between the notions of solving and checking (asserting that at least in some cases "solving" is significantly harder than "checking").

To illustrate the foregoing paragraph, consider various puzzles like jigsaw puzzles, mazes, crossword puzzles, Sudoku puzzles, and so on. In each of these puzzles, checking the correctness of a solution is very easy, whereas finding a solution is sometimes extremely hard.

As was mentioned in the various overviews, it is widely believed that finding solutions to search problems is, in general, harder than verifying the correctness of such solutions; that is, it is widely believed that $\mathcal{PC} \setminus \mathcal{PF} \neq \emptyset$. However, as also mentioned before, this is only a belief, not a fact. For further discussion see Section 2.7.

## 2.3 The Decision Version: Proving versus Verifying

As we shall see in Section 2.4 (and further in Section 3.3), the study of search problems (e.g., the $\mathcal{PC}$-vs-$\mathcal{PF}$ Question) can be "reduced" to the study of decision problems. Since the latter problems have a less cumbersome terminology, Complexity Theory tends to focus on them (and maintains its relevance to the study of search problems via the aforementioned reduction). Thus, the study of decision problems provides a convenient way for studying search problems. For example, the study of the complexity of deciding the satisfiability of Boolean formulae provides a convenient way for studying the complexity of finding satisfying assignments for such formulae.

We wish to stress, however, that decision problems are interesting and natural per se (i.e., beyond their role in the study of search problems). After all, some people do care about the truth, and so determining whether certain claims are true is a natural computational problem. Specifically, determining whether a given object (e.g., a Boolean formula) has some predetermined property (e.g., is satisfiable) constitutes an appealing computational problem. The P-vs-NP Question refers to the complexity of solving such problems for a wide and natural class of properties associated with the class NP. The latter class refers to properties that have "efficient proof systems" allowing for the verification of the claim that a given object has a predetermined property (i.e., is a member of a predetermined set). Jumping ahead, we mention that the P-vs-NP Question refers to the question of whether properties that have efficient proof systems can also be decided efficiently (without proofs). Let us clarify all of these notions.

Properties of objects are modeled as subsets of the set of all possible objects (i.e., a property is associated with the set of objects having this property). For example, the property of being a prime is associated with the set of prime numbers, and the property of being connected (resp., having a Hamiltonian path) is associated with the set of connected (resp., Hamiltonian) graphs. Thus, we focus on deciding membership in sets (as in Definition 1.2). The standard formulation of the P-vs-NP Question refers to the questionable equality of two natural classes of decision problems, denoted P and NP (and defined in Section 2.3.1 and Section 2.3.2, respectively).

### 2.3.1 The Class P as a Natural Class of Decision Problems

Needless to say, we are interested in the class of decision problems that are efficiently solvable. This class is traditionally denoted $\mathcal{P}$ (standing for Polynomial time). The following definition refers to the formulation of solving decision problems (provided in Definition 1.2).

**Definition 2.4** (efficiently solvable decision problems):

- *A decision problem $S \subseteq \{0, 1\}^*$ is* efficiently solvable *if there exists a polynomial-time algorithm $A$ such that, for every $x$, it holds that $A(x) = 1$ if and only if $x \in S$.*
- *We denote by $\mathcal{P}$ the class of decision problems that are efficiently solvable.*

Without loss of generality, for an algorithm $A$ as in the first item, it holds that $A(x) = 0$ whenever $x \notin S$, because we can modify any output different from 1 to 0. (Thus, $A$ solves the decision problem $S$ as per Definition 1.2.)

As in the case of Definition 2.2, we have defined a fundamental class of problems, which contains many natural problems (e.g., determining whether or not a given graph is connected), but we do not have a good understanding regarding its actual contents (i.e., we are unable to characterize many natural problems with respect to membership in this class). In fact, there are many natural decision problems that are not known to reside in $\mathcal{P}$, and a natural class containing a host of such problems is presented next. This class of decision problems is denoted NP (for reasons that will become evident in Section 2.6).

### 2.3.2 The Class NP and NP-Proof Systems

Whenever deciding on our own seems hard, it is natural to seek help (e.g., advice) from others. In the context of verifying that an object has a predetermined property (or belongs to a predetermined set), help may take the form of a proof, where proofs should be thought of as advice that can be evaluated for correctness. Indeed, a natural class of decision problems that arises is the class, denoted NP, of all sets such that membership (of each instance) in each set can be verified efficiently with the help of an adequate proof. Thus, we define NP as the class of decision problems that have efficiently verifiable proof systems. This definitional path requires clarifying the notion of a proof system.

Loosely speaking, we say that a set $S$ has a proof system if instances in $S$ have valid proofs of membership (i.e., proofs accepted as valid by the system), whereas instances not in $S$ have no valid proofs. Indeed, proofs are defined as strings that (when accompanying the instance) are accepted by the (efficient) verification procedure. That is, we say that $V$ is a verification procedure for membership in $S$ if it satisfies the following two conditions:

1. Completeness: True assertions have valid proofs (i.e., proofs accepted as valid by $V$). Bearing in mind that assertions refer to membership in $S$, this means that for every $x \in S$ there exists a string $y$ such that $V(x, y) = 1$; that is, $V$ accepts $y$ as a valid proof for the membership of $x$ in $S$.
2. Soundness: False assertions have no valid proofs. That is, for every $x \notin S$ and every string $y$ it holds that $V(x, y) = 0$, which means that $V$ rejects $y$ as a proof for the membership of $x$ in $S$.

We note that the soundness condition captures the "security" of the verification procedure, that is, its ability not to be fooled (by anything) into accepting a wrong assertion. The completeness condition captures the "viability" of the verification procedure, that is, its ability to be convinced of any valid assertion (when presented with an adequate proof).

We stress that, in general, proof systems are defined in terms of their verification procedures, which must satisfy adequate completeness and soundness conditions. Our focus here is on *efficient* verification procedures that utilize relatively short proofs (i.e., proofs that are of length that is polynomially bounded by the length of the corresponding assertion).[7]

Let us consider a couple of examples before turning to the actual definition (of efficiently verifiable proof systems). Starting with the set of Hamiltonian graphs, we note that this set has a verification procedure that, given a pair $(G, \pi)$, accepts if and only if $\pi$ is a Hamiltonian path in the graph $G$. In this case, $\pi$ serves as a proof that $G$ is Hamiltonian. Note that such proofs are relatively short (i.e., the path is actually shorter than the description of the graph) and are easy to verify. Needless to say, this proof system satisfies the

---

[7] **Advanced comment:** In continuation of footnote 3, we note that in this book we consider *deterministic* (polynomial-time) verification procedures, and consequently the completeness and soundness conditions that we state here are errorless. In contrast, we mention that various types of probabilistic (polynomial-time) verification procedures, as well as probabilistic completeness and soundness conditions, are also of interest (see Section 4.3.5 and [13, Chap. 9]). A common theme that underlies both treatments is that efficient verification is interpreted as meaning verification by a process that runs in time that is polynomial in the length of the assertion. In the current book, we use the equivalent formulation that considers the running time as a function of the total length of the assertion and the proof, but require that the latter has length that is polynomially bounded by the length of the assertion. (The latter issue is discussed in Section 2.5.)

aforementioned completeness and soundness conditions. Turning to the case of satisfiable Boolean formulae, given a formula $\phi$ and a truth assignment $\tau$, the verification procedure instantiates $\phi$ (according to $\tau$), and accepts if and only if simplifying the resulting Boolean expression yields the value `true`. In this case, $\tau$ serves as a proof that $\phi$ is satisfiable, and the alleged proofs are indeed relatively short and easy to verify.

**Definition 2.5** (efficiently verifiable proof systems)**:**

- *A decision problem* $S \subseteq \{0, 1\}^*$ *has an* efficiently verifiable proof system *if there exists a polynomial p and a polynomial-time* (verification) *algorithm V such that the following two conditions hold:*
  1. Completeness: *For every $x \in S$, there exists $y$ of length at most $p(|x|)$ such that $V(x, y) = 1$.*
     (Such a string $y$ is called an NP-witness for $x \in S$.)
  2. Soundness: *For every $x \notin S$ and every $y$, it holds that $V(x, y) = 0$.*
     *Thus, $x \in S$ if and only if there exists $y$ of length at most $p(|x|)$ such that $V(x, y) = 1$.*
     *In such a case, we say that $S$ has an NP-proof system, and refer to $V$ as its* verification procedure (or as the proof system itself).
- *We denote by $\mathcal{NP}$ the class of decision problems that have efficiently verifiable proof systems.*

We note that the term *NP-witness* is commonly used.[8] In some cases, $V$ (or the set of pairs accepted by $V$) is called a witness relation of $S$. We stress that the same set $S$ may have many different NP-proof systems (see Exercise 2.5), and that in some cases the difference is quite fundamental (see Exercise 2.6).

Typically, for natural decision problems in $\mathcal{NP}$, it is easy to show that these problems are in $\mathcal{NP}$ by using Definition 2.5. This is done by designing adequate NP-proofs of membership, which are typically quite straightforward, because natural decision problems are typically phrased as asking about the existence of a structure (or an object) that can be easily verified as valid. For example, SAT is defined as the set of satisfiable Boolean formulae, which means asking about the existence of satisfying assignments. Indeed, we can efficiently check whether a given assignment satisfies a given formula, which means that we have (a verification procedure for) an NP-proof system for SAT. Likewise, Hamiltonian graphs are defined as graphs containing simple paths that pass through all vertices.

---

[8] In most cases, this is done without explicitly defining $V$, which is understood from the context and/or by common practice. In many texts, $V$ is not called a proof system (nor a verification procedure of such a system), although this term is most adequate.

Note that for any search problem $R$ in $\mathcal{PC}$, the set of instances that have a solution with respect to $R$ (i.e., the set $S_R \overset{\text{def}}{=} \{x : R(x) \neq \emptyset\}$) is in $\mathcal{NP}$. Specifically, for any $R \in \mathcal{PC}$, consider the verification procedure $V$ such that $V(x, y) \overset{\text{def}}{=} 1$ if and only if $(x, y) \in R$, and note that the latter condition can be decided in poly($|x|$)-time. Thus, *any search problem in $\mathcal{PC}$ can be viewed as a problem of searching for* (efficiently verifiable) *proofs* (i.e., NP-witnesses for membership in the set of instances having solutions). On the other hand, any NP-proof system gives rise to a natural search problem in $\mathcal{PC}$, that is, the problem of searching for a valid proof (i.e., an NP-witness) for the given instance. (Specifically, the verification procedure $V$ yields the search problem that corresponds to $R = \{(x, y) : V(x, y) = 1\}$.) Thus, *$S \in \mathcal{NP}$ if and only if there exists $R \in \mathcal{PC}$ such that $S = \{x : R(x) \neq \emptyset\}$*.

The last paragraph suggests another easy way of showing that natural decision problems are in $\mathcal{NP}$: just thinking of the corresponding natural search problem. The point is that natural decision problems (in $\mathcal{NP}$) are phrased as referring to whether a solution exists for the corresponding natural search problem. (For example, in the case of SAT, the question is whether there exists a satisfying assignment to a given Boolean formula, and the corresponding search problem is finding such an assignment.) In all these cases, it is easy to check the correctness of solutions; that is, the corresponding search problem is in $\mathcal{PC}$, which implies that the decision problem is in $\mathcal{NP}$.

Observe that $\mathcal{P} \subseteq \mathcal{NP}$ holds: A verification procedure for claims of membership in a set $S \in \mathcal{P}$ may just ignore the alleged NP-witness and run the decision procedure that is guaranteed by the hypothesis $S \in \mathcal{P}$; that is, we may let $V(x, y) = A(x)$, where $A$ is the aforementioned decision procedure. Indeed, the latter verification procedure is quite an abuse of the term (because it makes no use of the proof); however, it is a legitimate one. As we shall shortly see, the P-vs-NP Question refers to the question of whether such proof-oblivious verification procedures can be used for every set that has some efficiently verifiable proof system. (Indeed, given that $\mathcal{P} \subseteq \mathcal{NP}$ holds, the P-vs-NP Question is whether or not $\mathcal{NP} \subseteq \mathcal{P}$.)

### 2.3.3 The P versus NP Question in Terms of Decision Problems

*Is it the case that NP-proofs are useless?* That is, is it the case that for every efficiently verifiable proof system, one can easily determine the validity of assertions without looking at the proof? If that were the case, then proofs would be meaningless, because they would offer no fundamental advantage over directly determining the validity of the assertion. The conjecture $\mathcal{P} \neq \mathcal{NP}$ asserts that proofs are useful: There exist sets in $\mathcal{NP}$ that cannot be decided by a polynomial-time algorithm, which means that for these sets, obtaining a proof of membership (for some instances) is useful (because we cannot efficiently determine membership in these sets by ourselves).

In the foregoing paragraph, we viewed $\mathcal{P} \neq \mathcal{NP}$ as asserting the advantage of obtaining proofs over deciding the truth by ourselves. That is, $\mathcal{P} \neq \mathcal{NP}$ asserts that (at least in some cases) verifying is easier than deciding. A slightly different perspective is that $\mathcal{P} \neq \mathcal{NP}$ asserts that finding proofs is harder than verifying their validity. This is the case because, for any set $S$ that has an NP-proof system, the ability to efficiently find proofs of membership with respect to this system (i.e., finding an NP-witness of membership in $S$ for any given $x \in S$) yields the ability to decide membership in $S$. Thus, for $S \in \mathcal{NP} \setminus \mathcal{P}$, it must be harder to find proofs of membership in $S$ than to verify the validity of such proofs (which can be done in polynomial time).

As was mentioned in the various overviews, it is widely believed that $\mathcal{P} \neq \mathcal{NP}$. For further discussion see Section 2.7.

## 2.4 Equivalence of the Two Formulations

As hinted several times, *the two formulations of the P-vs-NP Questions are equivalent.* That is, every search problem having efficiently checkable solutions is solvable in polynomial time (i.e., $\mathcal{PC} \subseteq \mathcal{PF}$) if and only if membership in any set that has an NP-proof system can be decided in polynomial time (i.e., $\mathcal{NP} \subseteq \mathcal{P}$). Recalling that $\mathcal{P} \subseteq \mathcal{NP}$ (whereas $\mathcal{PF}$ is not contained in $\mathcal{PC}$; see Exercise 2.2), we prove the following.

**Theorem 2.6:** $\mathcal{PC} \subseteq \mathcal{PF}$ *if and only if* $\mathcal{P} = \mathcal{NP}$.

**Proof:** Suppose, on the one hand, that the inclusion holds for the search version (i.e., $\mathcal{PC} \subseteq \mathcal{PF}$). We will show that for any set in $\mathcal{NP}$, this hypothesis implies the existence of an efficient algorithm for finding NP-witnesses for this set, which in turn implies that this set is in $\mathcal{P}$. Specifically, let $S$ be an arbitrary set in $\mathcal{NP}$, and $V$ be the corresponding verification procedure (i.e., satisfying the conditions in Definition 2.5). Without loss of generality, there exists a polynomial $p$ such that $V(x, y) = 1$ holds only if $|y| \leq p(|x|)$. Considering the (polynomially bounded) relation

$$R \stackrel{\text{def}}{=} \{(x, y) : V(x, y) = 1\}, \tag{2.1}$$

note that $R$ is in $\mathcal{PC}$ (since $V$ decides membership in $R$). Using the hypothesis $\mathcal{PC} \subseteq \mathcal{PF}$, it follows that the search problem of $R$ is solvable in polynomial

---

Input: $x$

Subroutine: a solver $A$ for the search problem of $R$.

Alternative 1: Output 1 if $A(x) \neq \perp$ and 0 otherwise.

Alternative 2: Output $V(x, A(x))$.

---

Figure 2.1. Solving $S$ by using a solver for $R$.

time. Denoting by $A$ the polynomial-time algorithm solving the search problem of $R$, we decide membership in $S$ in the obvious way: That is, on input $x$, we output 1 if and only if $A(x) \neq \perp$. Note that $A(x) \neq \perp$ holds if and only if $A(x) \in R(x)$, which in turn occurs if and only if $R(x) \neq \emptyset$ (equiv., $x \in S$).[9] Thus, $S \in \mathcal{P}$. Since we started with an arbitrary set in $\mathcal{NP}$, it follows $\mathcal{NP} \subseteq \mathcal{P}$ (and $\mathcal{NP} = \mathcal{P}$).

Suppose, on the other hand, that $\mathcal{NP} = \mathcal{P}$. We will show that for any search problem in $\mathcal{PC}$, this hypothesis implies an efficient algorithm for determining whether a given string $y'$ is a prefix of some solution to a given instance $x$ of this search problem, which in turn yields an efficient algorithm for finding solutions (for this search problem). Specifically, let $R$ be an arbitrary search problem in $\mathcal{PC}$. Considering the set

$$S'_R \overset{\text{def}}{=} \{\langle x, y' \rangle : \exists y'' \text{ s.t. } (x, y'y'') \in R\}, \tag{2.2}$$

note that $S'_R$ is in $\mathcal{NP}$ (because $R \in \mathcal{PC}$). Using the hypothesis $\mathcal{NP} \subseteq \mathcal{P}$, it follows that $S'_R$ is in $\mathcal{P}$. This yields a polynomial-time algorithm for solving the search problem of $R$, by extending a prefix of a potential solution bit by bit while using the decision procedure to determine whether or not the current prefix is valid. That is, on input $x$, we first check whether or not $\langle x, \lambda \rangle \in S'_R$ and output $\perp$ (indicating $R(x) = \emptyset$) in case $\langle x, \lambda \rangle \notin S'_R$. Otherwise, $\langle x, \lambda \rangle \in S'_R$, and we set $y' \leftarrow \lambda$. Next, we proceed in iterations, maintaining the invariant that $\langle x, y' \rangle \in S'_R$. In each iteration, we set $y' \leftarrow y'0$ if $\langle x, y'0 \rangle \in S'_R$ and $y' \leftarrow y'1$ if $\langle x, y'1 \rangle \in S'_R$. If none of these conditions hold (which happens after at most polynomially many iterations), then the current $y'$ satisfies $(x, y') \in R$. (An alternative termination condition amounts to checking explicitly whether the current $y'$ satisfies $(x, y') \in R$; see Figure 2.2.) Thus, for every $x \in S_R$ (i.e., $x$ such that $R(x) \neq \emptyset$), we output some string in $R(x)$. It follows that for an arbitrary $R \in \mathcal{PC}$, we have $R \in \mathcal{PF}$, and hence $\mathcal{PC} \subseteq \mathcal{PF}$. ∎

**Reflection.** The first part of the proof of Theorem 2.6 associates with each set $S$ in $\mathcal{NP}$ a natural relation $R$ (in $\mathcal{PC}$). Specifically, $R$ (as defined in Eq. (2.1))

---

[9] Indeed, an alternative decision procedure outputs 1 if and only if $(x, A(x)) \in R$, which in turn holds if and only if $V(x, A(x)) = 1$. The latter alternative appears as Alternative 2 in Figure 2.1.

---

Input: $x$

(Checking whether solutions exist)

    If $\langle x, \lambda \rangle \notin S'_R$ then halt with output $\bot$.

    (Comment: $\langle x, \lambda \rangle \notin S'_R$ if and only if $R(x) = \emptyset$.)

(Finding a solution (i.e., a string in $R(x) \neq \emptyset$))

    Initialize $y' \leftarrow \lambda$.

    While $(x, y') \notin R$ repeat

        If $\langle x, y'0 \rangle \in S'_R$ then $y' \leftarrow y'0$ else $y' \leftarrow y'1$.

        (Comment: Since $\langle x, y' \rangle \in S'_R$ but $(x, y') \notin R$,

        either $\langle x, y'0 \rangle$ or $\langle x, y'1 \rangle$ must be in $S'_R$.)

    Output $y'$ (which is indeed in $R(x)$).

---

Figure 2.2. Solving $R$ by using a solver for $S'_R$.

consists of all pairs $(x, y)$ such that $y$ is an NP-witness for membership of $x$ in $S$. Thus, the search problem of $R$ consists of finding such an NP-witness, when given $x$ as input. Indeed, $R$ is called the witness relation of $S$, and solving the search problem of $R$ allows for deciding membership in $S$. Thus, $R \in \mathcal{PC} \subseteq \mathcal{PF}$ implies $S \in \mathcal{P}$. In the second part of the proof, we associate with each $R \in \mathcal{PC}$ a set $S'_R$ (in $\mathcal{NP}$), but $S'_R$ is more "expressive" than the set $S_R \overset{\text{def}}{=} \{x : \exists y \text{ s.t. } (x, y) \in R\}$ (which is the natural NP-set arising from $R$). Specifically, $S'_R$ (as defined in Eq. (2.2)) consists of strings that encode pairs $(x, y')$ such that $y'$ is a prefix of some string in $R(x) = \{y : (x, y) \in R\}$. The key observation is that deciding membership in $S'_R$ allows for solving the search problem of $R$; that is, $S'_R \in \mathcal{P}$ implies $R \in \mathcal{PF}$.

**Conclusion.** Theorem 2.6 justifies the traditional focus on the decision version of the P-vs-NP Question. Indeed, given that both formulations of the question are equivalent, we may just study the less cumbersome one.

## 2.5 Technical Comments Regarding NP

The following comments are rather technical, and only the first one is used in the rest of this book.

**A Simplifying Convention.** We shall often assume that the length of solutions for any search problem in $\mathcal{PC}$ (resp., NP-witnesses for a set in $\mathcal{NP}$) is determined (rather than upper-bounded) by the length of the instance. That is, for any $R \in \mathcal{PC}$ (resp., verification procedure $V$ for a set in $\mathcal{NP}$), we shall assume that for some fixed polynomial $p$, if $(x, y) \in R$ (resp., $V(x, y) = 1$) then $|y| = p(|x|)$ rather than $|y| \leq p(|x|)$. This assumption can be justified by a trivial modification of $R$ (resp., $V$); see Exercise 2.7.

**Solving Problems in NP via Exhaustive Search.** Every problem in $\mathcal{PC}$ (resp., $\mathcal{NP}$) can be solved in exponential time (i.e., time $\exp(\mathrm{poly}(|x|))$ for input $x$). This can be done by an exhaustive search among all possible candidate solutions (resp., all possible candidate NP-witnesses). Thus, $\mathcal{NP} \subseteq \mathcal{EXP}$, where $\mathcal{EXP}$ denotes the class of decision problems that can be solved in exponential time (i.e., time $\exp(\mathrm{poly}(|x|))$ for input $x$).

**An Alternative Formulation.** Recall that when defining $\mathcal{PC}$ (resp., $\mathcal{NP}$), we have explicitly confined our attention to search problems of polynomially bounded relations (resp., NP-witnesses of polynomial length). In this case, a polynomial-time algorithm that decides membership of a given pair $(x, y)$ in a relation $R \in \mathcal{PC}$ (resp., check the validity of an NP-witness $y$ for membership of $x$ in $S \in \mathcal{NP}$) runs in time that is polynomial in the length of $x$. This observation leads to an alternative formulation of the class $\mathcal{PC}$ (resp., $\mathcal{NP}$), in which one allows solutions (resp., NP-witnesses) of arbitrary length but requires that the corresponding algorithms run in *time that is polynomial in the length of $x$ rather than polynomial in the length of $(x, y)$*. That is, by the alternative formulation a binary relation $R$ is in $\mathcal{PC}$ (resp., $S \in \mathcal{NP}$) if membership of $(x, y)$ in $R$ can be decided *in time that is polynomial in the length of $x$* (resp., the verification of a candidate NP-witness $y$ for membership of $x$ in $S$ is required to be performed in $\mathrm{poly}(|x|)$-time). Although this alternative formulation does not upper-bound the length of the solutions (resp., NP-witnesses), such an upper bound effectively follows in the sense that it suffices to inspect a $\mathrm{poly}(|x|)$-bit long prefix of the solution (resp., NP-witness) in order to determine its validity. Indeed, such a prefix is as good as the full-length solution (resp., NP-witness) itself. Thus, the alternative formulation is essentially equivalent to the original one.

## 2.6 The Traditional Definition of NP

Unfortunately, Definition 2.5 is not the most commonly used definition of $\mathcal{NP}$. Instead, traditionally, $\mathcal{NP}$ is defined as the class of sets that can be decided by a *fictitious* device called a non-deterministic polynomial-time machine (which explains the source of the notation NP). The reason that this class of fictitious devices is interesting is due to the fact that it captures (indirectly) the definition of NP-proof systems (i.e., Definition 2.5). Since the reader may come across the traditional definition of $\mathcal{NP}$ when studying different works, we feel obliged to provide the traditional definition as well as a proof of its equivalence to Definition 2.5.

**Definition 2.7** (non-deterministic polynomial-time Turing machines):

- *A non-deterministic Turing machine is defined as in Section 1.3.2, except that the transition function maps symbol-state pairs to subsets of triples* (rather than to a single triple) *in $\Sigma \times Q \times \{-1, 0, +1\}$. Accordingly, the configuration following a specific instantaneous configuration may be one of several possibilities, each determined by a different possible triple. Thus, the* computations of a non-deterministic machine *on a fixed input may result in different outputs.*

  *In the context of decision problems, one typically considers the question of whether or not there exists a computation that halts with output 1 after starting with a fixed input. This leads to the following notions:*
  - *We say that the* non-deterministic machine $M$ accepts $x$ *if there exists a computation of $M$, on input $x$, that halts with output 1.*
  - *The* set accepted by a non-deterministic machine *is the set of inputs that are accepted by the machine.*

- *A non-deterministic polynomial-time Turing machine is defined as one that halts after a number of steps that is no more than a fixed polynomial in the length of the input. Traditionally, $\mathcal{NP}$ is defined as the class of sets that are each accepted by some non-deterministic polynomial-time Turing machine.*

We stress that Definition 2.7 refers to a fictitious model of computation. Specifically, Definition 2.7 makes no reference to the number (or fraction) of possible computations of the machine (on a specific input) that yield a specific output.[10] Definition 2.7 only refers to whether or not computations leading to a certain output exist (for a specific input). The question of what the mere existence of such possible computations means (in terms of real life) is not addressed, because the model of a non-deterministic machine is not meant to provide a reasonable model of a (real-life) computer. The model is meant to capture something completely different (i.e., it is meant to provide an "elegant" definition of the class $\mathcal{NP}$, while relying on the fact that Definition 2.7 is equivalent to Definition 2.5).[11]

---

[10] **Advanced comment:** In contrast, the definition of a probabilistic machine refers to this number (or, equivalently, to the probability that the machine produces a specific output, when the probability is taken (essentially) uniformly over all possible computations). Thus, a probabilistic machine refers to a natural model of computation that can be realized provided we can equip the machine with a source of randomness. For details, see [13, Sec. 6.1].

[11] Whether or not Definition 2.7 is elegant is a matter of taste. For sure, many students find Definition 2.7 quite confusing; see further discussion in the teaching notes to this chapter.

Note that unlike other definitions in this book, Definition 2.7 makes explicit reference to a specific model of computation. Still, a similar (non-deterministic) extension can be applied to other models of computation by considering adequate non-deterministic computation rules. Also note that without loss of generality, we may assume that the transition function maps each possible symbol-state pair to exactly two triples (see Exercise 2.11).

**Theorem 2.8:** *Definition 2.5 is equivalent to Definition 2.7. That is, a set S has an NP-proof system if and only if there exists a non-deterministic polynomial-time machine that accepts S.*

**Proof:** Suppose, on the one hand, that the set $S$ has an NP-proof system, and let us denote the corresponding verification procedure by $V$. Let $p$ be a polynomial that determines the length of NP-witnesses with respect to $V$ (i.e., $V(x, y) = 1$ implies $|y| = p(|x|)$).[12] Consider the following non-deterministic polynomial-time machine, denoted $M$, that (on input $x$) first produces non-deterministically a potential NP-witness (i.e., $y \in \{0, 1\}^{p(|x|)}$) and then accepts if and only if this witness is indeed valid (i.e., $V(x, y) = 1$). That is, on input $x$, machine $M$ proceeds as follows:

1. Makes $m = p(|x|)$ non-deterministic steps, producing (non-deterministically) a string $y \in \{0, 1\}^m$.
2. Emulates $V(x, y)$ and outputs whatever it does.

We stress that the non-deterministic steps (taken in Step 1) may result in producing any $m$-bit string $y$. Recall that $x \in S$ if and only if there exists $y \in \{0, 1\}^{p(|x|)}$ such that $V(x, y) = 1$. It follows that $x \in S$ if and only if there exists a computation of $M$ on input $x$ that halts with output 1 (and thus $x \in S$ if and only if $M$ accepts $x$). This implies that the set accepted by $M$ equals $S$. Since $M$ is a non-deterministic polynomial-time machine, it follows that $S$ is in $\mathcal{NP}$ according to Definition 2.7.

Suppose, on the other hand, that there exists a non-deterministic polynomial-time machine $M$ that accepts the set $S$, and let $p$ be a polynomial upper-bounding the time complexity of $M$. Consider the following deterministic polynomial-time machine, denoted $M'$, that on input $(x, y)$ views $y$ as a description of the non-deterministic choices of machine $M$ on input $x$, and emulates the corresponding computation. That is, on input $(x, y)$, where $y$ has length $m = p(|x|)$, machine $M'$ emulates a computation of $M$ on input $x$ while using the bits of $y$ to determine the non-deterministic steps of $M$. Specifically, the $i^{\text{th}}$ step of $M$ on input $x$ is determined by the $i^{\text{th}}$ bit of $y$ such that the $i^{\text{th}}$

---

[12] See the simplifying convention in Section 2.5.

step of $M$ follows the first possibility (in the transition function) if and only if the $i^{\text{th}}$ bit of $y$ equals 1. Note that $x \in S$ if and only if there exists $y$ of length $p(|x|)$ such that $M'(x, y) = 1$. Thus, $M'$ gives rise to an NP-proof system for $S$, and so $S$ is in $\mathcal{NP}$ according to Definition 2.5. ■

## 2.7 In Support of P Being Different from NP

> Intuition and concepts constitute . . . the elements of all our knowledge,
> so that neither concepts without an intuition in some way corresponding
> to them, nor intuition without concepts, can yield knowledge.
>
> *Immanuel Kant (1724–1804)*

Kant speaks of the importance of *both* philosophical considerations (referred to as "concepts") and empirical considerations (referred to as "intuition") to science (referred to as (sound) "knowledge"). We shall indeed follow his lead.

It is widely believed that P is different from NP, that is, that $\mathcal{PC}$ contains search problems that are not efficiently solvable, and that there are NP-proof systems for sets that cannot be decided efficiently. This belief is supported by both philosophical and empirical considerations.

**Philosophical Considerations.** Both formulations of the P-vs-NP Question refer to natural questions about which we have strong conceptions. The notion of solving a (search) problem seems to presume that, at least in some cases (or in general), finding a solution is significantly harder than checking whether a presented solution is correct. This translates to $\mathcal{PC} \setminus \mathcal{PF} \neq \emptyset$. Likewise, the notion of a proof seems to presume that, at least in some cases (or in general), the proof is useful in determining the validity of the assertion, that is, that verifying the validity of an assertion may be made significantly easier when provided with a proof. This translates to $\mathcal{P} \neq \mathcal{NP}$, which also implies that it is significantly harder to find proofs than to verify their correctness, which again coincides with the daily experience of researchers and students.

**Empirical Considerations.** The class NP (or rather $\mathcal{PC}$) contains thousands of different problems for which no efficient solving procedure is known. Many of these problems have arisen in vastly different disciplines, and were the subject of extensive research of numerous different communities of scientists and engineers. These essentially independent studies have all failed to provide efficient algorithms for solving these problems, a failure that is extremely hard to attribute to sheer coincidence or to a streak of bad luck.

We mention that for many of the aforementioned problems, the best-known algorithms are not significantly faster than an exhaustive search (for a solution); that is, the complexity of the best-known algorithm is polynomially related to the complexity of an exhaustive search. Indeed, it is widely believed that for some problems in NP, no algorithm can be significantly faster than an exhaustive search.

The common belief (or conjecture) that $\mathcal{P} \neq \mathcal{NP}$ is indeed very appealing and intuitive. The fact that this natural conjecture is unsettled seems to be one of the sources of frustration of Complexity Theory. Our opinion, however, is that this feeling of frustration is out of place (and merely reflects a naive underestimation of the issues at hand). In contrast, the fact that Complexity Theory evolves around natural and simply stated questions that are so difficult to resolve makes its study very exciting.

Throughout the rest of this book, we will adopt the conjecture that P is different from NP. In a few places, we will explicitly use this conjecture, whereas in other places, we will present results that are interesting (if and) only if $\mathcal{P} \neq \mathcal{NP}$ (e.g., the entire theory of NP-completeness becomes uninteresting if $\mathcal{P} = \mathcal{NP}$).

## 2.8 Philosophical Meditations

Whoever does not value preoccupation with thoughts, can skip this chapter.

*Robert Musil, The Man without Qualities, Chap. 28*

The inherent limitations of our scientific knowledge were articulated by Kant, who argued that our knowledge cannot transcend our way of understanding. The "ways of understanding" are predetermined; they precede any knowledge acquisition and are the precondition to such acquisition. In a sense, Wittgenstein refined the analysis, arguing that knowledge must be formulated in a language, and the latter must be subject to a (sound) mechanism of assigning meaning. Thus, the inherent limitations of any possible "meaning-assigning mechanism" impose limitations on what can be (meaningfully) said.

Both philosophers spoke of the relation between the world and our thoughts. They took for granted (or rather assumed) that in the domain of well-formulated thoughts (e.g., logic), every valid conclusion can be effectively reached (i.e., every valid assertion can be effectively proved). Indeed, this naive assumption was refuted by Gödel. In a similar vain, Turing's work asserts that *there exist well-defined problems that cannot be solved by well-defined methods.*

We stress that Turing's assertion transcends the philosophical considerations of the first paragraph: It asserts that the limitations of our ability are due not only to the gap between the "world as is" and our model of it. In contrast, Turing's assertion refers to inherent limitations on any rational process, even when this process is applied to well-formulated information and is aimed at a well-formulated goal. Indeed, in contrast to naive presumptions, not every well-formulated problem can be (effectively) solved.

The $\mathcal{P} \neq \mathcal{NP}$ conjecture goes even beyond Turing's assertion. It limits the domain of the discussion to "fair" problems, that is, to problems for which valid solutions can be efficiently recognized as such. Indeed, there is something feigned in problems for which one cannot efficiently recognize valid solutions. Avoiding such feigned and/or unfair problems, $\mathcal{P} \neq \mathcal{NP}$ means that (even with this limitation) there exist problems that are inherently unsolvable in the sense that they cannot be solved *efficiently*. That is, in contrast to naive presumptions, *not every problem that refers to efficiently recognizable solutions can be solved efficiently*. In fact, the gap between the complexity of recognizing solutions and the complexity of finding them vouches for the meaningfulness of the notion of a problem.

# Exercises

*Exercise 2.1 (a quiz)*

1. What are the justifications for associating efficient computation with polynomial-time algorithms?
2. What are the classes $\mathcal{PF}$ and $\mathcal{PC}$?
3. What are the classes $\mathcal{P}$ and $\mathcal{NP}$?
4. List a few computational problems in $\mathcal{PF}$ (resp., $\mathcal{P}$).
5. Going beyond the list of the previous question, list a few problems in $\mathcal{PC}$ (resp., $\mathcal{NP}$).
6. What does $\mathcal{PC} \not\subseteq \mathcal{PF}$ mean in intuitive terms?
7. What does $\mathcal{P} \neq \mathcal{NP}$ mean in intuitive terms?
8. Is it the case that $\mathcal{PC} \not\subseteq \mathcal{PF}$ if and only if $\mathcal{P} \neq \mathcal{NP}$?
9. What are the justifications for believing that $\mathcal{P} \neq \mathcal{NP}$?

*Exercise 2.2 ($\mathcal{PF}$ contains problems that are not in $\mathcal{PC}$)* Show that $\mathcal{PF}$ contains some (unnatural) problems that are not in $\mathcal{PC}$.

*Guideline:* Consider the relation $R = \{(x, 1) : x \in \{0, 1\}^*\} \cup \{(x, 0) : x \in S\}$, where $S$ is some undecidable set. Note that $R$ is the disjoint union of two binary relations, denoted $R_1$ and $R_2$, where $R_1$ is in $\mathcal{PF}$ whereas $R_2$ is not in $\mathcal{PC}$. Furthermore, for every $x$ it holds that $R_1(x) \neq \emptyset$.

**Exercise 2.3** In contrast to Exercise 2.2, show that if $R \in \mathcal{PF}$ and each instance of $R$ has at most one solution (i.e., $|R(x)| \leq 1$ for every $x$), then $R \in \mathcal{PC}$.

**Exercise 2.4** Show that the following search problems are in $\mathcal{PC}$.

1. Finding a traveling salesman tour of length that does not exceed a given threshold (when also given a matrix of distances between cities);
2. Finding the prime factorization of a given natural number;
3. Solving a given system of quadratic equations over a finite field;
4. Finding a truth assignment that satisfies a given Boolean formula.

(For Item 2, use the fact that primality can be tested in polynomial time.)

**Exercise 2.5** Show that any $S \in \mathcal{NP}$ has many different NP-proof systems (i.e., verification procedures $V_1, V_2, \ldots$ such that $V_i(x, y) = 1$ does not imply $V_j(x, y) = 1$ for $i \neq j$).

*Guideline:* For $V$ and $p$ as in Definition 2.5, define $V_i(x, y) = 1$ if $|y| = p(|x|) + i$ and there exists a prefix $y'$ of $y$ such that $V(x, y') = 1$.

**Exercise 2.6** Relying on the fact that primality is decidable in polynomial time and assuming that there is no polynomial-time factorization algorithm, present two "natural but fundamentally different" NP-proof systems for the set of composite numbers.

*Guideline:* Consider the following verification procedures $V_1$ and $V_2$ for the set of composite numbers. Let $V_1(n, y) = 1$ if and only if $y = n$ and $n$ is not a prime, and $V_2(n, m) = 1$ if and only if $m$ is a non-trivial divisor of $n$. Show that valid proofs with respect to $V_1$ are easy to find, whereas valid proofs with respect to $V_2$ are hard to find.

**Exercise 2.7** Show that for every $R \in \mathcal{PC}$, there exists $R' \in \mathcal{PC}$ and a polynomial $p$ such that for every $x$ it holds that $R'(x) \subseteq \{0, 1\}^{p(|x|)}$, and $R' \in \mathcal{PF}$ if and only if $R \in \mathcal{PF}$. Formulate and prove a similar fact for NP-proof systems.

*Guideline:* Note that for every $R \in \mathcal{PC}$, there exists a polynomial $p$ such that for every $(x, y) \in R$ it holds that $|y| < p(|x|)$. Define $R'$ such that $R'(x) \stackrel{\text{def}}{=} \{y01^{p(|x|)-(|y|+1)} : (x, y) \in R\}$, and prove that $R' \in \mathcal{PF}$ if and only if $R \in \mathcal{PF}$.

**Exercise 2.8** In continuation of Exercise 2.7, show that for every set $S \in \mathcal{NP}$ and *every* sufficiently large polynomial $p$, there exists an NP-proof system $V$

such that all NP-witnesses to $x \in S$ are of length $p(|x|)$ (i.e., if $V(x, y) = 1$ then $|y| = p(|x|)$).

*Guideline:* Start with an NP-proof system $V_0$ for $S$ and a polynomial $p_0$ such that $V_0(x, y) = 1$ implies $|y| \leq p_0(|x|)$. For every polynomial $p > p_0$ (i.e., $p(n) > p_0(n)$ for all $n \in \mathbb{N}$), define $V$ such that $V(x, y'01^{p(|x|)-(|y'|+1)}) = 1$ if $V_0(x, y') = 1$ and $V(x, y) = 0$ otherwise.

***Exercise 2.9*** In continuation of Exercise 2.8, show that for every set $S \in \mathcal{NP}$ and *every* "nice" $\ell : \mathbb{N} \to \mathbb{N}$, there exists set $S' \in \mathcal{NP}$ such that (1) $S' \in \mathcal{P}$ if and only if $S \in \mathcal{P}$, and (2) there exists an NP-proof system $V'$ such that all NP-witnesses to $x \in S'$ are of length $\ell(|x|)$. Specifically, consider as nice any function $\ell : \mathbb{N} \to \mathbb{N}$ such that $\ell$ is monotonically non-decreasing, computable in polynomial time,[13] and satisfies $\ell(n) \leq \text{poly}(n)$ and $n \leq \text{poly}(\ell(n))$ (for every $n \in \mathbb{N}$). Note that the novelty here (wrt Exercise 2.8) is that $\ell$ may be a sub-linear function (e.g., $\ell(n) = \sqrt{n}$).

*Guideline:* For an adequate polynomial $p'$, consider $S' \stackrel{\text{def}}{=} \{x01^{p'(|x|)-|x|-1}\}$ and the NP-proof system $V'$ such that $V'(x01^{p'(|x|)-|x|-1}, y) = V(x, y)$ and $V'(x', y) = 0$ if $|x'| \notin \{p'(n) : n \in \mathbb{N}\}$. Now, use Exercise 2.8.

***Exercise 2.10*** Show that for every $S \in \mathcal{NP}$, there exists an NP-proof system $V$ such that the witness sets $W_x \stackrel{\text{def}}{=} \{y : V(x, y) = 1\}$ are disjoint.

*Guideline:* Starting with an NP-proof system $V_0$ for $S$, consider $V$ such that $V(x, y) = 1$ if $y = \langle x, y' \rangle$ and $V_0(x, y') = 1$ (and $V(x, y) = 0$ otherwise).

***Exercise 2.11*** Regarding Definition 2.7, show that if $S$ is accepted by some non-deterministic machine of time complexity $t$, then it is accepted by a non-deterministic machine of time complexity $O(t)$ that has a transition function that maps each possible symbol-state pair to exactly two triples.

*Guideline:* First note that a $k$-way (non-deterministic) choice can be emulated by $\log_2 k$ (non-deterministic) binary choices. (Indeed, this requires creating $O(k)$ new states for each such $k$-way choice.) Also note that one can introduce fictitious (non-deterministic) choices by duplicating the set of states of the machine.

---

[13] In fact, it suffices to require that the mapping $n \mapsto \ell(n)$ can be computed in time $\text{poly}(n)$.

# 3

# Polynomial-time Reductions

**Overview:** Reductions are procedures that use "functionally specified" subroutines. That is, the functionality of the subroutine is specified, but its operation remains unspecified and its running time is counted at unit cost. Thus, a reduction solves one computational problem by using oracle (or subroutine) calls to another computational problem. Analogously to our focus on efficient (i.e., polynomial-time) algorithms, here we focus on efficient (i.e., polynomial-time) reductions.

We present a general notion of (polynomial-time) reductions among computational problems, and view the notion of a "Karp-reduction" (also known as "many-to-one reduction") as an important special case that suffices (and is more convenient) in many cases. Reductions play a key role in the theory of NP-completeness, which is the topic of Chapter 4.

In the current chapter, we stress the fundamental nature of the notion of a reduction per se and highlight two specific applications: reducing search problems and optimization problems to decision problems. Furthermore, in these applications, it will be important to use the general notion of a reduction (i.e., "Cook-reduction" rather than "Karp-reduction"). We comment that the aforementioned reductions of search and optimization problems to decision problems further justify the common focus on the study of the decision problems.

**Organization.** We start by presenting the general notion of a polynomial-time reduction and important special cases of it (see Section 3.1). In Section 3.2, we present the notion of optimization problems and reduce such problems to corresponding search problems. In Section 3.3, we discuss the reduction of search problems to corresponding decision problems, while emphasizing the special case in which the search problem is

> reduced to the decision problem that is implicit in it. (In such a case, we
> say that the search problem is self-reducible.)

## Teaching Notes

We assume that many students have heard of reductions, but we fear that most have obtained a conceptually distorted view of their fundamental nature. In particular, we fear that reductions are identified with the theory of NP-completeness, whereas reductions have numerous other important applications that have little to do with NP-completeness (or completeness with respect to any other class). In particular, we believe that it is important to show that (natural) search and optimization problems can be reduced to (natural) decision problems.

**On Our Terminology.** We prefer the terms *Cook-reductions* and *Karp-reductions* over the terms "general (polynomial-time) reductions" and "many-to-one (polynomial-time) reductions." Also, we use the term *self-reducibility* in a non-traditional way; that is, we say that the search problem of $R$ is self-reducible if it can be reduced to the decision problem of $S_R = \{x : \exists y$ s.t. $(x, y) \in R\}$, whereas traditionally, *self-reducibility* refers to decision problems and is closely related to our notion of *downward self-reducible* (presented in Exercise 3.16).

**A Minor Warning.** In Section 3.3.2, which is an advanced section, we assume that the students have heard of NP-completeness. Actually, we only need the students to know the definition of NP-completeness. Yet the teacher may prefer postponing the presentation of this material to Section 4.1 (or even to a later stage).

## 3.1 The General Notion of a Reduction

Reductions are procedures that use "functionally specified" subroutines. That is, the functionality of the subroutine is specified, but its operation remains unspecified and its running time is counted at unit cost. Analogously to algorithms, which are modeled by Turing machines, reductions can be modeled as *oracle* (Turing) machines. A reduction solves one computational problem (which may be either a search problem or a decision problem) by using oracle (or subroutine) calls to another computational problem (which again may be either a search or a decision problem). Thus, such a reduction yields a (simple) transformation of algorithms that solve the latter problem into algorithms that solve the former problem.

### 3.1.1 The Actual Formulation

The notion of a general algorithmic reduction was discussed in Section 1.3.3 and formally defined in Section 1.3.6. These reductions, called Turing-reductions and modeled by oracle machines (cf. Section 1.3.6), made no reference to the time complexity of the main algorithm (i.e., the oracle machine). Here, we focus on efficient (i.e., polynomial-time) reductions, which are often called *Cook-reductions*. That is, we consider oracle machines (as in Definition 1.11) that run in time that is polynomial in the length of their input. We stress that the running time of an oracle machine is the number of steps made during its (own) computation, and that the oracle's reply on each query is obtained in a single step.

The key property of efficient reductions is that they allow for the transformation of efficient implementations of the subroutine (or the oracle) into efficient implementations of the task reduced to it. That is, as we shall see, if one problem is Cook-reducible to another problem and the latter is polynomial-time solvable, then so is the former.

The most popular case is that of reducing decision problems to decision problems, but we will also explicitly consider reducing search problems to search problems and reducing search problems to decision problems. Note that when reducing to a decision problem, the oracle is determined as the unique valid solver of the decision problem (since the function $f : \{0, 1\}^* \to \{0, 1\}$ solves the decision problem of membership in $S$ if, for every $x$, it holds that $f(x) = 1$ if $x \in S$ and $f(x) = 0$ otherwise). In contrast, when reducing to a search problem, the oracle is not uniquely determined because there may be many different valid solvers (since the function $f : \{0, 1\}^* \to \{0, 1\}^* \cup \{\bot\}$ solves the search problem of $R$ if, for every $x$, it holds that $f(x) \in R(x) \stackrel{\text{def}}{=} \{y : (x, y) \in R\}$ if $R(x) \neq \emptyset$ and $f(x) = \bot$ otherwise).[1] We capture both cases in the following definition.

**Definition 3.1** (Cook-reduction): *A problem* $\Pi$ *is* Cook-reducible *to a problem* $\Pi'$ *if there exists a polynomial-time oracle machine* $M$ *such that for every*

---

[1] Indeed, the solver is unique only if for every $x$ it holds that $|R(x)| \leq 1$.

*function f that solves Π′ it holds that $M^f$ solves Π, where $M^f(x)$ denotes the output of M on input x when given oracle access to f.*

Note that Π (resp., Π′) may be either a search problem or a decision problem (or even a yet-undefined type of a problem). At this point, the reader should verify that *if Π is Cook-reducible to Π′ and Π′ is solvable in polynomial time, then so is Π*; see Exercise 3.2 (which also asserts other properties of Cook-reductions).

We highlight the fact that a Cook-reduction of Π to Π′ yields a simple transformation of efficient algorithms that solve the problem Π′ into efficient algorithms that solve the problem Π. The transformation consists of combining the code (or description) of any algorithm that solves Π′ with the code of reduction, yielding a code of an algorithm that solves Π.

**An Important Example.** Observe that the second part of the proof of Theorem 2.6 is actually a Cook-reduction of the search problem of any $R$ in $\mathcal{PC}$ to a decision problem regarding a related set $S'_R = \{\langle x, y' \rangle : \exists y'' \text{ s.t. } (x, y'y'') \in R\}$, which is in $\mathcal{NP}$. Thus, that proof establishes the following result.

**Theorem 3.2:** *Every search problem in $\mathcal{PC}$ is Cook-reducible to some decision problem in $\mathcal{NP}$.*

We shall see a tighter relation between search and decision problems in Section 3.3; that is, in some cases, $R$ will be reduced to $S_R = \{x : \exists y \text{ s.t. } (x, y) \in R\}$ rather than to $S'_R$.

### 3.1.2 Special Cases

We shall consider two restricted types of Cook-reductions, where the first type applies only to decision problems and the second type applies only to search problems. In both cases, the reductions are restricted to making a single query.

**Restricted Reductions Among Decision Problems.** A Karp-reduction is a restricted type of a reduction (from one decision problem to another decision problem) that makes a single query, and furthermore replies with the very answer that it has received. Specifically, for decision problems $S$ and $S'$, we say that $S$ is Karp-reducible to $S'$ if there is a Cook-reduction of $S$ to $S'$ *that operates as follows*: On input $x$ (an instance for $S$), the reduction computes $x'$, makes query $x'$ to the oracle $S'$ (i.e., invokes the subroutine for $S'$ on input $x'$), and answers whatever the latter returns. This reduction is often represented by the polynomial-time computable mapping of $x$ to $x'$; that is, the standard definition of a Karp-reduction is actually as follows.

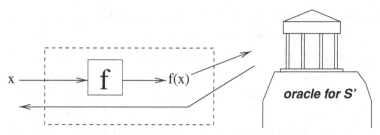

Figure 3.1. The Cook-reduction that arises from a Karp-reduction.

**Definition 3.3** (Karp-reduction): *A polynomial-time computable function f is called a* Karp-reduction *of S to S' if, for every x, it holds that $x \in S$ if and only if $f(x) \in S'$.*

Thus, syntactically speaking, a Karp-reduction is not a Cook-reduction, but it trivially gives rise to one (i.e., on input $x$, the oracle machine makes query $f(x)$, and returns the oracle answer; see Figure 3.1). Being slightly inaccurate but essentially correct, we shall say that Karp-reductions are special cases of Cook-reductions.

Needless to say, Karp-reductions constitute a very restricted case of Cook-reductions. Specifically, Karp-reductions refer only to reductions among decision problems, and are restricted to a single query (and to the way in which the answer is used). Still, Karp-reductions suffice for many applications (most importantly, for the theory of NP-completeness (when developed for decision problems)). On the other hand, due to purely technical (or syntactic) reasons, Karp-reductions are not adequate for reducing search problems to decision problems. Furthermore, Cook-reductions that make a single query are inadequate for reducing (hard) search problems to any decision problem (see Exercise 3.12).[2] We note that *even within the domain of reductions among decision problems, Karp-reductions are less powerful than Cook-reductions.* Specifically, whereas each decision problem is Cook-reducible to its complement, some decision problems are *not* Karp-reducible to their complement (see Exercises 3.4 and 5.10).

**Augmentation for Reductions Among Search Problems.** Karp-reductions may (and should) be augmented in order to handle reductions among search problems. The augmentation should provide a way of obtaining a solution for

---

[2] Cook-reductions that make a single query overcome the technical reason that makes Karp-reductions inadequate for reducing search problems to decision problems. (Recall that Karp-reductions are a special case of Cook-reductions that make a single query; cf. Exercise 3.11.)

the original instance from any solution for the reduced instance. Indeed, such a reduction of the search problem of $R$ to the search problem of $R'$ operates as follows: On input $x$ (an instance for $R$), the reduction computes $x'$, makes query $x'$ to the oracle $R'$ (i.e., invokes the subroutine for searching $R'$ on input $x'$) obtaining $y'$ such that $(x', y') \in R'$, and uses $y'$ to compute a solution $y$ to $x$ (i.e., $y \in R(x)$). Thus, such a reduction can be represented by two polynomial-time computable mappings, $f$ and $g$, such that $(x, g(x, y')) \in R$ for any $y'$ that is a solution of $f(x)$ (i.e., for $y'$ that satisfies $(f(x), y') \in R'$). Indeed, $f$ is a Karp-reduction (of $S_R = \{x : R(x) \neq \emptyset\}$ to $S_{R'} = \{x' : R'(x') \neq \emptyset\}$), but (unlike in the case of decision problems) the function $g$ may be non-trivial (i.e., we may not always have $g(x, y') = y'$). This type of reduction is called a Levin-reduction and, analogously to the case of a Karp-reduction, it is often identified with the two aforementioned mappings themselves (i.e., the (polynomial-time computable) mappings $f$ of $x$ to $x'$, and the (polynomial-time computable) mappings $g$ of $(x, y')$ to $y$).

**Definition 3.4** (Levin reduction): *A pair of polynomial-time computable functions, $f$ and $g$, is called a* Levin-reduction *of $R$ to $R'$ if $f$ is a Karp-reduction of $S_R = \{x : \exists y$ s.t. $(x, y) \in R\}$ to $S_{R'} = \{x' : \exists y'$ s.t. $(x', y') \in R'\}$ and for every $x \in S_R$ and $y' \in R'(f(x))$ it holds that $(x, g(x, y')) \in R$, where $R'(x') = \{y' : (x', y') \in R'\}$.*

Indeed, the (first) function $f$ preserves the existence of solutions; that is, for any $x$, it holds that $R(x) \neq \emptyset$ if and only if $R'(f(x)) \neq \emptyset$, since $f$ is a Karp-reduction of $S_R$ to $S_{R'}$. As for the second function (i.e., $g$), it maps any solution $y'$ for the reduced instance $f(x)$ to a solution for the original instance $x$ (where this mapping may also depend on $x$). We mention that it is natural also to consider a third function that maps solutions for $R$ to solutions for $R'$ (see Exercise 4.20).

Again, syntactically speaking, a Levin-reduction is not a Cook-reduction, but it trivially gives rise to one (i.e., on input $x$, the oracle machine makes query $f(x)$, and returns $g(x, y')$ if the oracle answers with $y' \neq \bot$ (and returns $\bot$ otherwise); see Figure 3.2).

### 3.1.3 Terminology and a Brief Discussion

Cook-reductions are often called general (polynomial-time) reductions, whereas Karp-reductions are often called many-to-one (polynomial-time) reductions. Indeed, throughout the current chapter, whenever we neglect to mention the type of a reduction, we actually mean a Cook-reduction.

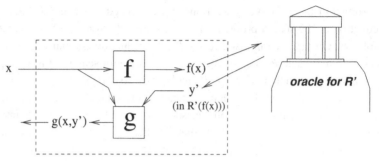

Figure 3.2. The Cook-reduction that arises from a Levin-reduction.

**Two Compound Notions.** The following terms, which refer to the existence of several reductions, are often used in advanced studies.

1. We say that two problems are computationally equivalent if they are reducible to each other. This means that the two problems are essentially as hard (or as easy). Note that computationally equivalent problems need not reside in the same complexity class.

   For example, as we shall see in Section 3.3, for many natural relations $R \in \mathcal{PC}$, the search problem of $R$ and the decision problem of $S_R = \{x : \exists y \text{ s.t. } (x, y) \in R\}$ are computationally equivalent, although (even syntactically) the two problems do not belong to the same class (i.e., $R \in \mathcal{PC}$ whereas $S_R \in \mathcal{NP}$). Also, each decision problem is computationally equivalent to its complement, although the two problems may not belong to the same class (see, e.g., Section 5.3).

2. We say that a *class of problems, C, is reducible to a problem $\Pi'$* if every problem in $C$ is reducible to $\Pi'$. We say that the class $C$ is reducible to the class $C'$ if for every $\Pi \in C$ there exists $\Pi' \in C'$ such that $\Pi$ is reducible to $\Pi'$.

   For example, Theorem 3.2 asserts that $\mathcal{PC}$ *is reducible to* $\mathcal{NP}$. Also note that $\mathcal{NP}$ is reducible to $\mathcal{PC}$ (see Exercise 3.9).

**On the Greater Flexibility of Cook-reductions.** The fact that we allow Cook-reductions (rather than confining ourselves to Karp-reductions) is essential to various important connections between decision problems and other computational problems. For example, as will be shown in Section 3.2, a natural class of optimization problems is reducible to $\mathcal{NP}$. Also recall that $\mathcal{PC}$ is reducible to $\mathcal{NP}$ (cf. Theorem 3.2). Furthermore, as will be shown in Section 3.3, many natural search problems in $\mathcal{PC}$ are reducible to a corresponding *natural* decision problem in $\mathcal{NP}$ (rather than merely to some problem in $\mathcal{NP}$). In all of these results, the reductions in use are (and must be) Cook-reductions.

Recall that we motivated the definition of Cook-reductions by referring to their natural ("positive") application, which offers a transformation of efficient implementations of the oracle into efficient algorithms for the reduced problem. Note, however, that once defined, reductions have a life of their own. In fact, the actual definition of a reduction does not refer to the aforementioned natural application, and reductions may be (and are) also used toward other applications. For further discussion, see Section 3.4.

## 3.2 Reducing Optimization Problems to Search Problems

Many search problems refer to a set of potential solutions, associated with each problem instance, such that different solutions are naturally assigned different "values" (resp., "costs"). For example, in the context of finding a clique in a given graph, the size of the clique may be considered the value of the solution. Likewise, in the context of finding a 2-partition of a given graph, the number of edges with both end points in the same side of the partition may be considered the cost of the solution. In such cases, one may be interested in finding a solution that has value exceeding some threshold (resp., cost below some threshold). Alternatively, one may seek a solution of maximum value (resp., minimum cost).

For simplicity, let us focus on the case of a value that we wish to maximize. Still, the two different aforementioned objectives (i.e., exceeding a threshold and optimization) give rise to two different (auxiliary) search problems related to the same relation $R$. Specifically, for a binary relation $R$ and a *value function* $f : \{0, 1\}^* \times \{0, 1\}^* \to \mathbb{R}$, we consider two search problems.

1. *Exceeding a threshold*: Given a pair $(x, v)$, the task is to find $y \in R(x)$ such that $f(x, y) \geq v$, where $R(x) = \{y : (x, y) \in R\}$. That is, we are actually referring to the search problem of the relation

$$R_f \overset{\text{def}}{=} \{(\langle x, v \rangle, y) : (x, y) \in R \land f(x, y) \geq v\}, \tag{3.1}$$

where $\langle x, v \rangle$ denotes a string that encodes the pair $(x, v)$.

2. *Maximization*: Given $x$, the task is to find $y \in R(x)$ such that $f(x, y) = v_x$, where $v_x$ is the maximum value of $f(x, y')$ over all $y' \in R(x)$. That is, we are actually referring to the search problem of the relation

$$R'_f \overset{\text{def}}{=} \{(x, y) \in R : f(x, y) = \max_{y' \in R(x)} \{f(x, y')\}\}. \tag{3.2}$$

(If $R(x) = \emptyset$, then we define $R'_f(x) = \emptyset$.)

Examples of value functions include the size of a clique in a graph, the amount of flow in a network (with link capacities), and so on. The task may be to find a clique of size exceeding a given threshold in a given graph or to find a maximum-size clique in a given graph. Note that in these examples, the "base" search problem (i.e., the relation $R$) is quite easy to solve, and the difficulty arises from the auxiliary condition on the value of a solution (presented in $R_f$ and $R'_f$). Indeed, one may trivialize $R$ (i.e., let $R(x) = \{0, 1\}^{\text{poly}(|x|)}$ for every $x$), and impose all necessary structure by the function $f$ (see Exercise 3.6).

We confine ourselves to the case that $f$ is (rational-valued and) polynomial-time computable, which in particular means that $f(x, y)$ can be represented by a rational number of length polynomial in $|x| + |y|$. We will show next that in this case, the two aforementioned search problems (i.e., of $R_f$ and $R'_f$) are computationally equivalent.

**Theorem 3.5:** *For any polynomial-time computable $f : \{0, 1\}^* \times \{0, 1\}^* \to \mathbb{Q}$ and a polynomially bounded binary relation $R$, let $R_f$ and $R'_f$ be as in Eq. (3.1) and Eq. (3.2), respectively. Then, the search problems of $R_f$ and $R'_f$ are computationally equivalent.*

Note that *for $R \in \mathcal{PC}$ and polynomial-time computable $f$, it holds that $R_f \in \mathcal{PC}$.* Combining Theorems 3.2 and 3.5, it follows that *in this case both $R_f$ and $R'_f$ are reducible to $\mathcal{NP}$.* We note, however, that even in this case it does not necessarily hold that $R'_f \in \mathcal{PC}$ (unless, of course, $\mathcal{P} = \mathcal{NP}$). See further discussion following the proof.

**Proof:** The search problem of $R_f$ is reduced to the search problem of $R'_f$ by finding an optimal solution (for the given instance) and comparing its value to the given threshold value. That is, we construct an oracle machine that solves $R_f$ by making a single query to $R'_f$. Specifically, on input $(x, v)$, the machine issues the query $x$ (to a solver for $R'_f$), obtaining the optimal solution $y$ (or an indication $\perp$ that $R(x) = \emptyset$), computes $f(x, y)$, and returns $y$ if $f(x, y) \geq v$. Otherwise (i.e., either $y = \perp$ or $f(x, y) < v$), the machine returns an indication that $R_f(\langle x, v \rangle) = \emptyset$.

Turning to the opposite direction, we reduce the search problem of $R'_f$ to the search problem of $R_f$ by first finding the optimal value $v_x = \max_{y \in R(x)}\{f(x, y)\}$ (by binary search on its possible values), and next finding a solution of value $v_x$. In both steps, we use oracle calls to $R_f$. For simplicity, we assume that $f$ assigns *positive* integer values (see Exercise 3.7), and let $\ell = \text{poly}(|x|)$ be such that $f(x, y) \leq 2^\ell - 1$ for every $y \in R(x)$. Then, on input $x$, we first find $v_x = \max\{f(x, y) : y \in R(x)\}$, by making oracle calls of the form $\langle x, v \rangle$. The point is that $v_x < v$ if and only if $R_f(\langle x, v \rangle) = \emptyset$, which in turn is indicated by the oracle answer $\bot$ (to the query $\langle x, v \rangle$). Making $\ell$ queries, we determine $v_x$ (see Exercise 3.8). Note that in case $R(x) = \emptyset$, all the answers will indicate that $R_f(\langle x, v \rangle) = \emptyset$, and we halt indicating that $R'_f(x) = \emptyset$ (which is indeed due to $R(x) = \emptyset$). Thus, we continue only if $v_x > 0$, which indicates that $R'_f(x) \neq \emptyset$. At this point, we make the query $(x, v_x)$, and halt returning the oracle's answer, which is a string $y \in R(x)$ such that $f(x, y) = v_x$. ∎

**Comments Regarding the Proof of Theorem 3.5.** The first direction of the proof uses the hypothesis that $f$ is polynomial-time computable, whereas the opposite direction only uses the fact that the optimal value lies in a finite space of exponential size that can be "efficiently searched." While the first direction is proved using a Levin-reduction, this seems impossible for the opposite direction (i.e., finding an optimal solution does not seem to be Levin-reducible to finding a solution that exceeds a threshold).

**On the Complexity of $R_f$ and $R'_f$.** Here, we focus on the natural case in which $R \in \mathcal{PC}$ and $f$ is polynomial-time computable. In this case, Theorem 3.5 asserts that $R_f$ and $R'_f$ are computationally equivalent. A closer look reveals, however, that $R_f \in \mathcal{PC}$ always holds, whereas $R'_f \in \mathcal{PC}$ does *not* necessarily hold. That is, the problem of finding a solution (for a given instance) that exceeds a given threshold is in the class $\mathcal{PC}$, whereas the problem of finding an optimal solution is not necessarily in the class $\mathcal{PC}$. For example, the problem of finding a clique of a given size $K$ in a given graph $G$ is in $\mathcal{PC}$, whereas the problem of finding a maximum-size clique in a given graph $G$ is not known (and is quite unlikely)[3] to be in $\mathcal{PC}$ (although it is Cook-reducible to $\mathcal{PC}$).

The foregoing discussion suggests that the class of problems that are reducible to $\mathcal{PC}$, which seems different from $\mathcal{PC}$ itself, is a natural and interesting class. Indeed, for every $R \in \mathcal{PC}$ and polynomial-time computable $f$, the former class contains $R'_f$.

## 3.3 Self-Reducibility of Search Problems

The results to be presented in this section further justify the focus on decision problems. Loosely speaking, these results show that for many natural relations

---

[3] See Exercise 5.14.

$R$, the question of whether or not the search problem of $R$ is efficiently solvable (i.e., is in $\mathcal{PF}$) is equivalent to the question of whether or not the "decision problem implicit in $R$" (i.e., $S_R = \{x : \exists y \text{ s.t. } (x, y) \in R\}$) is efficiently solvable (i.e., is in $\mathcal{P}$). In fact, we will show that these two computational problems (i.e., $R$ and $S_R$) are computationally equivalent. Note that the decision problem of $S_R$ is easily reducible to the search problem of $R$, and so our focus is on the other direction. That is, we are interested in relations $R$ for which the search problem of $R$ is reducible to the decision problem of $S_R$. In such a case, we say that $R$ is self-reducible.[4]

**Definition 3.6** (the decision implicit in a search and self-reducibility): *The decision problem implicit in the search problem of $R$ is deciding membership in the set $S_R = \{x : R(x) \neq \emptyset\}$, where $R(x) = \{y : (x, y) \in R\}$. The search problem of $R$ is called self-reducible if it can be reduced to the decision problem of $S_R$.*

Note that the search problem of $R$ and the problem of deciding membership in $S_R$ refer to the same instances: The search problem requires finding an adequate solution (i.e., given $x$ find $y \in R(x)$), whereas the decision problem refers to the question of whether such solutions exist (i.e., given $x$ determine whether or not $R(x)$ is non-empty). Thus, $S_R$ corresponds to the intuitive notion of a "decision problem implicit in $R$," because $S_R$ is a decision problem that one implicitly solves when solving the search problem of $R$. Indeed, for any $R$, *the decision problem of $S_R$ is easily reducible to the search problem for $R$* (see Exercise 3.10). It follows that *if a search problem $R$ is self-reducible, then it is computationally equivalent to the decision problem $S_R$.*

Note that the general notion of a reduction (i.e., Cook-reduction) seems inherent to the notion of self-reducibility. This is the case not only due to syntactic considerations, but is also the case for the following inherent reason. An oracle to any decision problem returns a single bit per invocation, while the intractability of a search problem in $\mathcal{PC}$ must be due to the lack of more than a "single bit of information" (see Exercise 3.12).

We shall see that self-reducibility is a property of many natural search problems (including all NP-complete search problems). This justifies the relevance of decision problems to search problems in a stronger sense than established

---

[4] Our usage of the term *self-reducibility* differs from the traditional one. Traditionally, a decision problem is called (downward) self-reducible if it is Cook-reducible to itself via a reduction that on input $x$ only makes queries that are smaller than $x$ (according to some appropriate measure on the size of instances). Under some natural restrictions (i.e., the reduction takes the disjunction of the oracle answers), such reductions yield reductions of search to decision (as discussed in the main text). For further details, see Exercise 3.16.

in Section 2.4: Recall that in Section 2.4, we showed that the fate of the search problem class $\mathcal{PC}$ (wrt $\mathcal{PF}$) is determined by the fate of the decision problem class $\mathcal{NP}$ (wrt $\mathcal{P}$). Here, we show that for many natural search problems in $\mathcal{PC}$ (i.e., self-reducible ones), the fate of such an individual problem $R$ (wrt $\mathcal{PF}$) is determined by the fate of the individual decision problem $S_R$ (wrt $\mathcal{P}$), where $S_R$ is the decision problem implicit in $R$. (Recall that $R \in \mathcal{PC}$ implies $S_R \in \mathcal{NP}$.) Thus, here we have "fate reductions" at the level of individual problems, rather than only at the level of classes of problems (as established in Section 2.4).

### 3.3.1 Examples

We now present a few search problems that are self-reducible. We start with SAT (see Appendix A.2), the set of satisfiable Boolean formulae (in CNF), and consider the search problem in which given a formula one should find a truth assignment that satisfies it. The corresponding relation is denoted $R_{\mathrm{SAT}}$; that is, $(\phi, \tau) \in R_{\mathrm{SAT}}$ if $\tau$ is a satisfying assignment to the formula $\phi$. Indeed, the decision problem implicit in $R_{\mathrm{SAT}}$ is SAT. Note that $R_{\mathrm{SAT}}$ is in $\mathcal{PC}$ (i.e., it is polynomially bounded, and membership of $(\phi, \tau)$ in $R_{\mathrm{SAT}}$ is easy to decide (by evaluating a Boolean expression)).

**Proposition 3.7** ($R_{\mathrm{SAT}}$ *is self-reducible*): *The search problem of $R_{\mathrm{SAT}}$ is reducible to* SAT.

Thus, the search problem of $R_{\mathrm{SAT}}$ is computationally equivalent to deciding membership in SAT. Hence, in studying the complexity of SAT, we also address the complexity of the search problem of $R_{\mathrm{SAT}}$.

**Proof:** We present an oracle machine that solves the search problem of $R_{\mathrm{SAT}}$ by making oracle calls to SAT. Given a formula $\phi$, we find a satisfying assignment to $\phi$ (in case such an assignment exists) as follows. First, we query SAT on $\phi$ itself, and return an indication that there is no solution if the oracle answer is 0 (indicating $\phi \notin$ SAT). Otherwise, we let $\tau$, initiated to the empty string, denote a prefix of a satisfying assignment of $\phi$. We proceed in iterations, where in each iteration we extend $\tau$ by one bit (as long as $\tau$ does not set all variables of $\phi$). This is done as follows: First we derive a formula, denoted $\phi'$, by setting the first $|\tau| + 1$ variables of $\phi$ according to the values $\tau 0$. We then query SAT on $\phi'$ (which means that we ask whether or not $\tau 0$ is a prefix of a satisfying assignment of $\phi$). If the answer is positive, then we set $\tau \leftarrow \tau 0$ else we set $\tau \leftarrow \tau 1$. This procedure relies on the fact that if $\tau$ is a prefix of a satisfying assignment of $\phi$ and $\tau 0$ is not a prefix of a satisfying assignment of $\phi$, then $\tau 1$ must be a prefix of a satisfying assignment of $\phi$.

We wish to highlight a key point that has been blurred in the foregoing description. Recall that the formula $\phi'$ is obtained by replacing some variables by constants, which means that $\phi'$ per se contains Boolean variables as well as Boolean constants. However, the standard definition of SAT disallows Boolean constants in its instances.[5] Nevertheless, $\phi'$ can be simplified such that the resulting formula contains no Boolean constants. This simplification is performed according to the straightforward Boolean rules: That is, the constant false can be omitted from any clause, but if a clause contains only occurrences of the constant false, then the entire formula simplifies to false. Likewise, if the constant true appears in a clause, then the entire clause can be omitted, and if all clauses are omitted, then the entire formula simplifies to true. Needless to say, if the simplification process yields a Boolean constant, then we may skip the query, and otherwise we just use the simplified form of $\phi'$ as our query.  ■

**Other Examples.** Reductions analogous to the one used in the proof of Proposition 3.7 can also be presented for other search problems (and not only for NP-complete ones). Two such examples are searching for a 3-coloring of a given graph and searching for an isomorphism between a given pair of graphs (where the first problem is known to be NP-complete and the second problem is believed not to be NP-complete). In both cases, the reduction of the search problem to the corresponding decision problem consists of iteratively extending a prefix of a valid solution, by making suitable queries in order to decide which extension to use. Note, however, that in these two cases, the process of getting rid of constants (representing partial solutions) is more involved. Specifically, in the case of Graph 3-Colorability (resp., Graph Isomorphism), we need to enforce a partial coloring of a given graph (resp., a partial isomorphism between a given pair of graphs); see Exercises 3.13 and 3.14, respectively.

**Reflection.** The proof of Proposition 3.7 (as well as the proofs of similar results) consists of two observations.

1. For every relation $R$ in $\mathcal{PC}$, it holds that the search problem of $R$ is reducible to the decision problem of $S_R' = \{\langle x, y' \rangle : \exists y'' \text{ s.t. } (x, y'y'') \in R\}$. Such a reduction is explicit in the proof of Theorem 2.6 and is implicit in the proof of Proposition 3.7.

---

[5] While the problem seems rather technical in the current setting (since it merely amounts to whether or not the definition of SAT allows Boolean constants in its instances), the analogous problem is far from being so technical in other cases (see Exercises 3.13 and 3.14).

2. For specific $R \in \mathcal{PC}$ (e.g., $S_{\text{SAT}}$), deciding membership in $S'_R$ is reducible to deciding membership in $S_R = \{x : \exists y \text{ s.t. } (x, y) \in R\}$. This is where the specific structure of SAT was used, allowing for a direct and natural transformation of instances of $S'_R$ to instances of $S_R$.

   We comment that if $S_R$ is NP-complete, then $S'_R$, which is always in $\mathcal{NP}$, is reducible to $S_R$ by the mere hypothesis that $S_R$ is NP-complete; this comment is elaborated in the following Section 3.3.2.

For an arbitrary $R \in \mathcal{PC}$, deciding membership in $S'_R$ is not necessarily reducible to deciding membership in $S_R$. Furthermore, deciding membership in $S'_R$ is not necessarily reducible to the search problem of $R$. (See Exercises 3.18, 3.19, and 3.20.)

In general, self-reducibility is a property of the search problem and not of the decision problem implicit in it. Furthermore, under plausible assumptions (e.g., the intractability of factoring), there exist relations $R_1, R_2 \in \mathcal{PC}$ having the same implicit-decision problem (i.e., $\{x : R_1(x) \neq \emptyset\} = \{x : R_2(x) \neq \emptyset\}$) such that $R_1$ is self-reducible but $R_2$ is not (see Exercise 3.21). However, for many natural decision problems, this phenomenon does not arise; that is, *for many natural NP-decision problems S, any NP-witness relation associated with S* (i.e., $R \in \mathcal{PC}$ such that $\{x : R(x) \neq \emptyset\} = S$) *is self-reducible*. For details, see the following Section 3.3.2.

### 3.3.2 Self-Reducibility of NP-Complete Problems

In this section, we assume that the reader has heard of NP-completeness. Actually, we only need the reader to know the definition of NP-completeness (i.e., a set $S$ is $\mathcal{NP}$-complete if $S \in \mathcal{NP}$ and every set in $\mathcal{NP}$ is reducible to $S$). Indeed, the reader may prefer to skip this section and return to it after reading Section 4.1 (or even later).

Recall that, in general, self-reducibility is a property of the search problem $R$ and not of the decision problem implicit in it (i.e., $S_R = \{x : R(x) \neq \emptyset\}$). In contrast, in the special case of NP-complete problems, self-reducibility holds for any witness relation associated with the (NP-complete) decision problem. That is, *all search problems that refer to finding NP-witnesses for any NP-complete decision problem are self-reducible.*

**Theorem 3.8:** *For every $R$ in $\mathcal{PC}$ such that $S_R$ is $\mathcal{NP}$-complete, the search problem of $R$ is reducible to deciding membership in $S_R$.*

In many cases, as in the proof of Proposition 3.7, the reduction of the search problem to the corresponding decision problem is quite natural. The following proof presents a generic reduction (which may be "unnatural" in some cases).

**Proof:** In order to reduce the search problem of $R$ to deciding $S_R$, we compose the following two reductions:

1. A reduction of the search problem of $R$ to deciding membership in $S'_R = \{\langle x, y' \rangle : \exists y'' \text{ s.t. } (x, y'y'') \in R\}$.
   As stated in Section 3.3.1 (in the paragraph titled "Reflection"), such a reduction is implicit in the proof of Proposition 3.7 (as well as being explicit in the proof of Theorem 2.6).
2. A reduction of $S'_R$ to $S_R$.
   This reduction exists by the hypothesis that $S_R$ is $\mathcal{NP}$-complete and the fact that $S'_R \in \mathcal{NP}$. (Note that we need not assume that this reduction is a Karp-reduction, and furthermore it may be an "unnatural" reduction).

The theorem follows. ∎

## 3.4 Digest and General Perspective

Recall that we presented (polynomial-time) reductions as (efficient) algorithms that use functionally specified subroutines. That is, an efficient reduction of problem $\Pi$ to problem $\Pi'$ is an efficient algorithm that solves $\Pi$ while making subroutine calls to any procedure that solves $\Pi'$. This presentation fits the "natural" ("positive") application of such a reduction; that is, *combining such a reduction with an efficient implementation of the subroutine* (that solves $\Pi'$), *we obtain an efficient algorithm for solving* $\Pi$.

We note that the existence of a polynomial-time reduction of $\Pi$ to $\Pi'$ actually means more than the latter implication. For example, a moderately inefficient algorithm for solving $\Pi'$ also yields something for $\Pi$; that is, if $\Pi'$ is solvable in time $t'$ then $\Pi$ is solvable in time $t$ such that $t(n) = \text{poly}(n) \cdot t'(\text{poly}(n))$; for example, if $t'(n) = n^{\log_2 n}$ then $t(n) = \text{poly}(n)^{1+\log_2 \text{poly}(n)} = n^{O(\log n)}$. Thus, *the existence of a polynomial-time reduction of $\Pi$ to $\Pi'$ yields a general upper bound on the time complexity of $\Pi$ in terms of the time complexity of $\Pi'$.*

We note that tighter relations between the complexity of $\Pi$ and $\Pi'$ can be established whenever the reduction satisfies additional properties. For example, suppose that $\Pi$ is polynomial-time reducible to $\Pi'$ by a reduction that makes queries of linear length (i.e., on input $x$ each query has length $O(|x|)$). Then, if $\Pi'$ is solvable in time $t'$ then $\Pi$ is solvable in time $t$ such that $t(n) = \text{poly}(n) \cdot t'(O(n))$; for example, if $t'(n) = 2^{\sqrt{n}}$ then $t(n) = 2^{O(\log n) + \sqrt{O(n)}} = 2^{O(\sqrt{n})}$. We further note that bounding other complexity measures of the reduction (e.g., its space complexity) allows for relating the corresponding complexities of the problems.

In contrast to the foregoing "positive" applications of polynomial-time reductions, the theory of NP-completeness (presented in Chapter 4) is famous for its "negative" application of such reductions. Let us elaborate. The fact that Π is polynomial-time reducible to Π' means that *if solving* Π' *is feasible, then solving* Π *is feasible*. The direct "positive" application starts with the hypothesis that Π' is feasibly solvable and infers that so is Π. In contrast, the "negative" application uses the counter-positive: It starts with the hypothesis that solving Π is infeasible and infers that the same holds for Π'.

# Exercises

### Exercise 3.1 *(a quiz)*

1. What are Cook-reductions?
2. What are Karp-reductions and Levin-reductions?
3. What is the motivation for defining all of these types of reductions?
4. Can any problem in $\mathcal{PC}$ be reduced to some problem in $\mathcal{NP}$?
5. What is self-reducibility and how does it relate to the previous question?
6. List five search problems that are self-reducible. (See Exercise 3.15.)

### Exercise 3.2 Verify the following properties of Cook-reductions:

1. Cook-reductions preserve efficient solvability: If Π is Cook-reducible to Π' and Π' is solvable in polynomial time, then so is Π.
2. Cook-reductions are transitive: If Π is Cook-reducible to Π' and Π' is Cook-reducible to Π'', then Π is Cook-reducible to Π''.
3. Cook-reductions generalize efficient decision procedures: If Π is solvable in polynomial time, then it is Cook-reducible to any problem Π'.

In continuation of the last item, show that a problem Π is solvable in polynomial time if and only if it is Cook-reducible to a trivial problem (e.g., deciding membership in the empty set).

### Exercise 3.3 Show that Karp-reductions (and Levin-reductions) are transitive.

### Exercise 3.4 Show that some decision problems are not Karp-reducible to their complement (e.g., the empty set is not Karp-reducible to $\{0, 1\}^*$).

A popular exercise of dubious nature is showing that any decision problem in $\mathcal{P}$ is Karp-reducible to any *non-trivial* decision problem, where the decision problem regarding a set $S$ is called non-trivial if $S \neq \emptyset$ and $S \neq \{0, 1\}^*$. It follows that every non-trivial set in $\mathcal{P}$ is Karp-reducible to its complement.

**Exercise 3.5 (Exercise 2.7, reformulated)** Show that for every search problem $R \in \mathcal{PC}$ there exists a polynomial $p$ and a search problem $R' \in \mathcal{PC}$ that is computationally equivalent to $R$ such that for every $x$ it holds that $R'(x) \subseteq \{0, 1\}^{p(|x|)}$. Formulate and prove a similar fact for NP-proof systems. Similarly, revisit Exercise 2.9.

**Exercise 3.6 (reducing search problems to optimization problems)** For every polynomially bounded relation $R$ (resp., $R \in \mathcal{PC}$), present a function $f$ (resp., a polynomial-time computable function $f$) such that the search problem of $R$ is computationally equivalent to the search problem in which given $(x, v)$ one has to find a $y \in \{0, 1\}^{\text{poly}(|x|)}$ such that $f(x, y) \geq v$.

*Guideline:* Let $f(x, y) = 1$ if $(x, y) \in R$ and $f(x, y) = 0$ otherwise.

**Exercise 3.7** In the proof of the second direction of Theorem 3.5, we made the simplifying assumption that $f$ assigns values that are both integral and positive.

1. Justify the aforementioned assumption by showing that for any rational-valued function $f$ there exists a function $g$ as in the assumption such that $R_f$ (resp., $R'_f$) is computationally equivalent to $R_g$ (resp., $R'_g$), where $R_f$, $R'_f$ and $R_g$, $R'_g$ are as in Theorem 3.5.
2. Extend the current proof of Theorem 3.5 so that it also applies to the general case in which $f$ is rational-valued.

Indeed, the two items provide alternative justifications for the simplifying assumption made in the said proof.

**Exercise 3.8 (an application of binary search)** Show that using $\ell$ binary queries of the form "is $z < v$" it is possible to determine the value of an integer $z$ that is a priori known to reside in the interval $[0, 2^{\ell} - 1]$.

*Guideline:* Consider a process that iteratively halves the interval in which $z$ is known to reside in.

**Exercise 3.9** Prove that $\mathcal{NP}$ is reducible to $\mathcal{PC}$.

*Guideline:* Consider the search problem defined in Eq. (2.1).

**Exercise 3.10** Prove that for any $R$, the decision problem of $S_R$ is easily reducible to the search problem for $R$, and that if $R$ is in $\mathcal{PC}$ then $S_R$ is in $\mathcal{NP}$.

*Guideline:* Consider a reduction that invokes the search oracle and answer 1 if and only if the oracle returns some string (rather than the "no solution" symbol).

**Exercise 3.11 (Cook-reductions that make a single query)** Let $M$ be a polynomial-time oracle machine that *makes at most one query*. Show that the computation of $M$ can be represented by two polynomial-time computable functions $f$ and $g$ such that $M^F(x) = g(x, F(f(x)))$, where $M^F(x)$ denotes the output of $M$ on input $x$ when given oracle access to the function $F$. Discuss the relationship between such Cook-reductions and Karp-reductions (resp., Levin-reductions).

**Exercise 3.12** Prove that if $R \in \mathcal{PC}$ is reducible to $S_R$ by a Cook-reduction that makes a logarithmic number of queries, then $R \in \mathcal{PF}$. Thus, self-reducibility for problems in $\mathcal{PC} \setminus \mathcal{PF}$ requires making more than logarithmically many queries. More generally, prove that if $R \in \mathcal{PC} \setminus \mathcal{PF}$ is Cook-reducible to any decision problem, then this reduction makes more than a logarithmic number of queries.

*Guideline:* Note that the oracle answers can be emulated by trying all possibilities, and that (for $R \in \mathcal{PC}$) the correctness of the output of the oracle machine can be efficiently tested.

**Exercise 3.13** Show that the standard search problem of Graph 3-Colorability[6] is self-reducible, where this search problem consists of finding a 3-coloring for a given input graph.

*Guideline:* Iteratively extend the current prefix of a 3-coloring of the graph by making adequate oracle calls to the decision problem of Graph 3-Colorability. Specifically, encode the question of whether or not $(\chi_1, \ldots, \chi_t) \in \{1, 2, 3\}^t$ is a prefix of a 3-coloring of the graph $G$ as a query regarding the 3-colorability of an auxiliary graph $G'$. Note that we merely need to check whether $G$ has a 3-coloring in which the equalities and inequalities induced by the (prefix of the) coloring $(\chi_1, \ldots, \chi_t)$ hold. This can be done by adequate gadgets (e.g., inequality is enforced by an edge between the corresponding vertices, whereas equality is enforced by an adequate subgraph that includes the relevant vertices as well as auxiliary vertices).

**Exercise 3.14** Show that the standard search problem of Graph Isomorphism[7] is self-reducible, where this search problem consists of finding an isomorphism between a given pair of graphs.

---

[6] See Appendix A.1.
[7] See Appendix A.1.

*Guideline:* Iteratively extend the current prefix of an isomorphism between the two $N$-vertex graphs by making adequate oracle calls to the decision problem of Graph Isomorphism. Specifically, encode the question of whether or not $(\pi_1, \ldots, \pi_t) \in [N]^t$ is a prefix of an isomorphism between $G_1 = ([N], E_1)$ and $G_2 = ([N], E_2)$ as a query regarding isomorphism between two auxiliary graphs $G_1'$ and $G_2'$. This can be done by attaching adequate gadgets to pairs of vertices that we wish to be mapped to each other (by the isomorphism). For example, we may connect each of the vertices in the $i^{\text{th}}$ pair to an auxiliary star consisting of $(N + i)$ vertices.

**Exercise 3.15** List five search problems that are self-reducible.

*Guideline:* Note that three such problems were mentioned in Section 3.3.1. Additional examples may include any NP-complete search problem (see Section 3.3.2) as well as any problem in $\mathcal{PF}$.

**Exercise 3.16 (downward self-reducibility)** We say that a set $S$ is downward self-reducible if there exists a Cook-reduction of $S$ to itself that only makes queries that are each shorter than the reduction's input (i.e., if on input $x$ the reduction makes the query $q$ then $|q| < |x|$).[8]

1. Show that SAT is downward self-reducible with respect to a natural encoding of CNF formulae. Note that this encoding should have the property that instantiating a variable in a formula results in a shorter formula.
   A harder exercise consists of showing that Graph 3-Colorability is downward self-reducible with respect to some reasonable encoding of graphs. Note that this encoding has to be selected carefully.

   *Guideline:* For the case of SAT use the fact that $\phi \in$ SAT if and only if either $\phi_0 \in$ SAT or $\phi_1 \in$ SAT, where $\phi_\sigma$ denotes the formula $\phi$ with the first variable instantiated to $\sigma$. For the case of Graph 3-Colorability, partition all possible 3-colorings according to whether or not they assign the first pair of unconnected vertices the same color. Enforce an inequality constraint by connecting the two vertices, and enforce an equality constraint by combining the two vertices (rather than by connecting them via a gadget that contains auxiliary vertices as suggested in the guideline to Exercise 3.13). Use an encoding that guarantees that any $(n + 1)$-vertex graph has a longer description than any $n$-vertex graph, and that adding edges decreases the description length.[9]

---

[8] Note that on some instances, the reduction may make no queries at all. (This option prevents a possible non-viability of the definition due to very short instances.)

[9] For example, encode any $n$-vertex graph that has $m$ edges as an $(n^3 - 2m \log_2 n)$-bit long string that contains the (adequately padded) list of all pairs of unconnected vertices.

2. Suppose that $S$ is downward self-reducible *by a reduction that outputs the disjunction of the oracle answers*.[10] Show that in this case, $S$ is characterized by a witness relation $R \in \mathcal{PC}$ (i.e., $S = \{x : R(x) \neq \emptyset\}$) that is self-reducible (i.e., the search problem of $R$ is Cook-reducible to $S$). Needless to say, it follows that $S \in \mathcal{NP}$.

*Guideline:* Define $R$ such that $(x_0, \langle x_1, \ldots, x_t \rangle)$ is in $R$ if $x_t \in S \cap \{0, 1\}^{O(1)}$ and, for every $i \in \{0, 1, \ldots, t - 1\}$, on input $x_i$ the self-reduction makes a set of queries that contains the string $x_{i+1}$. Prove that if $x_0 \in S$ then a sequence $(x_0, \langle x_1, \ldots, x_t \rangle) \in R$ exists (by forward induction (which selects for each $x_i \in S$ a query $x_{i+1}$ in $S$)). Next, prove that $(x_0, \langle x_1, \ldots, x_t \rangle) \in R$ implies $x_0 \in S$ (by backward induction from $x_t \in S$ (which infers from the hypothesis $x_{i+1} \in S$ that $x_i$ is in $S$)). Finally, prove that $R \in \mathcal{PC}$ (by noting that $t \leq |x_0|$).

Note that the notion of downward self-reducibility may be generalized in some natural ways. For example, we may also say that $S$ is downward self-reducible in case it is computationally equivalent via Karp-reductions to some set that is downward self-reducible (in the foregoing strict sense). Note that Part 2 still holds.

**Exercise 3.17 (compressing Karp-reductions)** In continuation of Exercise 3.16, we consider downward self-reductions that make at most one query (i.e., Cook-reductions of decision problems to themselves that make at most one query such that this query is shorter than the reduction's input). Note that compressing Karp-reductions are a special case, where the Karp-reduction $f$ is called compressing if $|f(x)| < |x|$ holds for all but finitely many $x$'s. Prove that if $S$ is downward self-reducible by a Cook-reduction that makes at most one query, then $S \in \mathcal{P}$.

*Guideline:* Consider first the special case of compressing Karp-reductions. Observe that for every $x$ and $i$ (which may depend on $x$), it holds that $x \in S$ if and only if $f^i(x) \in S$, where $f^i(x)$ denotes the Karp-reduction $f$ iterated $i$ times. When extending the argument to the general case, use Exercise 3.11.

**Exercise 3.18 (NP-problems that are not self-reducible)**

1. Prove that if a search problem $R$ is not self-reducible then (1) $R \notin \mathcal{PF}$ and (2) the set $S'_R = \{\langle x, y' \rangle : \exists y'' \text{ s.t. } (x, y'y'') \in R\}$ is not Cook-reducible to $S_R = \{x : \exists y \text{ s.t. } (x, y) \in R\}$.

---

[10] Note that this condition holds for both problems considered in the previous item.

2. Assuming that $\mathcal{P} \neq \mathcal{NP} \cap \text{co}\mathcal{NP}$, where $\text{co}\mathcal{NP} \overset{\text{def}}{=} \{\{0, 1\}^* \setminus S : S \in \mathcal{NP}\}$, show that there exists a search problem that is in $\mathcal{PC}$ but is not self-reducible.

*Guideline:* Given $S \in (\mathcal{NP} \cap \text{co}\mathcal{NP}) \setminus \mathcal{P}$, present relations $R_1, R_2 \in \mathcal{PC}$ such that $S = \{x : R_1(x) \neq \emptyset\} = \{x : R_2(x) = \emptyset\}$. Then, consider the relation $R = \{(x, 1y) : (x, y) \in R_1\} \cup \{(x, 0y) : (x, y) \in R_2\}$, and prove that $R \in \mathcal{PC} \setminus \mathcal{PF}$. Noting that $S_R = \{0, 1\}^*$, infer that $R$ is not self-reducible. (Actually, $R = R_1 \cup R_2$ will work, too.)

**Exercise 3.19 (extending generic solutions' prefixes versus $\mathcal{PC}$ and $\mathcal{PF}$)** In contrast to what one may guess, extending solutions' prefixes (equiv., deciding membership in $S'_R = \{\langle x, y' \rangle : \exists y'' \text{ s.t. } (x, y'y'') \in R\}$) may not be easy even if finding solutions is easy (i.e., $R \in \mathcal{PF}$). Specifically, assuming that $\mathcal{P} \neq \mathcal{NP}$, present a search problem $R$ in $\mathcal{PC} \cap \mathcal{PF}$ such that deciding $S'_R$ is not reducible to the search problem of $R$.

*Guideline:* Consider the relation $R = \{(x, 0x) : x \in \{0, 1\}^*\} \cup \{(x, 1y) : (x, y) \in R'\}$, where $R'$ is an arbitrary relation in $\mathcal{PC} \setminus \mathcal{PF}$, and note that $R \in \mathcal{PC}$. Prove that $R \in \mathcal{PF}$ but $S'_R \notin \mathcal{P}$.

**Exercise 3.20** In continuation of Exercise 3.18, present a *natural* search problem $R$ in $\mathcal{PC}$ such that if factoring integers is intractable, then the search problem $R$ (and so also $S'_R$) is not reducible to $S_R$.

*Guideline:* As in Exercise 2.6, consider the relation $R$ such that $(n, q) \in R$ if the integer $q$ is a non-trivial divisor of the integer $n$. Use the fact that the set of prime numbers is in $\mathcal{P}$.

**Exercise 3.21** In continuation of Exercises 3.18 and 3.20, show that under suitable assumptions there exists relations $R_1, R_2 \in \mathcal{PC}$ having the same implicit-decision problem (i.e., $\{x : R_1(x) \neq \emptyset\} = \{x : R_2(x) \neq \emptyset\}$) such that $R_1$ is self-reducible but $R_2$ is not. Specifically:

1. Prove the existence of such relations assuming that $\mathcal{P} \neq \mathcal{NP} \cap \text{co}\mathcal{NP}$;
2. Present natural relations assuming the intractability of factoring.

Hint: see Exercise 2.6.

**Exercise 3.22** Using Theorem 3.2, provide an alternative (presentation of the) proof of Theorem 3.8 without referring to the set $S'_R = \{\langle x, y' \rangle : \exists y'' \text{ s.t. } (x, y'y'') \in R\}$.[11]

---

[11] Indeed, this is merely a matter of presentation, since the proof of Theorem 3.2 refers to $S'_R$. Thus, when using Theorem 3.2, the decision problem (in $\mathcal{NP}$) to which we reduce $R$ is arbitrary only from the perspective of the theorem's statement (but not from the perspective of its proof).

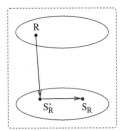 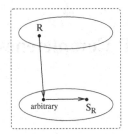 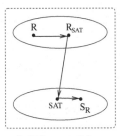

Figure 3.3. The three proofs of Theorem 3.8: The original proof of Theorem 3.8 is depicted on the left, the outline of Exercise 3.22 is in the middle, and the outline of Exercise 3.23 is on the right. The upper ellipses represent the class $\mathcal{PC}$, and the lower ellipses represent $\mathcal{NP}$.

*Guideline:* Theorem 3.2 implies that $R$ is Cook-reducible to some decision problem in $\mathcal{NP}$, which in turn is reducible to $S_R$ (due to the $\mathcal{NP}$-completeness of $S_R$).

**Exercise 3.23 (Theorem 3.8, revisited)** In continuation of Exercise 3.22, using Proposition 3.7 and the fact that $R_{\mathrm{SAT}}$ is $\mathcal{PC}$-complete (as per Definition 4.2), provide an alternative proof of Theorem 3.8 (again, without referring to the set $S_R'$). See Figure 3.3.

*Guideline:* Reduce the search problem of $R$ to deciding $S_R$, by composing the following three reductions: (1) a reduction of the search problem of $R$ to the search problem of $R_{\mathrm{SAT}}$, (2) a reduction of the search problem of $R_{\mathrm{SAT}}$ to SAT, and (3) a reduction of SAT to $S_R$.

# 4

# NP-Completeness

**Overview:** In light of the difficulty of settling the P-vs-NP Question, when faced with a hard problem H in NP, we cannot expect to prove that H is not in P (unconditionally), because this would imply $\mathcal{P} \neq \mathcal{NP}$. The best we can expect is a conditional proof that H is not in P, based on the assumption that NP is different from P. The contrapositive is proving that if H is in P, then so is any problem in NP (i.e., NP equals P). One possible way of proving such an assertion is showing that any problem in NP is polynomial-time reducible to H. This is the essence of the theory of NP-completeness.

In this chapter we prove the existence of NP-complete problems, that is, the existence of individual problems that "effectively encode" a wide class of seemingly unrelated problems (i.e., all problems in NP). We also prove that deciding the satisfiability of a given Boolean formula is NP-complete. Other NP-complete problems include deciding whether a given graph is 3-colorable and deciding whether a given graph contains a clique of a given size. The core of establishing the NP-completeness of these problems is showing that each of them can encode any other problem in NP. Thus, these demonstrations provide a method of encoding instances of any NP problem as instances of the target NP-complete problem.

**Organization.** We start by defining NP-complete problems (see Section 4.1) and demonstrating their existence (see Section 4.2). Next, in Section 4.3, we present several natural NP-complete problems, including circuit and formula satisfiability (i.e., CSAT and SAT), set cover, and Graph 3-Colorability. In Section 4.4, assuming that $\mathcal{P} \neq \mathcal{NP}$, we prove the existence of NP problems that are neither in P nor NP-complete.

# Teaching Notes

We are sure that many students have heard of NP-completeness before, but we suspect that most of them have missed some important conceptual points. Specifically, we fear that they have missed the point that the mere existence of NP-complete problems is amazing (let alone that these problems include natural ones such as SAT). We believe that this situation is a consequence of presenting the detailed proof of Cook's Theorem right after defining NP-completeness. In contrast, *we suggest starting with a proof that Bounded Halting is NP-complete.*

We suggest establishing the NP-completeness of SAT by a reduction from the circuit satisfaction problem (CSAT), after establishing the NP-completeness of the latter. Doing so allows us to decouple two important parts of the proof of the NP-completeness of SAT: the emulation of Turing machines by circuits and the emulation of circuits by formulae with auxiliary variables.

In view of the importance that we attach to search problems, we also address the NP-completeness of the corresponding search problems. While it could have been more elegant to derive the NP-completeness of the various decision problems by an immediate corollary to the NP-completeness of the corresponding search problems (see Exercise 4.2), we chose not to do so. Instead, we first derive the standard results regarding decision problems, and next augment this treatment in order to derive the corresponding results regarding search problems. We believe that our choice will better serve most students.

The purpose of Section 4.3.2 is to expose the students to a sample of NP-completeness results and proof techniques. We believe that this traditional material is insightful, but one may skip it if pressed for time.

We mention that the reduction presented in the proof of Proposition 4.10 is not the "standard" one, but is rather adapted from the FGLSS-reduction [10]. This is done in anticipation of the use of the FGLSS-reduction in the context of the study of the complexity of approximation (cf., e.g., [15] or [13, Sec. 10.1.1]). Furthermore, although this reduction creates a larger graph, we find it clearer than the "standard" reduction.

Section 4.3.5 provides a high-level discussion of some positive applications of NP-completeness. The core of this section is a brief description of three types of probabilistic proof systems and the role of NP-completeness in establishing three fundamental results regarding them. For further details on probabilistic proof systems, we refer the interested reader to [13, Chap. 9]. Since probabilistic proof systems provide natural extensions of the notion of an NP-proof system, which underlies our definition of $\mathcal{NP}$, we recommend Section 4.3.5 (with a possible augmentation based on [13, Chap. 9]) as the most appropriate choice of advanced material that may accompany the basic material covered in this book.

This chapter contains some additional advanced material that is not intended for presentation in class. One such example is the assertion of the existence of problems in NP that are neither in P nor NP-complete (i.e., Theorem 4.12). Indeed, we recommend either stating Theorem 4.12 without a proof or merely presenting the proof idea. Another example is Section 4.5, which seems unsuitable for most undergraduate students. Needless to say, Section 4.5 is definitely inappropriate for presentation in an undergraduate class, but it may be useful for guiding a discussion in a small group of interested students.

## 4.1 Definitions

Loosely speaking, a problem in NP is called NP-complete if any efficient algorithm for it can be converted into an efficient algorithm for any other problem in NP. Hence, if NP is different from P, then no NP-complete problem can be in P. The aforementioned conversion of an efficient algorithm for one NP-problem[1] into efficient algorithms for other NP-problems is actually performed by a reduction. Thus, a problem (in NP) is NP-complete if any problem in NP is efficiently reducible to it, which means that *each individual NP-complete problem "encodes" all problems in NP*.

The standard definition of NP-completeness refers to decision problems, but we will also present a definition of NP-complete (or rather $\mathcal{PC}$-complete) search problems. In both cases, NP-completeness of a problem $\Pi$ combines two conditions:

1. $\Pi$ is in the class (i.e., $\Pi$ being in $\mathcal{NP}$ or $\mathcal{PC}$, depending on whether $\Pi$ is a decision or a search problem).
2. Each problem in the class is reducible to $\Pi$. This condition is called NP-hardness.

Although a perfectly good definition of NP-hardness could have allowed arbitrary Cook-reductions, it turns out that Karp-reductions (resp., Levin-reductions) suffice for establishing the NP-hardness of all natural NP-complete decision (resp., search) problems. Consequently, NP-completeness is commonly defined using this restricted notion of a polynomial-time reduction.

**Definition 4.1** (NP-completeness of decision problems, restricted notion): *A set $S$ is $\mathcal{NP}$-complete if it is in $\mathcal{NP}$ and every set in $\mathcal{NP}$ is Karp-reducible to $S$.*

---

[1] I.e., a problem in NP.

A set is $\mathcal{NP}$-hard if every set in $\mathcal{NP}$ is Karp-reducible to it (i.e., the class $\mathcal{NP}$ is Karp-reducible to it). Indeed, there is no reason to insist on Karp-reductions (rather than using arbitrary Cook-reductions), except that the restricted notion suffices for all known demonstrations of NP-completeness and is easier to work with. An analogous definition applies to search problems.

**Definition 4.2** (NP-completeness of search problems, restricted notion): *A binary relation R is $\mathcal{PC}$-complete if it is in $\mathcal{PC}$ and every relation in $\mathcal{PC}$ is Levin-reducible to R.*

Throughout the book, we will sometimes abuse the terminology and refer to search problems as NP-complete (rather than $\mathcal{PC}$-complete). Likewise, we will say that a search problem is NP-hard (rather than $\mathcal{PC}$-hard) if every relation in $\mathcal{PC}$ is Levin-reducible to it. Note that *if R is $\mathcal{PC}$-complete, then $S_R$ is $\mathcal{NP}$-complete*, where $S_R = \{x : \exists y \text{ s.t. } (x, y) \in R\}$ (see Exercise 4.2).

We stress that the mere fact that we have defined a property (i.e., NP-completeness) does not mean that there exist objects that satisfy this property. *It is indeed remarkable that NP-complete problems do exist.* Such problems are "universal" in the sense that efficiently solving them allows for efficiently solving any other (reasonable) problem (i.e., problems in NP).

## 4.2 The Existence of NP-Complete Problems

We suggest not to confuse the mere existence of NP-complete problems, which is remarkable by itself, with the even more remarkable existence of "natural" NP-complete problems. The following proof delivers the first message and also focuses on the essence of NP-completeness, rather than on more complicated technical details. The essence of NP-completeness is that a single computational problem may "effectively encode" a wide class of seemingly unrelated problems.

**Theorem 4.3:** *There exist NP-complete relations and sets.*

**Proof:** The proof (as well as any other NP-completeness proofs) is based on the observation that some decision problems in $\mathcal{NP}$ (resp., search problems in $\mathcal{PC}$) are "rich enough" to encode all decision problems in $\mathcal{NP}$ (resp., all search problems in $\mathcal{PC}$). This fact is most obvious for the "generic" decision and search problems, denoted $S_u$ and $R_u$ (and defined next), which are used to derive the simplest proof of the current theorem.

We consider the following relation $R_u$ and the decision problem $S_u$ implicit in $R_u$ (i.e., $S_u = \{\overline{x} : \exists y \text{ s.t. } (\overline{x}, y) \in R_u\}$). Both problems refer to the same type of instances, which in turn have the form $\overline{x} = \langle M, x, 1^t \rangle$, where $M$ is a description of a (standard deterministic) Turing machine, $x$ is a string, and $t$ is a natural number. The number $t$ is given in unary (rather than in binary) in order to guarantee that bounds of the form poly($t$) are polynomial (rather than exponential) in the instance's length. (This implies that various complexity measures (e.g., time and length) that can be upper-bounded by a polynomial in $t$ yield upper bounds that are polynomial in the length of the instance (i.e., $|\langle M, x, 1^t \rangle|$, which is linearly related to $|M| + |x| + t$).) A solution to the instance $\overline{x} = \langle M, x, 1^t \rangle$ (of $R_u$) is a string $y$ (of length at most $t$)$^2$ such that $M$ accepts the input pair $(x, y)$ within $t$ steps.

---

**Definition.** *The relation* $R_u$ *consists of pairs* $(\langle M, x, 1^t \rangle, y)$ *such that* $M$ *accepts the input pair* $(x, y)$ *within $t$ steps, where* $|y| \leq t$.

The corresponding set $S_u \stackrel{\text{def}}{=} \{\overline{x} : \exists y \text{ s.t. } (\overline{x}, y) \in R_u\}$ consists of triples $\langle M, x, 1^t \rangle$ such that machine $M$ accepts some input of the form $(x, \cdot)$ within $t$ steps.

---

It is easy to see that $R_u$ is in $\mathcal{PC}$ and that $S_u$ is in $\mathcal{NP}$. Indeed, $R_u$ is recognizable by a universal Turing machine, which on input $(\langle M, x, 1^t \rangle, y)$ emulates ($t$ steps of) the computation of $M$ on $(x, y)$. Note that this emulation can be conducted in poly($|M| + |x| + t$) = poly($|(\langle M, x, 1^t \rangle, y)|$) steps, and recall that $R_u$ is polynomially bounded (by its very definition). (The fact that $S_u \in \mathcal{NP}$ follows similarly.)$^3$ We comment that u indeed stands for *universal* (i.e., universal machine), and the proof extends to any reasonable model of computation (which has adequate universal machines).

We now turn to show that $R_u$ and $S_u$ are NP-hard in the adequate sense (i.e., $R_u$ is $\mathcal{PC}$-hard and $S_u$ is $\mathcal{NP}$-hard). We first show that any set in $\mathcal{NP}$ is Karp-reducible to $S_u$. Let $S$ be a set in $\mathcal{NP}$ and let us denote its witness relation by $R$; that is, $R$ is in $\mathcal{PC}$ and $x \in S$ if and only if there exists $y$ such that $(x, y) \in R$. Let $p_R$ be a polynomial bounding the length of solutions in $R$ (i.e., $|y| \leq p_R(|x|)$ for every $(x, y) \in R$), let $M_R$ be a polynomial-time machine deciding membership (of alleged $(x, y)$ pairs) in $R$, and let $t_R$ be a polynomial bounding its running time. Then, the desired Karp-reduction maps an instance

---

$^2$ Instead of requiring that $|y| \leq t$, one may require that $M$ is "canonical" in the sense that it reads its entire input before halting. Thus, if $|y| > t$, then such a canonical machine $M$ does not halt (let alone accept) within $t$ steps when given the input pair $(x, y)$.

$^3$ Alternatively, $S_u \in \mathcal{NP}$ follows from $R_u \in \mathcal{PC}$, because for every $R \in \mathcal{PC}$ it holds that $S_R = \{x : \exists y \text{ s.t. } (x, y) \in R\}$ is in $\mathcal{NP}$.

$x$ (for $S$) to the instance $\langle M_R, x, 1^{t_R(|x|+p_R(|x|))} \rangle$ (for $S_u$); that is,

$$x \mapsto f(x) \stackrel{\text{def}}{=} \langle M_R, x, 1^{t_R(|x|+p_R(|x|))} \rangle. \tag{4.1}$$

Note that this mapping can be computed in polynomial time, and that $x \in S$ if and only if $f(x) = \langle M_R, x, 1^{t_R(|x|+p_R(|x|))} \rangle \in S_u$. Details follow.

First, note that the mapping $f$ does depend (of course) on $S$, and so it may depend on the fixed objects $M_R$, $p_R$ and $t_R$ (which depend on $S$). Thus, computing $f$ on input $x$ calls for printing the fixed string $M_R$, copying $x$, and printing a number of 1's that is a fixed polynomial in the length of $x$. Hence, $f$ is polynomial-time computable. Second, recall that $x \in S$ if and only if there exists $y$ such that $|y| \le p_R(|x|)$ and $(x, y) \in R$. Since $M_R$ accepts $(x, y) \in R$ within $t_R(|x| + |y|)$ steps, it follows that $x \in S$ if and only if there exists $y$ such that $|y| \le p_R(|x|)$ and $M_R$ accepts $(x, y)$ within $t_R(|x| + |y|)$ steps.[4] It follows that $x \in S$ if and only if $f(x) \in S_u$.

We now turn to the search version. For reducing the search problem of any $R \in \mathcal{PC}$ to the search problem of $R_u$, we use essentially the same reduction. On input an instance $x$ (for $R$), we make the query $\langle M_R, x, 1^{t_R(|x|+p_R(|x|))} \rangle$ to the search problem of $R_u$ and return whatever the latter returns. Note that if $x \notin S$, then the answer will be "no solution," whereas for every $x$ and $y$ it holds that $(x, y) \in R$ if and only if $(\langle M_R, x, 1^{t_R(|x|+p_R(|x|))} \rangle, y) \in R_u$. Thus, a Levin-reduction of $R$ to $R_u$ consists of the pair of functions $(f, g)$, where $f$ is the foregoing Karp-reduction and $g(x, y) = y$. Note that, indeed, for every $(f(x), y) \in R_u$, it holds that $(x, g(x, y)) = (x, y) \in R$. ∎

**Digest: Generic Reductions.** The reduction presented in the proof of Theorem 4.3 is called "generic" because it (explicitly) refers to any (generic) NP-problem. That is, we actually presented a scheme for the design of reductions from any set $S$ in $\mathcal{NP}$ (resp., relation $R$ in $\mathcal{PC}$) to the set $S_u$ (resp., relation $R_u$). When plugging in a specific set $S$ (resp., relation $R$), or rather by providing the corresponding machine $M_R$ and polynomials $p_R, t_R$, we obtain a specific Karp-reduction $f$ (as described in the proof). Note that the fact that we not only provide a Karp-reduction of each $S \in \mathcal{NP}$ to $S_u$ but also provide a scheme for deriving such reductions, is more than required in the definition of NP-completeness.[5]

---

[4] This presentation assumes that $p_R$ and $t_R$ are monotonically non-decreasing, which holds without loss of generality.

[5] **Advanced comment:** We comment that it is hard to conceive of a demonstration of NP-completeness that does not yield a scheme for the design of reductions from any given

**Digest: the Role of $1^t$ in the Definition of $R_u$.** The role of including $1^t$ in the description of the problem instance is to allow placement of $R_u$ in $\mathcal{PC}$ (resp., $S_u$ in $\mathcal{NP}$). In contrast, consider the relation $R_u'$ that consists of pairs $(\langle M, x, t \rangle, y)$ such that $M$ accepts $\langle x, y \rangle$ within $t$ steps. Indeed, the difference between $R_u$ and $R_u'$ is that in $R_u$ the time bound $t$ appears in unary notation, whereas in $R_u'$ it appears in binary. Note that although $R_u'$ is $\mathcal{PC}$-hard (see Exercise 4.3), it is not in $\mathcal{PC}$ (because membership in $R_u'$ cannot be decided in polynomial time (see [13, §4.2.1.2])). Going even further, we note that omitting $t$ altogether from the problem instance yields a search problem that is not solvable at all. That is, consider the relation $R_H \stackrel{\text{def}}{=} \{(\langle M, x \rangle, y) : M(x, y) = 1\}$ (which is related to the Halting Problem). Indeed, the search problem of any relation in $\mathcal{PC}$ is Karp-reducible to the search problem of $R_H$, but $R_H$ is not solvable at all (i.e., there exists no algorithm that halts on every input such that on input $\overline{x} = \langle M, x \rangle$ the algorithm outputs a string $y$ in $R_H(\overline{x})$ if such a $y$ exists).

## Bounded Halting and Non-Halting

We note that the problem shown to be NP-complete in the proof of Theorem 4.3 is related to the following two problems, called Bounded Halting and Bounded Non-Halting. Fixing any programming language, the instance to each of these problems consists of a program $\pi$ and a time bound $t$ (presented in unary).

1. The decision version of Bounded Halting consists of determining whether or not *there exists an input* (of length at most $t$) *on which the program $\pi$ halts in $t$ steps*, whereas the search problem consists of finding such an input.
2. The decision version of Bounded Non-Halting consists of determining whether or not *there exists an input* (of length at most $t$) *on which the program $\pi$ does **not** halt in $t$ steps*, whereas the search problem consists of finding such an input.

It is easy to prove that both problems are NP-complete (see Exercise 4.4). Note that the two (decision) problems are not complementary (i.e., $(\pi, 1^t)$ may be a yes-instance of both decision problems).[6]

---

NP-problem to the target NP-complete problem. On the other hand, our scheme requires knowledge of a machine $M_R$ and polynomials $p_R, t_R$ that correspond to the given relation $R$, rather than only knowledge of the relation $R$ itself. But, again, it is hard to conceive of an alternative (i.e., how is $R$ to be represented to us otherwise?).

[6] Indeed, $(\pi, 1^t)$ can not be a no-instance of both decision problems, but this does not make the problems complementary. In fact, the two decision problems yield a three-way partition of the

The decision version of Bounded Non-Halting refers to a fundamental computational problem in the area of program verification, specifically, to the problem of *determining whether a given program halts within a given time bound on all inputs of a given length.*[7] We have mentioned Bounded Halting because it is often referred to in the literature, but we believe that Bounded Non-Halting is much more relevant to the project of program verification (because one seeks programs that halt on all inputs (i.e., no-instances of Bounded Non-Halting), rather than programs that halt on some input).

**Reflection.** The fact that Bounded Non-Halting is probably intractable (i.e., is intractable provided that $\mathcal{P} \neq \mathcal{NP}$) is even more relevant to the project of program verification than the fact that the Halting Problem is undecidable. The reason is that the latter problem (as well as other related undecidable problems) refers to arbitrarily long computations, whereas the former problem refers to an explicitly bounded number of computational steps. Specifically, Bounded Non-Halting is concerned with the *existence of an input that causes the program to violate a certain condition* (i.e., halting) *within a given time bound.*

In light of the foregoing discussion, the common practice of "bashing" Bounded (Non-)Halting as an "unnatural" problem seems very odd at an age in which computer programs play such a central role. (Nevertheless, we will use the term "natural" in this traditionally and odd sense in the next title, which actually refers to natural computational problems that seem unrelated to computation.)

## 4.3 Some Natural NP-Complete Problems

Having established the mere existence of NP-complete problems, we now turn to proving the existence of NP-complete problems that do not (explicitly) refer to computation in the problem's definition. We stress that thousands of such problems are known (and a list of several hundreds can be found in [11]).

---

instances $(\pi, 1^t)$: (1) pairs $(\pi, 1^t)$ such that for *every input* $x$ (of length at most $t$) the computation of $\pi(x)$ halts within $t$ steps, (2) pairs $(\pi, 1^t)$ for which such halting occurs on *some inputs but not on all inputs*, and (3) pairs $(\pi, 1^t)$ such that there *exists no input* (of length at most $t$) on which $\pi$ halts in $t$ steps. Note that instances of type (1) are exactly the no-instances of Bounded Non-Halting, whereas instances of type (3) are exactly the no-instances of Bounded Halting.

[7] The length parameter need not equal the time bound. Indeed, a more general version of the problem refers to two bounds, $\ell$ and $t$, and to whether the given program halts within $t$ steps on each possible $\ell$-bit input. It is easy to prove that the problem remains NP-complete also in the case that the instances are restricted to having parameters $\ell$ and $t$ such that $t = p(\ell)$, for any fixed polynomial $p$ (e.g., $p(n) = n^2$, rather than $p(n) = n$ as used in the main text).

We will prove that deciding the satisfiability of Boolean formulae is NP-complete (i.e., Cook's Theorem), and also present some combinatorial problems that are NP-complete. This presentation is aimed at providing a (small) sample of natural NP-completeness results, as well as some tools toward proving NP-completeness of new problems of interest. We start by making a comment regarding the latter issue.

The reduction presented in the proof of Theorem 4.3 is called "generic" because it (explicitly) refers to any (generic) NP-problem. That is, we actually presented a scheme for the design of reductions from any desired NP-problem to the single problem proved to be NP-complete. Indeed, in doing so, we have followed the definition of NP-completeness. However, once we know some NP-complete problems, a different route is open to us. We may establish the NP-completeness of a new problem by reducing a known NP-complete problem to the new problem. This alternative route is indeed a common practice, and it is based on the following simple proposition.

**Proposition 4.4:** *If an NP-complete problem $\Pi$ is reducible to some problem $\Pi'$ in NP, then $\Pi'$ is NP-complete. Furthermore, reducibility via Karp-reductions* (resp., Levin-reductions) *is preserved.*

That is, if an $\mathcal{NP}$-complete decision problem $S$ is Karp-reducible to a decision problem $S' \in \mathcal{NP}$, then $S'$ is $\mathcal{NP}$-complete. Similarly, if a $\mathcal{PC}$-complete search problem $R$ is Levin-reducible to a search problem $R' \in \mathcal{PC}$, then $R'$ is $\mathcal{PC}$-complete.

**Proof:** The proof boils down to asserting the transitivity of reductions. Specifically, the NP-hardness of $\Pi$ means that every problem in NP is reducible to $\Pi$, which in turn is reducible to $\Pi'$ (by the hypothesis). Thus, by transitivity of reduction (see Exercise 3.3), every problem in NP is reducible to $\Pi'$, which means that $\Pi'$ is NP-hard and the proposition follows.  ∎

### 4.3.1 Circuit and Formula Satisfiability: CSAT and SAT

We consider two related computational problems, CSAT and SAT, which refer (in the decision version) to the satisfiability of Boolean circuits and formulae, respectively. (We refer the reader to the definition of Boolean circuits, formulae, and CNF formulae (see §1.4.1.1 and §1.4.3.1).)

We suggest establishing the NP-completeness of SAT by a reduction from the circuit satisfaction problem (CSAT), after establishing the NP-completeness of the latter. Doing so allows the decoupling of two important parts of the proof of the NP-completeness of SAT: the emulation of Turing machines by circuits and the emulation of circuits by formulae with auxiliary variables.

### 4.3.1.1 The NP-Completeness of CSAT

Recall that (bounded fan-in) Boolean circuits are directed acyclic graphs with internal vertices, called gates, labeled by Boolean operations (of arity either 2 or 1), and external vertices called terminals that are associated with either inputs or outputs. When setting the inputs of such a circuit, all internal nodes are assigned values in the natural way, and this yields a value to the output(s), called an evaluation of the circuit on the given input. The evaluation of circuit $C$ on input $z$ is denoted $C(z)$. We focus on circuits with a single output, and let CSAT denote the set of satisfiable Boolean circuits; that is, a circuit $C$ is in CSAT if there exists an input $z$ such that $C(z) = 1$. We also consider the related relation $R_{\mathrm{CSAT}} = \{(C, z) : C(z) = 1\}$.

**Theorem 4.5** (NP-completeness of CSAT): *The set* (resp., relation) CSAT (resp., $R_{\mathrm{CSAT}}$) *is $\mathcal{NP}$-complete* (resp., $\mathcal{PC}$-complete).

**Proof:** It is easy to see that CSAT $\in \mathcal{NP}$ (resp., $R_{\mathrm{CSAT}} \in \mathcal{PC}$). Thus, we turn to showing that these problems are NP-hard. We will focus on the decision version (but also discuss the search version).

We will present (again, but for the last time in this book) a generic reduction, where here we reduce any NP-problem to CSAT. The reduction is based on the observation, mentioned in Section 1.4.1 (see also Exercise 1.15), that the computation of polynomial-time algorithms can be emulated by polynomial-size circuits. We start with a description of the basic idea.

In the current context, we wish to emulate the computation of a fixed machine $M$ on input $(x, y)$, *where $x$ is fixed and $y$ varies* (but $|y| = \mathrm{poly}(|x|)$ and the total number of steps of $M(x, y)$ is polynomial in $|x| + |y|$). Thus, $x$ will be "hard-wired" into the circuit, whereas $y$ will serve as the input to the circuit. The circuit itself, denoted $C_x$, will consists of "layers" such that each layer will represent an instantaneous configuration of the machine $M$, and the relation between consecutive configurations in a computation of this machine will be captured by ("uniform") local gadgets in the circuit. The number of layers will depend on $|x|$ as well as on the polynomial that upper-bounds the running time of $M$, and an additional gadget will be used to detect whether the last configuration is accepting. Thus, only the first layer of the circuit $C_x$ (which will represent an initial configuration with input prefixed by $x$) will depend on $x$. (See Figure 4.1.) The punch line is that determining whether, for a given $x$, there exists a $y \in \{0, 1\}^{\mathrm{poly}(|x|)}$ such that $M(x, y) = 1$ (in a given number of steps) will be reduced to whether there exists a $y$ such that $C_x(y) = 1$. Performing this reduction for any machine $M_R$ that corresponds to any $R \in \mathcal{PC}$ (as in the proof of Theorem 4.3), we establish the fact that CSAT is NP-complete. Details follow.

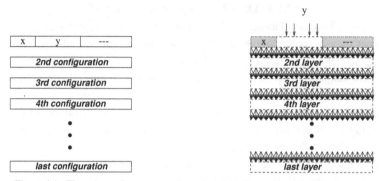

Figure 4.1. The schematic correspondence between the configurations in the computation of $M(x, y)$ (on the left) and the evaluation of the circuit $C_x$ on input $y$ (on the right), where $x$ is fixed and $y$ varies. The value of $x$ (as well as a sequence of blanks) is hard-wired (marked gray) in the first layer of $C_x$, and directed edges connect consecutive layers.

Recall that we wish to reduce an arbitrary set $S \in \mathcal{NP}$ to CSAT. Let $R$, $p_R$, $M_R$, and $t_R$ be as in the proof of Theorem 4.3 (i.e., $R$ is the witness relation of $S$, whereas $p_R$ bounds the length of the NP-witnesses, $M_R$ is the machine deciding membership in $R$, and $t_R$ is its polynomial time bound). Without loss of generality (and for simplicity), suppose that $M_R$ is a one-tape Turing machine.[8] We will construct a Karp-reduction that maps an instance $x$ (for $S$) to a circuit, denoted $f(x) \stackrel{\text{def}}{=} C_x$, such that $C_x(y) = 1$ if and only if $M_R$ accepts the input $(x, y)$ within $t_R(|x| + p_R(|x|))$ steps. Thus, it will follow that $x \in S$ if and only if there exists $y \in \{0, 1\}^{p_R(|x|)}$ such that $C_x(y) = 1$ (i.e., if and only if $C_x \in$ CSAT). The circuit $C_x$ will depend on $x$ as well as on $M_R$, $p_R$, and $t_R$. (We stress that $M_R$, $p_R$, and $t_R$ are fixed, whereas $x$ varies and is thus explicit in our notation.)

Before describing the circuit $C_x$, let us consider a possible computation of $M_R$ on input $(x, y)$, where $x$ is fixed and $y$ represents a generic string of length $p_R(|x|)$. Such a computation proceeds for (at most) $t = t_R(|x| + p_R(|x|))$ steps, and corresponds to a sequence of (at most) $t + 1$ instantaneous configurations, each of length $t$. Each such configuration can be encoded by $t$ pairs of symbols, where the first symbol in each pair indicates the contents of a cell and the second symbol indicates either a state of the machine or the fact that the machine is not located in this cell. Thus, each pair is a member of $\Sigma \times (Q \cup \{\bot\})$, where $\Sigma$ is the finite "work alphabet" of $M_R$, and $Q$ is its finite set of internal states, which does not contain the special symbol $\bot$ (which is used as indication that the machine is not present at a cell). The initial configuration consists of $\langle x, y \rangle$

[8] See Exercise 1.12.

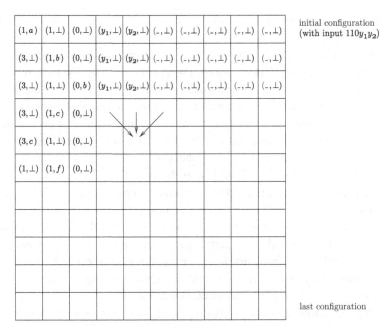

| $(1,a)$ | $(1,\bot)$ | $(0,\bot)$ | $(y_1,\bot)$ | $(y_2,\bot)$ | $(\text{-},\bot)$ | $(\text{-},\bot)$ | $(\text{-},\bot)$ | $(\text{-},\bot)$ | $(\text{-},\bot)$ |
|---|---|---|---|---|---|---|---|---|---|
| $(3,\bot)$ | $(1,b)$ | $(0,\bot)$ | $(y_1,\bot)$ | $(y_2,\bot)$ | $(\text{-},\bot)$ | $(\text{-},\bot)$ | $(\text{-},\bot)$ | $(\text{-},\bot)$ | $(\text{-},\bot)$ |
| $(3,\bot)$ | $(1,\bot)$ | $(0,b)$ | $(y_1,\bot)$ | $(y_2,\bot)$ | $(\text{-},\bot)$ | $(\text{-},\bot)$ | $(\text{-},\bot)$ | $(\text{-},\bot)$ | $(\text{-},\bot)$ |
| $(3,\bot)$ | $(1,c)$ | $(0,\bot)$ | | | | | | | |
| $(3,c)$ | $(1,\bot)$ | $(0,\bot)$ | | | | | | | |
| $(1,\bot)$ | $(1,f)$ | $(0,\bot)$ | | | | | | | |
| | | | | | | | | | |
| | | | | | | | | | |
| | | | | | | | | | |
| | | | | | | | | | |
| | | | | | | | | | |

initial configuration (with input $110y_1y_2$)

last configuration

Figure 4.2. An array representing ten consecutive computation steps on input $110y_1y_2$. Blank characters are marked by a hyphen (-), whereas the indication that the machine is not present in the cell is marked by $\bot$. The state of the machine in each configuration is represented in the cell in which it resides, where the set of states of this machine equals {a, b, c, d, e, f}. The three arrows represent the determination of an entry by the three entries that reside above it. The machine underlying this example accepts the input if and only if the input contains a zero.

as input, and is padded by blanks to a total length of $t$, whereas the decision of $M_R(x, y)$ can be read from (the leftmost cell of) the last configuration.[9] We view these $t + 1$ possible configurations as rows in an array, where the $i^{\text{th}}$ row describes the instantaneous configuration of $M(x, y)$ after $i - 1$ steps (and repeats the previous row in the case that the computation of $M(x, y)$ halts before making $i - 1$ steps). For every $i > 1$, the values of the entries in the $i^{\text{th}}$ row are determined by the entries of the $(i - 1)^{\text{st}}$ row (which resides just above the $i^{\text{th}}$ row), where this determination reflects the transition function of $M_R$. Furthermore, the value of each entry in the said row is determined by the values of (up to) three entries that reside in the row above it (see Exercise 4.5). Thus, the aforementioned computation is represented by a $(t + 1) \times t$ array, depicted in Figure 4.2, where each entry encodes one out of a constant

[9] We refer to the output convention presented in Section 1.3.2, by which the output is written in the leftmost cells and the machine halts at the cell to its right.

number of possibilities, which in turn can be encoded by a constant-length bit string.

The actual description of $C_x$. The circuit $C_x$ has a structure that corresponds to the aforementioned array (see, indeed, Figure 4.1). Specifically, each row in the array is represented by a corresponding layer in the circuit $C_x$ such that each entry in the array is represented by a *constant* number of gates in $C_x$. When $C_x$ is evaluated at $y$, these gates will be assigned values that encode the contents of the corresponding entry in the array that describes the computation of $M_R(x, y)$. In particular, the entries of the first row of the array are "encoded" (in the first layer of $C_x$) by hard-wiring the reduction's input (i.e., $x$) and feeding the circuit's input (i.e., $y$) to the adequate input terminals. That is, the circuit has $p_R(|x|)$ ("real") input terminals (corresponding to $y$), and the hard-wiring of constants to the other $O(t) - p_R(|x|)$ gates (of the first layer) that represent the first row is done by simple gadgets (as in Figure 1.3). Indeed, the additional hard-wiring in the first layer corresponds to the other fixed elements of the initial configuration (i.e., the blank symbols, and the encoding of the initial state and of the initial location; cf. Figure 4.2). The entries of subsequent rows will be "encoded" in corresponding layers of $C_x$ (or rather computed at evaluation time). Specifically, the values that encode an entry in the array will be computed by using *constant-size* circuits that determine the value of an entry based on the three relevant entries that are encoded in the layer above it. Recall that each entry is encoded by a constant number of gates (in the corresponding layer), and thus these constant-size circuits merely compute the constant-size function described in Exercise 4.5. In addition, the circuit $C_x$ has a few extra gates that check the values of the entries of the last row in order to determine whether or not it encodes an accepting configuration.[10]

---

Advanced comment. We note that although the foregoing construction of $C_x$ capitalizes on various specific details of the (one-tape) Turing machine model, it can be easily adapted to other natural models of efficient computation (by showing that in such models, the transformation from one configuration to the subsequent one can be emulated by a (polynomial-time constructible) circuit). Alternatively, we recall the Cobham-Edmonds Thesis asserting that any problem that is solvable in polynomial time (on some "reasonable" model) can be solved in polynomial time by a (one-tape) Turing machine.

---

[10] In continuation of footnote 9, we note that it suffices to check the values of the two leftmost entries of the last row. We assumed here that the circuit propagates a halting configuration to the last row. Alternatively, we may check for the existence of an accepting/halting configuration in the entire array, since this condition is quite simple.

The complexity of the mapping of $x$ to $f(x) = C_x$. Given $x$, the circuit $C_x$ can be constructed in polynomial time, by encoding $x$ in an appropriate manner (in the first layer) and generating a "highly uniform" gridlike circuit of size $s$, where $s = O(t_R(|x| + p_R(|x|))^2)$. Specifically, the gates of the first layer are determined by $x$ such that each gate is determined by at most a single bit of $x$, whereas the constant-size circuits connecting consecutive layers only depend on the transition function of $M_R$ (which is fixed in the context of reducing $S$ to CSAT). Finally, note that the total number of gates is quadratically related to $t_R(|x| + p_R(|x|))$, which is a fixed polynomial in $|x|$ (again, because $p_R$ and $t_R$ are fixed (polynomials) in the context of reducing $S$ to CSAT).

The validity of the mapping of $x$ to $f(x) = C_x$. By its construction, the circuit $C_x$ emulates $t_R(|x| + p_R(|x|))$ steps of computation of $M_R$ on input $(x, \cdot)$. Thus, indeed, $C_x(y) = 1$ if and only if $M_R$ accepts the input $(x, y)$ while making at most $t_R(|x| + p_R(|x|))$ steps. Recalling that $S = \{x : \exists y \text{ s.t. } |y| = p_R(|x|) \wedge (x, y) \in R\}$ and that $M_R$ decides membership in $R$ in time $t_R$, we infer that $x \in S$ if and only if $f(x) = C_x \in$ CSAT. Furthermore, $(x, y) \in R$ if and only if $(f(x), y) \in R_{\text{CSAT}}$.

It follows that $f$ is a Karp-reduction of $S$ to CSAT, and, for $g(x, y) \overset{\text{def}}{=} y$, it holds that $(f, g)$ is a Levin-reduction of $R$ to $R_{\text{CSAT}}$. The theorem follows. ∎

#### 4.3.1.2 The NP-Completeness of SAT

Recall that Boolean formulae are special types of Boolean circuits (i.e., circuits having a tree structure).[11] We further restrict our attention to formulae given in conjunctive normal form (CNF). We denote by SAT the set of satisfiable CNF formulae (i.e., a CNF formula $\phi$ is in SAT if there exists a truth assignment $\tau$ such that $\phi(\tau) = 1$). We also consider the related relation $R_{\text{SAT}} = \{(\phi, \tau) : \phi(\tau) = 1\}$.

**Theorem 4.6** (NP-completeness of SAT): *The set* (resp., *relation*) SAT (resp., $R_{\text{SAT}}$) *is* $\mathcal{NP}$-*complete* (resp., $\mathcal{PC}$-*complete*).

**Proof:** Since the set of possible instances of SAT is a subset of the set of instances of CSAT, it is clear that SAT $\in \mathcal{NP}$ (resp., $R_{\text{SAT}} \in \mathcal{PC}$). To prove that SAT is NP-hard, we reduce CSAT to SAT (and use Proposition 4.4). The reduction boils down to introducing auxiliary variables in order to "cut" the computation of an arbitrary ("deep") circuit into a conjunction of related computations of "shallow" circuits (i.e., depth-2 circuits) of unbounded fan-in, which in turn may be presented as a CNF formula. The aforementioned

---

[11] For an alternative definition, see Appendix A.2.

auxiliary variables hold the *possible* values of the internal gates of the original circuit, and the clauses of the CNF formula enforce the consistency of these values with the corresponding gate operation. For example, if $\text{gate}_i$ and $\text{gate}_j$ feed into $\text{gate}_k$, which is a $\wedge$-gate, then the corresponding auxiliary variables $g_i, g_j, g_k$ should satisfy the Boolean condition $g_k \equiv (g_i \wedge g_j)$, which can be written as a 3CNF formula with four clauses. Details follow.

We start by Karp-reducing CSAT to SAT. Given a Boolean circuit $C$, with $n$ input terminals and $m$ gates, we first construct $m$ *constant-size* formulae on $n + m$ variables, where the first $n$ variables correspond to the input terminals of the circuit and the other $m$ variables correspond to its gates. The $i^{\text{th}}$ formula will depend on the variable that correspond to the $i^{\text{th}}$ gate and the 1 or 2 variables that correspond to the vertices that feed into this gate (i.e., 2 vertices in case of $\wedge$-gate or $\vee$-gate and a single vertex in case of a $\neg$-gate, where these vertices may be either input terminals or other gates). This (constant-size) formula will be satisfied by a truth assignment if and only if this assignment matches the gate's functionality (i.e., feeding this gate with the corresponding values results in the corresponding output value). Note that these *constant-size* formulae can be written as constant-size CNF formulae (in fact, as 3CNF formulae).[12] Taking the conjunction of these $m$ formulae and the variable associated with the (gate that feeds into the) output terminal, we obtain a formula $\phi$ in CNF. An example, where $n = 3$ and $m = 4$, is presented in Figure 4.3.

To summarize, the reduction maps the circuit $C$ to a CNF formula $\phi$ such that

$$\phi(x_1, \ldots, x_n, g_1, \ldots, g_m) = \left( \bigwedge_{i=1}^{m} \phi_i(x_1, \ldots, x_n, g_1, \ldots, g_m) \right) \wedge g_m \quad (4.2)$$

where the Boolean variables $x_1, \ldots, x_n$ represent the possible values of the input terminals of $C$, the Boolean variables $g_1, \ldots, g_n$ represent possible values of the corresponding gates of $C$, and $\phi_i$ is a constant-size CNF formula that depends only on 2 or 3 of the aforementioned variables (as explained in the previous paragraphs).

Note that $\phi$ can be constructed in polynomial time from the circuit $C$; that is, the mapping of $C$ to $\phi = f(C)$ is polynomial-time computable. We claim that $C$ is in CSAT if and only if $\phi$ is in SAT. The two directions of this claim are proved next.

---

[12] Recall that any Boolean function can be written as a CNF formula having size that is exponential in the length of its input (cf. Exercise 1.17), which in this case is a constant (i.e., either 2 or 3). Indeed, note that the Boolean functions that we refer to here depend on 2 or 3 Boolean variables (since they indicate whether or not the corresponding values respect the gate's functionality).

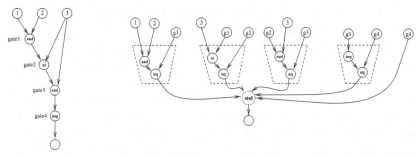

Figure 4.3. Using auxiliary variables (i.e., the $g_i$'s) to "cut" a depth-5 circuit (into a CNF). The dashed regions will be replaced by equivalent CNF formulae. The (small) dashed circle, representing an unbounded fan-in and-gate, is the conjunction of all constant-size circuits (which enforce the functionalities of the original gates) and the variable that represents the (gate that feeds the) output terminal in the original circuit.

1. Suppose that for some string $s$ it holds that $C(s) = 1$. Then, assigning to the $i^{\text{th}}$ auxiliary variable (i.e., $g_i$) the value that is assigned to the $i^{\text{th}}$ gate of $C$ when evaluated on $s$, we obtain (together with $s$) a truth assignment that satisfies $\phi$. This is the case because such an assignment satisfies all $m$ constant-size CNF formulae (i.e., all $\phi_i$'s), as well as the variable $g_m$ associated with the output of $C$.

2. On the other hand, if the truth assignment $\tau$ satisfies $\phi$, then the first $n$ bit values in $\tau$ correspond to an input on which $C$ evaluates to 1. This is the case because the $m$ constant-size CNF formulae (i.e., the $\phi_i$'s) guarantee that the variables of $\phi$ are assigned values that correspond to the evaluation of $C$ on the first $n$ bits of $\tau$, while the fact that $g_m$ has value $\texttt{true}$ guarantees that this evaluation of $C$ yields the value 1. (Recall that $g_m$ must have value $\texttt{true}$ in any assignment that satisfies $\phi$, whereas the value of $g_m$ represents the value of the output of $C$ on the foregoing input.)

Thus, we have established that $f$ is a Karp-reduction of CSAT to SAT. Note that the mapping (of the truth assignment $\tau$ to its $n$-bit prefix) used in Item 2 is the second mapping required by the definition of a Levin-reduction. Thus, augmenting $f$ with the aforementioned second mapping yields a Levin-reduction of $R_{\text{CSAT}}$ to $R_{\text{SAT}}$. ∎

**Digest and Perspective.** The fact that the second mapping required by the definition of a Levin-reduction is explicit in the proof of the validity of the corresponding Karp-reduction is a fairly common phenomenon. Actually (see

Exercise 4.20), typical presentations of Karp-reductions provide two auxiliary polynomial-time computable mappings (in addition to the main mapping of instances from one problem (e.g., CSAT) to instances of another problem (e.g., SAT)): The first auxiliary mapping is of solutions for the preimage instance (e.g., of CSAT) to solutions for the image instance of the reduction (e.g., of SAT), whereas the second mapping goes the other way around. For example, the proof of the validity of the Karp-reduction of CSAT to SAT, denoted $f$, specified two additional mappings $h$ and $g$ such that $(C, s) \in R_{\text{CSAT}}$ implies $(f(C), h(C, s)) \in R_{\text{SAT}}$ and $(f(C), \tau) \in R_{\text{SAT}}$ implies $(C, g(C, \tau)) \in R_{\text{CSAT}}$. Specifically, in the proof of Theorem 4.6, we used $h(C, s) = (s, a_1, \ldots, a_m)$ where $a_i$ is the value assigned to the $i^{\text{th}}$ gate in the evaluation of $C(s)$, and $g(C, \tau)$ being the $n$-bit prefix of $\tau$. (Note that only the main mapping (i.e., $f$) and the second auxiliary mapping (i.e., $g$) are required in the definition of a Levin-reduction.)

**3SAT.** Observe that the formulae resulting from the Karp-reduction presented in the proof of Theorem 4.6 are actually 3CNF formulae; that is, each such formula is in conjunctive normal form (CNF) and *each of its clauses contains at most three literals*. Thus, the foregoing reduction actually establishes the NP-completeness of 3SAT (i.e., SAT restricted to CNF formula with up to three literals per clause). Alternatively, one may Karp-reduce SAT (i.e., satisfiability of CNF formula) to 3SAT (i.e., satisfiability of 3CNF formula) by replacing long clauses with conjunctions of three-variable clauses (using auxiliary variables; see Exercise 4.6). Either way, we get the following result, where the "furthermore" part is proved by an additional reduction.

**Proposition 4.7:** *3SAT is NP-complete. Furthermore, the problem remains NP-complete also if we restrict the instances such that each variable appears in at most three clauses.*

**Proof:** The "furthermore part" is proved by a reduction from 3SAT. We just replace each occurrence of a Boolean variable by a *new copy* of this variable, and add clauses to enforce that all these copies are assigned the same value. Specifically, if variable $z$ occurs $t$ times in the original 3CNF formula $\phi$, then we introduce $t$ new variables (i.e., its "copies"), denoted $z^{(1)}, \ldots, z^{(t)}$, and replace the $i^{\text{th}}$ occurrence of $z$ in $\phi$ by $z^{(i)}$. In addition, we add the clauses $z^{(i+1)} \vee \neg z^{(i)}$ for $i = 1 \ldots, t$ (where $t + 1$ is understood as 1). Thus, each variable appears at most three times in the new formula. Note that the clause $z^{(i+1)} \vee \neg z^{(i)}$ is logically equivalent to $z^{(i)} \Rightarrow z^{(i+1)}$, and thus the conjunction of the aforementioned $t$ clauses is logically equivalent to $z^{(1)} \Leftrightarrow z^{(2)} \Leftrightarrow \cdots \Leftrightarrow z^{(t)}$. The validity of the reduction follows. ∎

**Related Problems.** Note that instances of SAT can be viewed as systems of Boolean conditions over Boolean variables. Such systems can be emulated by various types of systems of arithmetic conditions, implying the NP-hardness of solving the latter types of systems. Examples include systems of *integer* linear inequalities (see Exercise 4.8) and systems of quadratic equalities (see Exercise 4.10).

In contrast to the foregoing, we mention that SAT restricted to CNF formula with up to *two* literals per clause is solvable in polynomial time (see Exercise 4.7). Thus, whereas deciding the satisfiability of 3CNF formulae (i.e., $3\text{SAT}$) is $\mathcal{NP}$-complete, the corresponding problem for 2CNF formulae, denoted $2\text{SAT}$, is in $\mathcal{P}$. The same phenomena arise also with respect to other natural problems (e.g., 3-colorability versus 2-colorability), but we suggest not attributing too much significance to this fact.

### 4.3.2 Combinatorics and Graph Theory

The purpose of this section is to expose the reader to a sample of NP-completeness results and proof techniques (i.e., the design of reductions among computational problems). We present just a few of the many appealing combinatorial problems that are known to be NP-complete.

As in §4.3.1.2, the NP-completeness of new problems is proved by showing that their instances can encode instances of problems that are already known to be NP-complete (e.g., SAT-instances can encode CSAT-instances). Typically, these encodings operate in a local manner, mapping small components of the original instance to local gadgets in the produced instance. Indeed, these problem-specific gadgets are the core of the encoding scheme.

Throughout this section, we focus on the decision versions of the various problems and adopt a more informal style. Specifically, we will present a typical decision problem as a problem of deciding whether a given instance, which belongs to a set of relevant instances, is a "yes-instance" or a "no-instance" (rather than referring to deciding membership of arbitrary strings in a set of yes-instances). For further discussion of this style and its rigorous formulation, see Section 5.1. We will also omit showing that these decision problems are in NP; indeed, for natural problems in NP, showing membership in NP is typically straightforward.

**Set Cover.** We start with the Set Cover problem, in which an instance consists of a collection of finite sets $S_1, \ldots, S_m$ and an integer $K$ and the question (for decision) is whether or not there exist (at most)[13] $K$ sets that cover $\bigcup_{i=1}^{m} S_i$ (i.e., indices $i_1, \ldots, i_K$ such that $\bigcup_{j=1}^{K} S_{i_j} = \bigcup_{i=1}^{m} S_i$).

**Proposition 4.8:** Set Cover *is NP-complete.*

**Proof:** We present a Karp-reduction of SAT to Set Cover. For a CNF formula $\phi$ with $m$ clauses and $n$ variables, we consider the sets $S_{1,t}$, $S_{1,f}, .., S_{n,t}, S_{n,f} \subseteq \{1, \ldots, m\}$ such that $S_{i,t}$ (resp., $S_{i,f}$) is the set of the indices of the clauses (of $\phi$) that are satisfied by setting the $i^{\text{th}}$ variable to true (resp., false). That is, if the $i^{\text{th}}$ variable appears unnegated in the $j^{\text{th}}$ clause then $j \in S_{i,t}$, whereas if the $i^{\text{th}}$ variable appears negated in the $j^{\text{th}}$ clause then $j \in S_{i,f}$. Indeed, $S_{i,t} \cup S_{i,f}$ equals the set of clauses containing an occurrence of the $i^{\text{th}}$ variable, and the union of all these $2n$ sets equals $[m] \stackrel{\text{def}}{=} \{1, \ldots, m\}$. In order to force any cover to contain either $S_{i,t}$ or $S_{i,f}$, we augment the universe with $n$ additional elements and add the $i^{\text{th}}$ such element to both $S_{i,t}$ and $S_{i,f}$. Thus, the reduction proceeds as follows.

1. On input a CNF formula $\phi$ (with $n$ variables and $m$ clauses), the reduction computes the sets $S_{1,t}, S_{1,f}, .., S_{n,t}, S_{n,f}$ such that $S_{i,t}$ (resp., $S_{i,f}$) is the set of the indices of the clauses in which the $i^{\text{th}}$ variable appears unnegated (resp., negated).

2. The reduction outputs the instance $f(\phi) \stackrel{\text{def}}{=} ((S_1, .., S_{2n}), n)$, where for $i = 1, \ldots, n$ it holds that $S_{2i-1} = S_{i,t} \cup \{m+i\}$ and $S_{2i} = S_{i,f} \cup \{m+i\}$.

Note that $f(\phi)$ is a yes-instance of Set Cover if and only if the collection $(S_1, .., S_{2n})$ contains a sub-collection of $n$ sets that covers $[m+n]$. Observing that $f$ is computable in polynomial time, we complete the proof by showing that $f$ is a valid Karp-reduction of SAT to Set Cover.

Assume, on the one hand, that $\phi$ is satisfied by $\tau_1 \cdots \tau_n$. Then, for every $j \in [m]$ there exists an $i \in [n]$ such that setting the $i^{\text{th}}$ variable to $\tau_i$ satisfies the $j^{\text{th}}$ clause, and so $j \in S_{2i-\tau_i}$. It follows that the collection $\{S_{2i-\tau_i} : i = 1, \ldots, n\}$ covers $\{1, \ldots, m+n\}$, because $\{S_{2i-\tau_i} \cap [m] : i = 1, \ldots, n\}$ covers $\{1, \ldots, m\}$ while $\{S_{2i-\tau_i} \setminus [m] : i = 1, \ldots, n\}$ covers $\{m+1, \ldots, m+n\}$. Thus, $\phi \in$ SAT implies that $f(\phi)$ is a yes-instance of Set Cover.

On the other hand, for every $i \in [n]$, each cover of $\{m+1, \ldots, m+n\} \subset \{1, \ldots, m+n\}$ must include either $S_{2i-1}$ or $S_{2i}$, because these are the only sets that cover the element $m+i$. Thus, a cover of $\{1, \ldots, m+n\}$ using $n$ of the $S_j$'s

---

[13] Clearly, in the case of Set Cover, the two formulations (i.e., asking for exactly $K$ sets or at most $K$ sets) are computationally equivalent; see Exercise 4.13.

must contain, for every $i$, either $S_{2i-1}$ or $S_{2i}$ but not both. Setting $\tau_i$ accordingly (i.e., $\tau_i = 1$ if and only if $S_{2i-1}$ is in the cover) implies that $\{S_{2i-\tau_i} : i = 1, \ldots, n\}$ (or rather $\{S_{2i-\tau_i} \cap [m] : i = 1, \ldots, n\}$) covers $\{1, \ldots, m\}$. It follows that $\tau_1 \cdots \tau_n$ satisfies $\phi$, because for every $j \in [m]$ there exists an $i \in [n]$ such that $j \in S_{2i-\tau_i}$ (which implies that setting the $i^{\text{th}}$ variable to $\tau_i$ satisfies the $j^{\text{th}}$ clause). Thus, if $f(\phi)$ is a yes-instance of Set Cover (i.e., there is a cover of $[m+n]$ that uses $n$ of the $S_j$'s), then $\phi \in$ SAT. ∎

**Exact Cover and 3XC.** The Exact Cover problem is similar to the Set Cover problem, except that here the sets that are used in the cover are not allowed to intersect. That is, each element in the universe should be covered by *exactly* one set in the cover. Restricting the set of instances to sequences of 3-sets (i.e., sets of size three), we get the restricted problem called 3-Exact Cover (3XC), in which it is unnecessary to specify the number of sets to be used in the exact cover (since this number must equal the size of the universe divided by three). The problem 3XC is rather technical, but it is quite useful for demonstrating the NP-completeness of other problems (by reducing 3XC to them); see, for example, Exercises 4.17 and 4.18.

**Proposition 4.9:** 3-Exact Cover *is NP-complete.*

Indeed, it follows that the Exact Cover (in which sets of arbitrary size are allowed) is NP-complete. This follows both for the case that the number of sets in the desired cover is unspecified and for the various cases in which this number is upper-bounded and/or lower-bounded in terms of an integer that is part of the instance (as in Set Cover).

**Proof:** The reduction is obtained by composing four reductions, which involve three intermediate computational problems. The first of these problems is a *restricted case* of 3SAT, denoted r3SAT, in which each *literal* appears in at most *two* clauses. Note that, by Proposition 4.7, 3SAT is NP-complete even when the instances are restricted such that each *variable* appears in at most *three* clauses. Actually, the reduction presented in the proof of Proposition 4.7 can be slightly modified in order to reduce 3SAT to r3SAT (see Exercise 4.11).[14]

The second intermediate problem that we consider is a *restricted version* of Set Cover, denoted 3SC, in which each set has at most three elements. (Indeed, as in the general case of Set Cover, an instance consists of a sequence of finite sets as well as an integer $K$, and the question is whether there exists a

---

[14] Alternatively, a closer look at the reduction presented in the proof of Proposition 4.7 reveals that it always produces instances of r3SAT. This alternative presupposes that copies are created also when the original variable appears three times in the original formula.

cover with at most $K$ sets.) We reduce r3SAT to 3SC by using the (very same) reduction presented in the proof of Proposition 4.8, while observing that the size of each set in the reduced instance is at most three (i.e., one more than the number of occurrences of the corresponding literal in clauses of the original formula).

Next, we reduce 3SC to the following *restricted version* of Exact Cover, denoted 3XC', in which each set has *at most* three elements. An instance of 3XC' consists of a sequence of finite sets as well as an integer $K$, and the question is whether there exists an *exact* cover with at most $K$ sets. The reduction maps an instance $((S_1, \ldots, S_m), K)$ of 3SC to the instance $(C', K)$ such that $C'$ is a collection of all subsets of each of the sets $S_1, \ldots, S_m$. Since each $S_i$ has size at most three, we introduce at most seven non-empty subsets per each such set, and the reduction can be computed in polynomial time. The reader may easily verify the validity of this reduction (see Exercise 4.12).

Finally, we reduce 3XC' to 3XC. Consider an instance $((S_1, \ldots, S_m), K)$ of 3XC', and suppose that $\bigcup_{i=1}^m S_i = [n]$. If $n > 3K$ then this is definitely a no-instance, which can be mapped to a dummy no-instance of 3XC, and so we assume that $x \stackrel{\text{def}}{=} 3K - n \geq 0$. Intuitively, $x$ represents the "excess" covering ability of a hypothetical *exact* cover that consists of $K$ sets, each having three elements. Thus, we augment the set system with $x$ new elements, denoted $n + 1, \ldots, 3K$, and replace each $S_i$ such that $|S_i| < 3$ by a sub-collection of 3-sets such that each 3-set contains $S_i$ as well as an adequate number of elements from $\{n + 1, \ldots, 3K\}$, such that the sub-collection associated with $S_i$ contains a set for each possible $(3 - |S_i|)$-set of $\{n + 1, \ldots, 3K\}$. That is, in case $|S_i| = 2$, the set $S_i$ is replaced by the sub-collection $(S_i \cup \{n + 1\}, \ldots, S_i \cup \{3K\})$, whereas a singleton $S_i$ is replaced by the sets $S_i \cup \{j_1, j_2\}$ for every $j_1 < j_2$ in $\{n + 1, \ldots, 3K\}$. In addition, we add all possible 3-subsets of $\{n + 1, \ldots, 3K\}$. This completes the description of the last reduction, the validity of which is left as an exercise (see Exercise 4.12).

Let us conclude. We have introduced the intermediate problems r3SAT, 3SC, and 3XC', and presented a sequence of Karp-reductions leading from 3SAT to 3XC via these intermediate problems. Specifically, we reduced 3SAT to r3SAT, then reduced r3SAT to 3SC, next reduced 3SC to 3XC', and finally reduced 3XC' to 3XC. Composing these four reductions, we obtain a Karp-reduction of 3SAT to 3XC, and the proposition follows.  ∎

**Vertex Cover, Independent Set, and Clique.** Turning to graph theoretic problems (see Appendix A.1), we start with the Vertex Cover problem, which is a special case of the Set Cover problem. The instances consist of pairs $(G, K)$, where $G = (V, E)$ is a simple graph and $K$ is an integer, and the problem is whether or not there exists a set of (at most) $K$ vertices that is incident to all graph edges (i.e., each edge in $G$ has at least one end point in this set). Indeed, this instance of Vertex Cover can be viewed as an instance of Set Cover by considering the collection of sets $(S_v)_{v \in V}$, where $S_v$ denotes the set of edges incident at vertex $v$ (i.e., $S_v = \{e \in E : v \in e\}$). Thus, the NP-hardness of Set Cover follows from the NP-hardness of Vertex Cover (but this implication is unhelpful for us here, since we already know that Set Cover is NP-hard and we wish to prove that Vertex Cover is NP-hard). We also note that the Vertex Cover problem is computationally equivalent to the Independent Set and Clique problems (see Exercise 4.14), and thus it suffices to establish the NP-hardness of one of these problems.

**Proposition 4.10:** *The problems* Vertex Cover, Independent Set *and* Clique *are NP-complete.*

**Proof:** We show a reduction from 3SAT to Independent Set.[15] On input a 3CNF formula $\phi$ with $m$ clauses and $n$ variables, we construct a graph with $7m$ vertices, denoted $G_\phi$, as follows:

- The vertices are grouped in $m$ equal-size sets, each corresponding to one of the clauses, and edges are placed among all vertices that belong to each of these 7-sets (thus obtaining $m$ disjoint 7-vertex cliques). The 7-set corresponding to a specific clause contains seven vertices that correspond to the seven truth assignments (to the three variables in the clause) that *satisfy the clause*. That is, the vertices in the graph correspond to partial assignments such that the seven vertices that belong to the $i^{th}$ 7-set correspond to the seven partial assignments that instantiate the variables in the $i^{th}$ clause in a way that satisfies this clause. For example, if the $i^{th}$ clause equals $x_{j_1} \vee x_{j_2} \vee \neg x_{j_3}$, then the $i^{th}$ 7-set consists of vertices that correspond to the seven Boolean functions $\tau$ that are defined on $\{j_1, j_2, j_3\} \subset [n]$ and satisfy $\tau(j_1) \vee \tau(j_2) \vee \neg\tau(j_3)$.

- In addition to the edges that are internal to these $m$ 7-sets (which form 7-vertex cliques), we add an edge between each pair of vertices that corresponds to partial assignments that are *mutually inconsistent*. That is, if a specific (satisfying) assignment to the variables of the $i^{th}$ clause is inconsistent with some (satisfying) assignment to the variables of the $j^{th}$ clause, then we connect the corresponding vertices by an edge. In particular, no

---

[15] **Advanced comment:** The following reduction is not the "standard" one (see Exercise 4.15), but is rather adapted from the FGLSS-reduction (see [10]). This is done in anticipation of the use of the FGLSS-reduction in the context of the study of the complexity of approximation (cf., e.g., [15] or [13, Sec. 10.1.1]).

edges are placed between 7-sets that represent clauses that share no common variable. (In contrast, the edges that are internal to the $m$ 7-sets may be viewed as a special case of the edges connecting mutually inconsistent partial assignments.)

To summarize, on input $\phi$, the reduction outputs the pair $(G_\phi, m)$, where $G_\phi$ is the aforementioned graph and $m$ is the number of clauses in $\phi$.

We stress that each 7-set of the graph $G_\phi$ contains only vertices that correspond to partial assignments that satisfy the corresponding clause; that is, the single partial assignment that does not satisfy this clause is not represented as a vertex in $G_\phi$. Recall that the edges placed among vertices represent partial assignments that are mutually inconsistent. Thus, each truth assignment $\tau$ to the entire formula $\phi$ yields an independent set in $G_\phi$, which contains all the vertices that correspond to partial assignments that are consistent with $\tau$ and satisfy the corresponding clauses. Indeed, the size of this independent set equals the number of clauses that are satisfied by the assignment $\tau$. These observations underlie the validity of the reduction, which is argued next.

Suppose, on the one hand, that $\phi$ is satisfiable by the truth assignment $\tau$. Consider the partial assignments, to the $m$ clauses, that are derived from $\tau$. We claim that these partial assignments correspond to an independent set of size $m$ in $G_\phi$. The claim holds because these $m$ partial assignments satisfy the corresponding $m$ clauses (since $\tau$ satisfies $\phi$) and are mutually consistent (because they are all derived from $\tau$). It follows that the these $m$ partial assignments correspond to $m$ vertices (residing in different 7-sets), and there are no edges between these vertices. Thus, $\phi \in$ SAT implies that $G_\phi$ has an independent set of size $m$.

On the other hand, any independent set of size $m$ in $G_\phi$ must contain exactly one vertex in each of the $m$ 7-sets, because no independent set may contain two vertices that reside in the same 7-set. Furthermore, each independent set in $G_\phi$ induces a (possibly partial) truth assignment to $\phi$, because the partial assignments "selected" in the various 7-sets must be consistent (or else an edge would have existed among the corresponding vertices). Recalling that an independent set that contains a vertex from a specific 7-set induces a partial truth assignment that satisfies the corresponding clause, it follows that an independent set that contains a vertex of each 7-set induces a truth assignment that satisfies $\phi$. Thus, if $G_\phi$ has an independent set of size $m$ then $\phi \in$ SAT. ∎

**Graph 3-Colorability (G3C).** In this problem, the instances are graphs and the question is whether or not the graph's vertices can be colored using three colors such that neighboring vertices are not assigned the same color.

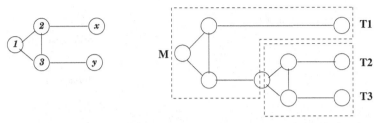

Figure 4.4. The clause gadget and its sub-gadget. The left-hand side depicts the sub-gadget and a generic legal 3-coloring of it. Note that if $x = y$, in this 3-coloring, then $x = y = 1$. The clause gadget is shown on the right-hand side. For any legal 3-coloring of this gadget it holds that if the three terminals of the gadget are assigned the same color, $\chi$, then M is also assigned the color $\chi$.

**Proposition 4.11:** Graph 3-Colorability *is NP-complete.*

**Proof:** We reduce 3SAT to G3C by mapping a 3CNF formula $\phi$ to the graph $G_\phi$ that consists of two special ("designated") vertices, a gadget per each variable of $\phi$, a gadget per each clause of $\phi$, and edges connecting some of these components as follows:

- The two designated vertices are called ground and false, and are connected by an edge that ensures that they must be given different colors in any legal 3-coloring of $G_\phi$. We will refer to the color assigned to the vertex ground (resp., false) by the name ground (resp., false). The third color will be called true.

- The gadget associated with variable $x$ is a pair of vertices, associated with the two literals of $x$ (i.e., $x$ and $\neg x$). These vertices are connected by an edge, and each of them is also connected to the vertex ground. Thus, in any legal 3-coloring of $G_\phi$ one of the vertices associated with the variable is colored true and the other is colored false.

- The gadget associated with a clause $C$ is depicted in Figure 4.4. It contains a master vertex, denoted **M**, and three terminal vertices, denoted **T1**, **T2**, and **T3**. The master vertex is connected by edges to the vertices ground and false, and thus in any legal 3-coloring of $G_\phi$ the master vertex must be colored true. The gadget has the property that it is possible to color the terminals with any combination of the colors true and false, except for coloring all terminals with false. That is, in any legal 3-coloring of $G_\phi$, if no terminal of a clause gadget is colored ground, then at least one of these terminals is colored true.

The terminals of the gadget associated with clause $C$ will be *identified* with the vertices (of variable gadgets) that are associated with the corresponding

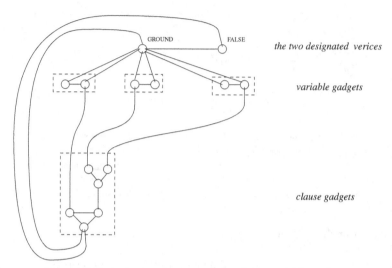

Figure 4.5. A single clause gadget and the relevant variables gadgets.

literals appearing in $C$. This means that each clause gadget shares its terminals with the corresponding variable gadgets, and that the various clause gadgets are not vertex-disjoint but may rather share some terminals (i.e., those associated with literals that appear in several clauses).[16] See Figure 4.5.

The aforementioned association forces each terminal to be colored either true or false (in any legal 3-coloring of $G_\phi$). By the foregoing discussion it follows that in any legal 3-coloring of $G_\phi$, at least one terminal of each clause gadget must be colored true.

Verifying the validity of the reduction is left as an exercise (see Exercise 4.16).  ∎

**Digest.** The reductions presented in the current section are depicted in Figure 4.6, where bold arrows indicate reductions presented explicitly in the proofs of the various propositions (indicated by their index). Note that r3SAT and 3SC are only mentioned inside the proof of Proposition 4.9.

### 4.3.3 Additional Properties of the Standard Reductions

We mention that the standard reductions used to establish natural NP-completeness results have several additional properties or can be modified

---

[16] Alternatively, we may use disjoint gadgets and "connect" each terminal with the corresponding literal (in the corresponding vertex gadget). Such a connection (i.e., an auxiliary gadget) should force the two end points to have the same color in any legal 3-coloring of the graph.

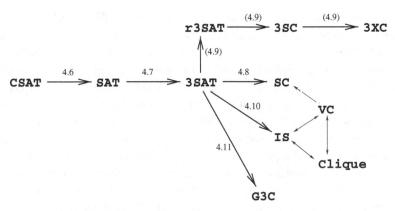

Figure 4.6. The (non-generic) reductions presented in Section 4.3.

to have such properties. These properties include an efficient transformation of solutions in the direction of the reduction (see Exercise 4.20), the preservation of the number of solutions (see Exercise 4.21), and being invertible in polynomial time (see Exercise 4.22 as well as Exercise 4.23). Furthermore, these reductions are relatively "simple" in the sense that they can be computed by restricted classes of polynomial-time algorithms (e.g., algorithms of logarithmic space complexity).

The foregoing assertions are easiest to verify for the generic reductions presented in the proofs of Theorems 4.3 and 4.5. These reductions satisfy all additional properties (without any modification). Turning to the non-generic reductions (depicted in Figure 4.6), we note that they all satisfy all additional properties with the exception of the preservation of the number of solutions (see Exercise 4.21). However, in each of the cases that our reduction does not satisfy the latter property, an alternative reduction that does satisfy it is known.

We also mention the fact that all known NP-complete sets are (effectively) isomorphic in the sense that every two such sets are isomorphic via a polynomial-time computable and invertible mapping (see Exercise 4.24).

### 4.3.4 On the Negative Application of NP-Completeness

Since its discovery in the early 1970s, NP-completeness has been used as the main tool by which the intrinsic complexity of certain problems is demonstrated. Recall that if an NP-complete problem is in P, then all problems in NP are in P (i.e., $\mathcal{P} = \mathcal{NP}$). Hence, demonstrating the NP-completeness of a problem yields very strong evidence for its intractability.

We mention that NP-completeness means more than intractability in the strict computational sense (i.e., that no efficient algorithm may solve the

problem). It also means that the problem at hand (or the underlying question) has a very rich structure and that the underlying question has no simple
answer. To see why this is the case, consider a question that refers to objects of
a certain type (e.g., territorial maps) and a property that some of these objects
have (e.g., being 3-colorable). The question at hand may call for a *simple* characterization of the objects that satisfy the property, but if the corresponding
decision problem is NP-complete,[17] then no such characterization is likely to
exist. We stress that the quest for a "simple" characterization could have had
nothing to do with computation, but "simple" characterizations yield efficient
decision procedures and so NP-completeness is relevant. Furthermore, the NP-
completeness of a problem means that the objects underlying the desired characterization are complex enough to encode all NP-problems. Indeed, diverse
scientific disciplines, which were unsuccessfully struggling with some of their
internal questions, came to realize that these questions are inherently difficult since they are closely related to computational problems that are NP-
complete.

Lastly, let us note that demonstrating the NP-completeness of a problem is
not the end of the story. Since the problem originates in reality, it does not go
away once we realize that it is (probably) hard to solve. However, the problem
we consider is never identical to the problem we need to solve in reality; the
former is just a model (or abstraction) of the latter. Thus, the fact that our
abstraction turns out to yield an NP-complete problem calls for a refinement of
our modeling. A careful reconsideration may lead us to realize that we only care
about a subset of all possible instances or that we may relax the requirements
from the desired solutions. Such relaxations lead to notions of average-case
complexity and approximation, which are indeed the subject of considerable
study. The interested reader is referred to [13, Chap. 10].

### 4.3.5 Positive Applications of NP-Completeness

Throughout this chapter, we have referred to the negative implication of NP-
completeness, that is, the fact that it provides evidence to the intractability
of problems. Indeed, the definition of NP-complete problems was motivated
by the intention to use it as a vehicle for proving the hardness of natural
computational problems (which reside in NP). Furthermore, we really do not
expect to use NP-completeness for the straightforward positive applications of
reductions that were discussed in Section 3.4. *So what can the current section
title actually mean?*

---

[17] This is indeed the case with respect to determinig whether a given territorial map is 3-colorable.

The answer is that we may use NP-complete problems as a vehicle to demonstrate properties of all problems in NP. For example, in Section 2.5, we proved that $\mathcal{NP} \subseteq \mathcal{EXP}$ by referring to an exhaustive search among all possible NP-witnesses (for a given instance, with respect to any problem in $\mathcal{NP}$). An alternative proof can first establish that SAT $\in \mathcal{EXP}$ and then use the fact that membership in $\mathcal{EXP}$ is preserved under Cook-reductions. The benefit in this approach is that it is more natural to consider an exhaustive search for SAT. However, this positive application is in line with the applications discussed in Section 3.4, although $\mathcal{EXP}$ is not considered a class of efficient problems.

Nevertheless, positive applications that are farther from the applications discussed in Section 3.4 have played an important role in the study of "probabilistic proof systems" (to be surveyed shortly). In three important cases, fundamental results regarding (all decision problems in) $\mathcal{NP}$ were derived by first establishing the result for SAT (or G3C), and then invoking the $\mathcal{NP}$-completeness of SAT (resp., G3C) in order to derive the same result for each problem in $\mathcal{NP}$. The benefit in this methodology is that the simple and natural structure of SAT (resp., G3C) facilitates the establishing of the said result for it.

Following is a brief description of three types of probabilistic proof systems and the role of NP-completeness in establishing three fundamental results regarding them. The reader is warned that the rest of the current section is advanced material, and furthermore that following this text requires some familiarity with the notion of randomized algorithms. On the other hand, the interested reader is referred to [13, Chap. 9] for further details.

**A General Introduction to Probabilistic Proof Systems.** The glory attributed to the creativity involved in finding proofs causes us to forget that it is the less-glorified process of verification that gives proofs their value. Conceptually speaking, proofs are secondary to the verification procedure; indeed, proof systems are defined in terms of their verification procedures. The notion of a verification procedure presupposes the notion of computation and, furthermore, the notion of efficient computation. Associating efficient computation with polynomial-time procedures, we obtain a fundamental class of proof systems, called NP-proof systems; see, indeed, Definition 2.5. We stress that that NP-proofs provide a satisfactory formulation of (efficiently verifiable) proof systems, provided that one associates efficient procedures with *deterministic* polynomial-time procedures. However, we can gain a lot if we are willing to take a somewhat non-traditional step and allow *probabilistic* verification procedures.

We shall consider three types of probabilistic proof systems. As in the case of NP-proof systems, in each of the following types of proof systems, explicit bounds are imposed on the computational complexity of the verification procedure, which in turn is personified by the notion of a verifier. The real novelty, in the case of probabilistic proof systems, is that the verifier is allowed to toss coins and *rule by statistical evidence*. Thus, these probabilistic proof systems carry a probability of error; yet this probability is explicitly bounded and, furthermore, can be reduced by successive application of the proof system.

**Interactive Proof Systems.** As we shall see, randomized and interactive verification procedures, giving rise to *interactive proof systems*, seem much more powerful (i.e., "expressive") than their deterministic counterparts. Loosely speaking, an interactive proof system is a game between a computationally bounded verifier and a computationally unbounded prover whose goal is to convince the verifier of the validity of some assertion. Specifically, the verifier is probabilistic and its time complexity is polynomial in the length of the assertion. It is required that if the assertion holds, then the verifier must always accept (when interacting with an appropriate prover strategy). On the other hand, if the assertion is false, then the verifier must reject with probability at least $\frac{1}{2}$, no matter what strategy is employed by the prover. Thus, a "proof" in this context is not a fixed and static object, but rather a randomized (and dynamic) process in which the verifier interacts with the prover. Intuitively, one may think of this interaction as consisting of "tricky" questions asked by the verifier, to which the prover has to reply "convincingly."

A fundamental result regarding interactive proof systems is their existence for any set in $\mathrm{co}\mathcal{NP} \stackrel{\text{def}}{=} \{\overline{S} : S \in \mathcal{NP}\}$, where $\overline{S} \stackrel{\text{def}}{=} \{0, 1\}^* \setminus S$. This result should be contrasted with the common belief that some sets in $\mathrm{co}\mathcal{NP}$ do *not* have NP-proof systems (i.e., $\mathcal{NP} \neq \mathrm{co}\mathcal{NP}$; cf. Section 5.3). Interestingly, the fact that any set in $\mathrm{co}\mathcal{NP}$ has an interactive proof system is established by presenting such a proof system for $\overline{\text{SAT}}$ (and deriving a proof system for any $\overline{S} \in \mathrm{co}\mathcal{NP}$ by using the Karp-reduction of $\overline{S}$ to $\overline{\text{SAT}}$, which is the very Karp-reduction of $S$ to SAT).[18] The construction of an interactive proof system for $\overline{\text{SAT}}$ relies on an "arithmetization" of CNF formulae, and hence we clearly benefit from the fact that this specific and natural problem (i.e., SAT) is NP-complete.

**Zero-knowledge Proof Systems.** Interactive proof systems provide the stage for a meaningful introduction of *zero-knowledge proofs*, which are of great

---

[18] **Advanced comment:** Actually, the result can be extended to show that a decision problem has an interactive proof system if and only if it is in $\mathcal{PSPACE}$, where $\mathcal{PSPACE}$ denotes the class of problems that are solvable in polynomial space complexity. We mention that this extension also relies on the use of a natural complete problem, which is also amenable to arithmetization.

theoretical and practical interest (especially in cryptography). Loosely speaking, zero-knowledge proofs are interactive proofs that yield nothing (to the verifier) beyond the fact that the assertion is indeed valid. For example, a *zero-knowledge proof* that a certain Boolean formula is satisfiable does not reveal a satisfying assignment to the formula nor any partial information regarding such an assignment (e.g., whether the first variable can assume the value true). Whatever the verifier can efficiently compute after interacting with a zero-knowledge prover can be efficiently computed from the assertion itself (without interacting with anyone). Thus, zero-knowledge proofs exhibit an extreme contrast between being convinced of the validity of a statement and learning anything in addition (while receiving such a convincing proof).

A fundamental result regarding zero-knowledge proof systems is their existence, under reasonable complexity assumptions, for any set in $\mathcal{NP}$. Interestingly, this result is established by presenting such a proof system for Graph 3-Colorability (i.e., G3C), and by deriving a proof system for any $S \in \mathcal{NP}$ by using the Karp-reduction of $S$ to SAT. The construction of a zero-knowledge proof system for G3C is facilitated by the simple structure of the problem, specifically, the fact that verifying the (global) claim that a specific 3-partition is a valid 3-coloring amounts to verifying a polynomial number of local constraints (i.e., that the colors assigned to the end points of each edge are different).

**Probabilistically Checkable Proof Systems.** NP-proofs can be efficiently transformed into a (redundant) form that offers a trade-off between the number of locations examined in the NP-proof and the confidence in its validity. These redundant proofs are called *probabilistically checkable proofs* (abbreviated PCPs), and have played a key role in the study of approximation problems.

Loosely speaking, a PCP-system consists of a probabilistic polynomial-time verifier having access to an oracle that represents a proof in redundant form. Typically, the verifier accesses only few of the oracle bits, where these bit positions are determined by the outcome of the verifier's coin tosses. Again, it is required that if the assertion holds, then the verifier must always accept (when given access to an adequate oracle), whereas, if the assertion is false, then the verifier must reject with probability at least $\frac{1}{2}$, no matter which oracle is used.

A fundamental result regarding PCP-systems is that any set in $\mathcal{NP}$ has a PCP-system in which the verifier issues only a *constant* number of (binary!) queries. Again, the fact that any set in $\mathcal{NP}$ has such a PCP-system is established by presenting such a proof system for SAT (and deriving a similar proof system for any $S \in \mathcal{NP}$ by using the Karp-reduction of $S$ to SAT). The construction for SAT relies, again, on an arithmetization of CNF formulae, where this arithmetization is different from the one used in the construction of interactive proof systems for $\overline{\text{SAT}}$.

## 4.4 NP Sets That Are Neither in P nor NP-Complete

As stated in Section 4.3, thousands of problems have been shown to be NP-complete (cf. [11, Apdx.], which contains a list of more than three hundred main entries). Things have reached a situation in which people seem to expect any NP-set to be either NP-complete or in $\mathcal{P}$. This naive view is wrong: *Assuming* $\mathcal{NP} \neq \mathcal{P}$, *there exist sets in* $\mathcal{NP}$ *that are neither NP-complete nor in* $\mathcal{P}$, *where here NP-hardness also allows Cook-reductions.*

**Theorem 4.12:** *Assuming* $\mathcal{NP} \neq \mathcal{P}$, *there exists a set T in* $\mathcal{NP} \setminus \mathcal{P}$ *such that some sets in* $\mathcal{NP}$ *are not Cook-reducible to T.*

Theorem 4.12 asserts that if $\mathcal{NP} \neq \mathcal{P}$, then $\mathcal{NP}$ is partitioned into three non-empty classes: the class $\mathcal{P}$, the class of problems to which $\mathcal{NP}$ is Cook-reducible, and the rest, denoted $\mathcal{NPI}$ (where "I" stands for "intermediate"). We already know that the first two classes are not empty, and Theorem 4.12 establishes the non-emptiness of $\mathcal{NPI}$ under the condition that $\mathcal{NP} \neq \mathcal{P}$, which is actually a necessary condition (because if $\mathcal{NP} = \mathcal{P}$ then every set in $\mathcal{NP}$ is Cook-reducible to any other set in $\mathcal{NP}$).

The following proof of Theorem 4.12 presents an unnatural decision problem in $\mathcal{NPI}$. We mention that some natural decision problems (e.g., some that are computationally equivalent to factoring) are conjectured to be in $\mathcal{NPI}$. We also mention that if $\mathcal{NP} \neq \text{co}\mathcal{NP}$, where $\text{co}\mathcal{NP} = \{\{0, 1\}^* \setminus S : S \in \mathcal{NP}\}$, then $\Delta \stackrel{\text{def}}{=} \mathcal{NP} \cap \text{co}\mathcal{NP} \subseteq \mathcal{P} \cup \mathcal{NPI}$ holds (as a corollary to Theorem 5.7). Thus, if $\mathcal{NP} \neq \text{co}\mathcal{NP}$ then $\Delta \setminus \mathcal{P}$ is a (natural) subset of $\mathcal{NPI}$, and the non-emptiness of $\mathcal{NPI}$ follows provided that $\Delta \neq \mathcal{P}$. Recall that Theorem 4.12 establishes the non-emptiness of $\mathcal{NPI}$ under the seemingly weaker assumption that $\mathcal{NP} \neq \mathcal{P}$.

**Proof Sketch:**[19] The basic idea is to modify an arbitrary set in $\mathcal{NP} \setminus \mathcal{P}$ so as to fail all possible reductions (from $\mathcal{NP}$ to the modified set), as well as all possible polynomial-time decision procedures (for the modified set). Specifically, starting with $S \in \mathcal{NP} \setminus \mathcal{P}$, we derive $S' \subset S$ such that on the one hand there is no polynomial-time reduction of $S$ to $S'$ while on the other hand $S' \in \mathcal{NP} \setminus \mathcal{P}$.

---

[19] For an alternative presestation, see [1, sec 3.3].

The process of modifying $S$ into $S'$ proceeds in iterations, alternatively failing a potential reduction (by dropping sufficiently many strings from the rest of $S$) and failing a potential decision procedure (by including sufficiently many strings from the rest of $S$). Specifically, each potential reduction of $S$ to $S'$ can be failed by dropping finitely many elements from the current $S'$, whereas each potential decision procedure can be failed by keeping finitely many elements of the current $S'$. These two assertions are based on the following two corresponding facts:

1. Any polynomial-time reduction (of any set not in $\mathcal{P}$) to any finite set (e.g., a finite subset of $S$) must fail, because only sets in $\mathcal{P}$ are Cook-reducible to a finite set. Thus, for any finite set $F_1$ and any potential reduction (i.e., a polynomial-time oracle machine), there exists an input $x$ on which this reduction to $F_1$ fails.[20]

2. For every finite set $F_2$, any polynomial-time decision procedure for $S \setminus F_2$ must fail, because $S$ is Cook-reducible to $S \setminus F_2$. Thus, for any potential decision procedure (i.e., a polynomial-time algorithm), there exists an input $x$ on which this procedure fails.[21]

As stated, the process of modifying $S$ into $S'$ proceeds in iterations, alternatively failing a potential reduction (by dropping finitely many strings from the rest of $S$) and failing a potential decision procedure (by including finitely many strings from the rest of $S$). This can be done efficiently because *it is inessential to determine the first possible points of alternation* (in which sufficiently many strings were dropped (resp., included) to fail the next potential reduction (resp., decision procedure)). It suffices to guarantee that adequate points of alternation (albeit highly non-optimal ones) can be efficiently determined. Thus, $S'$ is the intersection of $S$ and some set in $\mathcal{P}$, which implies that $S' \in \mathcal{NP}$. Following are some comments regarding the implementation of the foregoing idea.

The first issue is that the foregoing plan calls for an ("effective") enumeration of all polynomial-time oracle machines (resp., polynomial-time algorithms). However, none of these sets can be enumerated (by an algorithm). Instead, we

---

[20] We mention that the proof relies on additional observations regarding this failure. Specifically, the aforementioned reduction fails while the only queries that are answered positively are those residing in $F_1$. Furthermore, the aforementioned failure is due to a finite set of queries (i.e., the set of all queries made by the reduction when invoked on an input that is smaller or equal to $x$). Thus, for every finite set $F_1 \subset S' \subseteq S$, any reduction of $S$ to $S'$ can be failed by dropping a finite number of elements from $S'$ and without dropping elements of $F_1$.

[21] Again, the proof relies on additional observations regarding this failure. Specifically, this failure is due to a finite "prefix" of $S \setminus F_2$ (i.e., the set $\{z \in S \setminus F_2 : z \leq x\}$). Thus, for every finite set $F_2$, any polynomial-time decision procedure for $S \setminus F_2$ can be failed by keeping a finite subset of $S \setminus F_2$.

enumerate all corresponding machines along with all possible polynomials, and for each pair $(M, p)$ we consider executions of machine $M$ with time bound specified by the polynomial $p$. That is, we use the machine $M_p$ obtained from the pair $(M, p)$ by suspending the execution of $M$ on input $x$ after $p(|x|)$ steps. We stress that we do not know whether machine $M$ runs in polynomial time, but the computations of any polynomial-time machine is "covered" by some pair $(M, p)$.

Next, let us clarify the process in which reductions and decision procedures are ruled out. We present a construction of a "filter" set $F$ in $\mathcal{P}$ such that the final set $S'$ will equal $S \cap F$. Recall that we need to select $F$ such that each polynomial-time reduction of $S$ to $S \cap F$ fails, and each polynomial-time procedure for deciding $S \cap F$ fails. The key observation is that for every finite $F'$ each polynomial-time reduction of $S$ to $(S \cap F) \cap F'$ fails, whereas for every finite $F'$ each polynomial-time procedure for deciding $(S \cap F) \setminus F'$ fails. Furthermore, each of these failures occurs on some input, and such an input can be determined by finite portions of $S$ and $F$. Thus, we alternate between failing possible reductions and decision procedures on some inputs, while not trying to determine the "optimal" points of alternation but, rather, determining points of alternation in an efficient manner (which in turn allows for efficiently deciding membership in $F$). Specifically, we let $F = \{x : f(|x|) \equiv 1 \bmod 2\}$, where $f : \mathbb{N} \to \{0\} \cup \mathbb{N}$ will be defined such that (i) each of the first $f(n) - 1$ machines is failed by some input of length at most $n$, and (ii) the value $f(n)$ can be computed in poly($n$)-time.

The value of $f(n)$ is defined by the following process that performs exactly $n^3$ computation steps (where cubic time is a rather arbitrary choice). The process proceeds in (an a priori unknown number of) iterations, where in the $i + 1^{\text{st}}$ iteration we try to find an input on which the $i + 1^{\text{st}}$ (modified) machine fails. Specifically, in the $i + 1^{\text{st}}$ iteration we scan all inputs, in lexicographic order, until we find an input on which the $i + 1^{\text{st}}$ (modified) machine fails, where this machine is an oracle machine if $i + 1$ is odd and a standard machine otherwise. If we detect a failure of the $i + 1^{\text{st}}$ machine, then we increment $i$ and proceed to the next iteration. When we reach the allowed number of steps (i.e., $n^3$ steps), we halt outputting the current value of $i$ (i.e., the current $i$ is output as the value of $f(n)$). Needless to say, this description is heavily based on determining whether or not the $i + 1^{\text{st}}$ machine fails on specific inputs. Intuitively, these inputs will be much shorter than $n$, and so performing these decisions in time $n^3$ (or so) is not out of the question – see next paragraph.

In order to determine whether or not a failure (of the $i + 1^{\text{st}}$ machine) occurs on a particular input $x$, we need to emulate the computation of this machine on input $x$, as well as determine whether $x$ is in the relevant set (which is either $S$ or $S' = S \cap F$). Recall that if $i + 1$ is even, then we need to fail a standard machine (which attempts to decide $S'$), and otherwise we need to fail an oracle machine (which attempts to reduce $S$ to $S'$). Thus, for even $i + 1$ we need to determine whether $x$ is in $S' = S \cap F$, whereas for odd $i + 1$ we need to determine whether $x$ is in $S$ as well as whether some other strings (which appear as queries) are in $S'$. Deciding membership in $S \in \mathcal{NP}$ can be done in exponential time (by using the exhaustive search algorithm that tries all possible NP-witnesses). Indeed, this means that when computing $f(n)$ we may only complete the treatment of inputs that are of logarithmic (in $n$) length, but anyhow in $n^3$ steps we cannot hope to reach (in our lexicographic scanning) strings of length greater than $3 \log_2 n$. As for deciding membership in $F$, this requires an ability to compute $f$ on adequate integers. That is, we may need to compute the value of $f(n')$ for various integers $n'$, but as noted, $n'$ will be much smaller than $n$ (since $n' \leq \text{poly}(|x|) \leq \text{poly}(\log n)$). Thus, the value of $f(n')$ is just computed recursively (while counting the recursive steps in our total number of steps).[22] The point is that when considering an input $x$, we may need the values of $f$ only on $\{1, \ldots, p_{i+1}(|x|)\}$, where $p_{i+1}$ is the polynomial bounding the running time of the $i + 1^{\text{st}}$ (modified) machine, and obtaining such a value takes at most $p_{i+1}(|x|)^3$ steps. We conclude that the number of steps performed toward determining whether or not a failure (of the $i + 1^{\text{st}}$ machine) occurs on the input $x$ is upper-bounded by an (exponential) function of $|x|$.

As hinted in the foregoing paragraph, the procedure will complete $n^3$ steps well before examining inputs of length greater than $3 \log_2 n$, but this does not matter. What matters is that $f$ *is unbounded* (see Exercise 4.25). Furthermore, by construction, $f(n)$ is computed in $\text{poly}(n)$-time. ◻

**Comment.** The proof of Theorem 4.12 actually establishes that *for every decidable set $S \notin \mathcal{P}$, there exists $S' \notin \mathcal{P}$ such that $S'$ is Karp-reducible to $S$ but $S$ is not Cook-reducible to $S'$.*[23] Thus, if $\mathcal{P} \neq \mathcal{NP}$ then there exists an infinite sequence of sets $S_1, S_2, \ldots$ in $\mathcal{NP} \setminus \mathcal{P}$ such that $S_{i+1}$ is Karp-reducible to $S_i$ but $S_i$ is not Cook-reducible to $S_{i+1}$. Furthermore, $S_1$ may be $\mathcal{NP}$-complete. That is, there exists an infinite sequence of problems (albeit unnatural ones), all in $\mathcal{NP}$, such that each problem is "easier" than the previous ones (in the sense that it can be reduced to any of the previous problems while none of these problems can be reduced to it).

---

[22] We do not bother to present a more efficient implementation of this process. That is, we may afford to recompute $f(n')$ every time we need it (rather than store it for later use).

[23] The said Karp-reduction (of $S'$ to $S$) maps $x$ to itself if $x \in F$ and otherwise maps $x$ to a fixed no-instance of $S$.

# 4.5 Reflections on Complete Problems

> This book will perhaps only be understood by those who have them-
> selves already thought the thoughts which are expressed in it – or similar
> thoughts. It is therefore not a text-book. Its object would be attained if it
> afforded pleasure to one who read it with understanding.
>
> *Ludwig Wittgenstein, Tractatus Logico-Philosophicus*

Indeed, this section should be viewed as an invitation to meditate together
on questions of the type: *What enables the existence of complete problems?*
Accordingly, the style is intentionally naive and imprecise; this entire section
may be viewed as an open-ended exercise, asking the interested reader to
consider substantiations of the vague text.[24]

We know that NP-complete problems exist. The question we ask here is
what aspects in our modeling of problems enable the existence of complete
problems. We should, of course, bear in mind that completeness refers to a
class of problems; the complete problem should "encode" each problem in the
class and be itself in the class. Since the first aspect, hereafter referred to as
encodability of a class, is amazing enough (at least to a layman), we start by
asking what enables it. We identify two fundamental paradigms, regarding the
modeling of problems, that seem essential to the encodability of any (infinite)
class of problems:

1. Each problem refers to an infinite set of possible instances.
2. The specification of each problem uses a finite description (e.g., an algorithm
   that enumerates all the possible solutions for any given instance).[25]

These two paradigms seem somewhat conflicting, yet put together they suggest the definition of a universal problem. Specifically, this problem refers to
instances of the form $(D, x)$, where $D$ is a description of a problem and $x$ is
an instance to that problem, and a solution to the instance $(D, x)$ is a solution
to $x$ with respect to the problem (described by) $D$. Intuitively, this universal
problem can encode any other problem (provided that problems are modeled
in a way that conforms with the foregoing paradigms): Solving the universal
problem allows for solving any other problem.[26]

---

[24] We warn that this exercise may be unsuitable for most undergraduate students.

[25] This seems the most naive notion of a description of a problem. An alternative notion of a
description refers to an algorithm that recognizes all valid instance-solution pairs (as in the
definition of NP). However, at this point, we also allow "non-effective" descriptions (as giving
rise to the Halting Problem).

[26] Recall, however, that the universal problem is not (algorithmically) solvable. Thus, both parts
of the implication are false (i.e., this problem is not solvable and, needless to say, there exist

Note that the foregoing universal problem is actually complete with respect to the class of all problems, but it is not complete with respect to any class that contains only (algorithmically) solvable problems (because this universal problem is not solvable). Turning our attention to classes of solvable problems, we seek versions of the universal problem that are complete for these classes. One archetypical difficulty that arises is that, given a description $D$ (as part of the instance to the universal problem), we cannot tell whether or not $D$ is a description of a problem in a predetermined class $C$ (because this decision problem is unsolvable).[27] This fact is relevant because if the universal problem requires solving instances that refer to a problem not in $C$, then intuitively it cannot be itself in $C$.

Before turning to the resolution of the foregoing difficulty, we note that the aforementioned modeling paradigms are pivotal to the theory of computation at large. In particular, so far we have made no reference to any complexity consideration. Indeed, a complexity consideration is the key to resolving the foregoing difficulty: The idea is modifying any description $D$ into a description $D'$ such that $D'$ is always in $C$, and $D'$ agrees with $D$ in the case that $D$ is in $C$ (i.e., in this case they described exactly the same problem). We stress that in the case that $D$ is not in $C$, the corresponding problem $D'$ may be arbitrary (as long as it is in $C$). Such a modification is possible with respect to many Complexity theoretic classes. We consider two different types of classes, where in both cases the class is defined in terms of the time complexity of algorithms that do something related to the problem (e.g., recognize valid solutions, as in the definition of NP).

1. *Classes defined by a single time-bound function $t$* (e.g., $t(n) = n^3$). In this case, any algorithm $D$ is modified to the algorithm $D'$ that, on input $x$, emulates (up to) $t(|x|)$ steps of the execution of $D(x)$. The modified version of the universal problem treats the instance $(D, x)$ as $(D', x)$. This version can encode any problem in the said class $C$ (corresponding to time complexity $t$).

But will this (version of the universal) problem be itself in $C$? The answer depends both on the efficiency of emulation in the corresponding computational model and on the growth rate of $t$. For example, for triple-exponential $t$, the answer will be definitely yes, because $t(|x|)$ steps

unsolvable problems). Indeed, the notion of a problem is rather vague at this stage; it certainly extends beyond the set of all solvable problems.

[27] Here we ignore the possibility of using promise problems, which do enable for avoiding such instances without requiring anybody to recognize them. Indeed, using promise problems resolves this difficulty, but the issues discussed following the next paragraph remain valid.

can be emulated in poly($t(|x|)$)-time (in any reasonable model) while $t(|(D, x)|) > t(|x| + 1) > \text{poly}(t(|x|))$. On the other hand, in most reasonable models, the emulation of $t(|x|)$ steps requires more than $O(t(|x|))$ time, whereas for any polynomial $t$ it holds that $t(n + O(1))$ is smaller than $2 \cdot t(n)$.

2. *Classes defined by a family of infinitely many functions of different growth rate* (e.g., polynomials). We can, of course, select a function $t$ that grows faster than any function in the family and proceed as in the prior case, but then the resulting universal problem will definitely not be in the class.

   Note that in the current case, a complete problem will indeed be striking because, in particular, it will be associated with one function $t_0$ that grows more moderately than some other functions in the family (e.g., a fixed polynomial grows more moderately than other polynomials). Seemingly this means that the algorithm describing the universal machine should be faster in terms of the actual number of steps than some algorithms that describe some other problems in the class. This impression presumes that the instances of both problems are (approximately) of the same length, and so we intensionally violate this presumption by artificially increasing the length of the description of the instances to the universal problem. For example, if $D$ is associated with the time bound $t_D$, then the instance $(D, x)$ to the universal problem is presented as, say, $(D, x, 1^{t_0^{-1}(t_D(|x|)^2)})$, where the square compensates for the overhead of the emulation (and in the case of NP we used $t_0(n) = n$).

We believe that the last item explains the existence of NP-complete problems. But *what about the NP-completeness of SAT?*

We first note that the NP-hardness of CSAT is an immediate consequence of the fact that Boolean circuits can emulate algorithms.[28] This fundamental fact is rooted in the notion of an algorithm (which postulates the simplicity of a single computational step) and holds for any reasonable model of computation. Thus, for every $D$ and $x$, the problem of finding a string $y$ such that $D(x, y) = 1$ is "encoded" as finding a string $y$ such that $C_{D,x}(y) = 1$, where $C_{D,x}$ is a Boolean circuit that is easily derived from $(D, x)$. In contrast to the fundamental fact underlying the NP-hardness of CSAT, the NP-hardness of SAT relies on a clever trick that allows for encoding instances of CSAT as instances of SAT.

As stated, the NP-completeness of SAT is proved by encoding instances of CSAT as instances of SAT. Similarly, the NP-completeness of other new problems is proved by encoding instances of problems that are already known to

---

[28] The fact that CSAT is in NP is a consequence of the fact that the circuit evaluation problem is solvable in polynomial time.

be NP-complete. Typically, these encodings operate in a local manner, mapping small components of the original instance to local gadgets in the produced instance. Indeed, these problem-specific gadgets are the core of the encoding phenomenon. Presented with such a gadget, it is typically easy to verify that it works. Thus, *one may not be surprised by most of these individual gadgets, but the fact that they exist for thousands of natural problems is definitely amazing.*

# Exercises

### Exercise 4.1 (a quiz)

1. What are NP-complete (search and decision) problems?
2. Is it likely that the problem of finding a perfect matching in a given graph is NP-complete?
3. Prove the existence of NP-complete problems.
4. How does the complexity of solving one NP-complete problem effect the complexity of solving any problem in $\mathcal{NP}$ (resp., $\mathcal{PC}$)?
5. In continuation of the previous question, assuming that some NP-complete problem can be solved in time $t$, upper-bound the complexity of solving any problem in $\mathcal{NP}$ (resp., $\mathcal{PC}$).
6. List five NP-complete problems.
7. Why does the fact that SAT is Karp-reducible to Set Cover imply that Set Cover is NP-complete?
8. Are there problems in $\mathcal{NP} \setminus \mathcal{P}$ that are not NP-complete?

**Exercise 4.2 ($\mathcal{PC}$-completeness implies $\mathcal{NP}$-completeness)** Show that if the search problem $R$ is $\mathcal{PC}$-complete, then $S_R$ is $\mathcal{NP}$-complete, where $S_R = \{x : \exists y \text{ s.t. } (x, y) \in R\}$.

**Exercise 4.3** Prove that any $R \in \mathcal{PC}$ is Levin-reducible to $R'_u$, where $R'_u$ consists of pairs $(\langle M, x, t \rangle, y)$ such that $M$ accepts the input pair $(x, y)$ within $t$ steps (and $|y| \leq t$). Recall that $R'_u \notin \mathcal{PC}$ (see [13, §4.2.1.2]).

*Guideline:* A minor modification of the reduction used in the proof of Theorem 4.3 will do.

**Exercise 4.4** Prove that Bounded Halting and Bounded Non-Halting are NP-complete, where the problems are defined as follows. The instance consists of a pair $(M, 1^t)$, where $M$ is a Turing machine and $t$ is an integer. The decision version of Bounded Halting (resp., Bounded Non-Halting) consists of determining whether or not there exists an input (of length at most $t$) on which $M$ halts (resp., does *not* halt) in $t$ steps, whereas the search problem consists of finding such an input.

*Guideline:* Either modify the proof of Theorem 4.3 or present a reduction of (say) the search problem of $R_u$ to the search problem of Bounded (Non-) Halting. (Indeed, the exercise is more straightforward in the case of Bounded Halting.)

**Exercise 4.5** In the proof of Theorem 4.5, we claimed that the value of each entry in the "array of configurations" of a machine $M$ is determined by the values of the three entries that reside in the row above it (as in Figure 4.2). Present a function $f_M : \Gamma^3 \to \Gamma$, where $\Gamma = \Sigma \times (Q \cup \{\bot\})$, that substantiates this claim.

*Guideline:* For example, for every $\sigma_1, \sigma_2, \sigma_3 \in \Sigma$, it holds that $f_M((\sigma_1, \bot), (\sigma_2, \bot), (\sigma_3, \bot)) = (\sigma_2, \bot)$. More interestingly, if the transition function of $M$ maps $(\sigma, q)$ to $(\tau, p, +1)$ then, for every $\sigma_1, \sigma_2, \sigma_3 \in Q$, it holds that $f_M((\sigma, q), (\sigma_2, \bot), (\sigma_3, \bot)) = (\sigma_2, p)$ and $f_M((\sigma_1, \bot), (\sigma, q), (\sigma_3, \bot)) = (\tau, \bot)$.

**Exercise 4.6** Present and analyze a reduction of SAT to 3SAT.

*Guideline:* For a clause $C$, consider auxiliary variables such that the $i^{\text{th}}$ variable indicates whether one of the first $i$ literals is satisfied, and replace $C$ by a 3CNF formula that uses the original variables of $C$ as well as the auxiliary variables. For example, the clause $\vee_{i=1}^{t} x_i$ is replaced by the conjunction of 3CNF formulae that are logically equivalent to the formulae $(y_2 \equiv (x_1 \vee x_2))$, $(y_i \equiv (y_{i-1} \vee x_i))$ for $i = 3, \dots, t$, and $y_t$. We comment that this is not the standard reduction, but we find it conceptually more appealing. (The standard reduction replaces the clause $\vee_{i=1}^{t} x_i$ by the conjunction of the 3CNF formula $(x_1 \vee x_2 \vee y_2), ((\neg y_{i-1}) \vee x_i \vee y_i)$ for $i = 3, \dots, t$, and $\neg y_t$.)

**Exercise 4.7 (efficient solvability of 2SAT)** In contrast to the NP-completeness of 3SAT, prove that 2SAT (i.e., the satisfiability of 2CNF formulae) is in $\mathcal{P}$.

*Guideline:* Consider the following forcing process for CNF formulae. If the formula contains a singleton clause (i.e., a clause having a single literal), then the corresponding variable is assigned the only value that satisfies the clause, and the formula is simplified accordingly (possibly yielding a constant formula, which is either true or false). The process is repeated until the formula is either a constant or contains only non-singleton clauses. Note that a formula $\phi$ is satisfiable if and only if the formula obtained from $\phi$ by the forcing process is satisfiable. Now, consider the following algorithm for solving the search problem associated with $2\text{SAT}$.

1. Choose an arbitrary variable in $\phi$. For each $\sigma \in \{0, 1\}$, denote by $\phi_\sigma$ the formula obtained from $\phi$ by assigning this variable the value $\sigma$ and applying the forcing process to the resulting formula.

   Note that $\phi_\sigma$ is either a Boolean constant or a 2CNF formula (which is a conjunction of some clauses of $\phi$).
2. If, for some $\sigma \in \{0, 1\}$, the formula $\phi_\sigma$ equals the constant true, then we halt with a satisfying assignment for the original formula.
3. If both assignments yield the constant false (i.e., for every $\sigma \in \{0, 1\}$ the formula $\phi_\sigma$ equals false), then we halt asserting that the original formula is unsatisfiable.
4. Otherwise (i.e., for each $\sigma \in \{0, 1\}$, the formula $\phi_\sigma$ is a (non-constant) 2CNF formula), we select $\sigma \in \{0, 1\}$ arbitrarily, set $\phi \leftarrow \phi_\sigma$, and go to Step 1.

Proving the correctness of this algorithm boils down to observing that the arbitrary choice made in Step 4 is immaterial. Indeed, this observation relies on the fact that we refer to 2CNF formulae, which implies that the forcing process either yields a constant or a 2CNF formula (which is a conjunction of some clauses of the original $\phi$).

***Exercise 4.8 (Integer Linear Programming)*** Prove that the following problem is NP-hard.[29] An instance of the problem is a system of linear inequalities (say, with integer constants), and the problem is to determine whether the system has an integer solution. A typical instance of this decision problem follows.

$$x + 2y - z \geq 3$$

$$-3x - z \geq -5$$

$$x \geq 0$$

$$-x \geq -1$$

*Guideline:* Reduce from SAT. Specifically, consider an arithmetization of the input CNF by replacing $\vee$ with addition and $\neg x$ by $1 - x$. Thus, each clause gives rise to an inequality (e.g., the clause $x \vee \neg y$ is replaced by the inequality

---

[29] Proving that the problem is in NP requires showing that if a system of linear inequalities has an integer solution, then it has an integer solution in which all numbers are of length that is polynomial in the length of the description of the system. Such a proof is beyond the scope of the current textbook.

$x + (1 - y) \geq 1$, which simplifies to $x - y \geq 0$). Enforce a 0-1 solution by introducing inequalities of the form $x \geq 0$ and $-x \geq -1$, for every variable $x$.

**Exercise 4.9 (Maximum Satisfiability of Linear Systems over GF(2))** Prove that the following problem is NP-complete. An instance of the problem consists of a system of linear equations over GF(2) and an integer $k$, and the problem is to determine whether there exists an assignment that satisfies at least $k$ equations. (Note that the problem of determining whether there exists an assignment that satisfies all of the equations is in $\mathcal{P}$.)

*Guideline:* Reduce from 3SAT, using the following arithmetization. Replace each clause that contains $t \leq 3$ literals by $2^t - 1$ linear GF(2) equations that correspond to the different non-empty subsets of these literals, and assert that their sum (modulo 2) equals one; for example, the clause $x \vee \neg y$ is replaced by the equations $x + (1 - y) = 1, x = 1$, and $1 - y = 1$. Identifying $\{\texttt{false}, \texttt{true}\}$ with $\{0, 1\}$, prove that if the original clause is satisfied by a Boolean assignment $\overline{v}$ then exactly $2^{t-1}$ of the corresponding equations are satisfied by $\overline{v}$, whereas if the original clause is unsatisfied by $\overline{v}$ then none of the corresponding equations is satisfied by $\overline{v}$.

**Exercise 4.10 (Satisfiability of Quadratic Systems over GF(2))** Prove that the following problem is NP-complete. An instance of the problem consists of a system of quadratic equations over GF(2), and the problem is to determine whether there exists an assignment that satisfies all the equations. Note that the result also holds for systems of quadratic equations over the reals (by adding conditions that force values in $\{0, 1\}$).

*Guideline:* Start by showing that the corresponding problem for cubic equations is NP-complete, by a reduction from 3SAT that maps the clause $x \vee \neg y \vee z$ to the equation $(1 - x) \cdot y \cdot (1 - z) = 0$. Reduce the problem for cubic equations to the problem for quadratic equations by introducing auxiliary variables; that is, given an instance with variables $x_1, \ldots, x_n$, introduce the auxiliary variables $x_{i,j}$'s and add equations of the form $x_{i,j} = x_i \cdot x_j$.

**Exercise 4.11 (restricted versions of 3SAT)** Prove that the following restricted version of 3SAT, denoted r3SAT, is NP-complete. An instance of the problem consists of a 3CNF formula such that each *literal* appears in at most *two* clauses, and the problem is to determine whether this formula is satisfiable.

*Guideline:* Recall that Proposition 4.7 establishes the NP-completeness of a version of 3SAT in which the instances are restricted such that each *variable* appears in at most *three* clauses. So it suffices to reduce this restricted problem to r3SAT. This reduction is based on the fact that if all (three) occurrences of a variable are of the same type (i.e., they are all negated or all non-negated), then this variable can be assigned a value that satisfies all clauses in which it appears (and so the variable and the clauses in which it appear can be omitted from the instance). Thus, the desired reduction consists of applying the foregoing simplification to all relevant variables. Alternatively, a closer look at the reduction used in the proof of Proposition 4.7 reveals the fact that this reduction maps any 3CNF formula to a 3CNF formula in which each literal appears in at most two clauses.

**Exercise 4.12** Verify the validity of the three main reductions presented in the proof of Proposition 4.9; that is, we refer to the reduction of r3SAT to 3SC, the reduction of 3SC to 3XC′, and the reduction of 3XC′ to 3XC.

**Exercise 4.13** Show that the following two variants of Set Cover are computationally equivalent. In both variants, an instance consists of a collection of finite sets $S_1, \ldots, S_m$ and an integer $K$. In the first variant we seek a vertex cover of size *at most* $K$, whereas in the second variant we seek a vertex cover of size *exactly* $K$. Consider both the decision and search versions of both variants, and note that $K \leq m$ may not hold.

**Exercise 4.14 (Clique and Independent Set)** An instance of the Independent Set problem consists of a pair $(G, K)$, where $G$ is a graph and $K$ is an integer, and the question is whether or not the graph $G$ contains an independent set (i.e., a set with no edges between its members) of size (at least) $K$. The Clique problem is analogous. Prove that both problems are computationally equivalent via Karp-reductions to the Vertex Cover problem.

**Exercise 4.15 (an alternative proof of Proposition 4.10)** Consider the following sketch of a reduction of 3SAT to Independent Set. On input a 3CNF formula $\phi$ with $m$ clauses and $n$ variables, we construct a graph $G_\phi$ consisting of $m$ triangles (corresponding to the (three literals in the) $m$ clauses) augmented with edges that link conflicting literals. That is, if $x$ appears as the $i_1^{th}$ literal of the $j_1^{th}$ clause and $\neg x$ appears as the $i_2^{th}$ literal of the $j_2^{th}$ clause, then we draw an edge between the $i_1^{th}$ vertex of the $j_1^{th}$ triangle and the $i_2^{th}$ vertex of the $j_2^{th}$ triangle. Prove that $\phi \in 3SAT$ if and only if $G_\phi$ has an independent set of size $m$.

**Exercise 4.16** Verify the validity of the reduction presented in the proof of Proposition 4.11.

**Exercise 4.17 (Subset Sum)** Prove that the following problem is NP-complete. The instance consists of a list of $n + 1$ integers, denoted $a_1, \ldots, a_n, b$, and the question is whether or not a subset of the $a_i$'s sums up to $b$ (i.e., exists $I \subseteq [n]$

such that $\sum_{i \in I} a_i = b$). Establish the NP-completeness of this problem, called Subset Sum, by a reduction from 3XC.

*Guideline:* Given an instance $(S_1, \ldots, S_m)$ of 3XC, where (without loss of generality) $S_1, \ldots, S_m \subseteq [3k]$, consider the following instance of Subset Sum that consists of a list of $m + 1$ integers such that $b = \sum_{j=1}^{3k} (m + 1)^j$ and $a_i = \sum_{j \in S_i} (m + 1)^j$ for every $i \in [m]$. (Some intuition may be gained by writing all integers in base $m + 1$.)

**Exercise 4.18** Prove that the following problem is NP-complete. The instance consists of a list of permutations over $[n]$, denoted $\pi_1, \ldots, \pi_m$, a target permutation $\pi$ (over $[n]$), and an integer $t$ presented in unary (i.e., $1^t$). The question is whether or not there exists a sequence, $i_1, \ldots, i_\ell \in [m]$, such that $\ell \leq t$ and $\pi = \pi_{i_\ell} \circ \cdots \circ \pi_{i_2} \circ \pi_{i_1}$, where $\circ$ denotes the composition of permutations. Establish the NP-completeness of this problem by a reduction from 3XC.

*Guideline:* Given an instance $(S_1, \ldots, S_m)$ of 3XC, where (without loss of generality) $S_1, \ldots, S_m \subseteq [3k]$, consider the following instance $((\pi_1, \ldots, \pi_m), \pi, 1^k)$ of the permutation problem (over $[6k]$). The target permutation $\pi$ is the involution (over $[6k]$) that satisfies $\pi(2i) = 2i - 1$ for every $i \in [3k]$. For $j = 1, \ldots, m$, the $j^{\text{th}}$ permutation in the list (i.e., $\pi_j$) is the involution that satisfies $\pi(2i) = 2i - 1$ if $i \in S_j$ and $\pi(2i) = 2i$ (as well as $\pi(2i - 1) = 2i - 1$) otherwise.

**Exercise 4.19** The fact that SAT and CSAT are NP-complete implies that Graph 3-Colorability and Clique can be reduced to SAT and CSAT (via a generic reduction). In this exercise, however, we ask for simple and direct reductions.

1. Present a simple reduction of Graph 3-Colorability to 3SAT.

   *Guideline:* Introduce three Boolean variables for each vertex such that $x_{i,j}$ indicates whether vertex $i$ is colored with the $j^{\text{th}}$ color. Construct clauses that enforce that each vertex is colored by a single color, and that no adjacent vertices are colored with the same color.

2. Present a simple reduction of Clique to CSAT.

   *Guideline:* Introduce a Boolean input for each vertex such that this input indicates whether the vertex is in the clique. The circuit should check that all pairs of inputs that are set to 1 correspond to pairs of vertices that are adjacent in the graph, and check that the number of variables that are set to 1 exceeds the given threshold. This calls for constructing a circuit that counts. Constructing a corresponding Boolean formula is left as an advanced exercise.

**Exercise 4.20 (an augmented form of Levin-reductions)** In continuation of the discussion in the main text, consider the following augmented form of Levin-reductions. Such a reduction of $R$ to $R'$ consists of three polynomial-time mappings $(f, h, g)$ such that ($f$ is a Karp-reduction of $S_R$ to $S_{R'}$ and)[30] the following two conditions hold:

1. For every $(x, y) \in R$ it holds that $(f(x), h(x, y)) \in R'$.
2. For every $(f(x), y') \in R'$ it holds that $(x, g(x, y')) \in R$.

(We note that this definition is actually the one used by Levin in [21], except that he restricted $h$ and $g$ to depend only on their second argument.)

Prove that such a reduction implies both a Karp-reduction and a Levin-Reduction, and show that all reductions presented in this chapter satisfy this augmented requirement.

**Exercise 4.21 (parsimonious reductions)** Let $R, R' \in \mathcal{PC}$ and let $f$ be a Karp-reduction of $S_R = \{x : R(x) \neq \emptyset\}$ to $S_{R'} = \{x : R'(x) \neq \emptyset\}$. We say that $f$ is parsimonious (with respect to $R$ and $R'$) if for every $x$ it holds that $|R(x)| = |R'(f(x))|$. For each of the reductions presented in this chapter, determine whether or not it is parsimonious.[31]

**Exercise 4.22 (polynomial-time invertible reductions)** Show that, under a suitable (but natural) encoding of the problems' instances, all Karp-reductions presented in this chapter are one-to-one and polynomial-time invertible; that is, show that for every such reduction $f$ there exists a polynomial-time algorithm that, on any input in the image of $f$, returns the unique preimage under $f$. Note that, without loss of generality, when given a string that is not in the image of $f$, the inverting algorithm returns a special symbol.

**Exercise 4.23 (on polynomial-time invertible reductions (following [2]))** In continuation of Exercise 4.22, we consider a general condition on sets that implies that any Karp-reduction to them can be modified into a one-to-one and polynomial-time invertible Karp-reduction. Loosely speaking, a set is markable if it is feasible to "mark" any instance $x$ by a label $\alpha$ such that the resulting instance $M(x, \alpha)$ preserves the "membership bit" of $x$ (wrt the set) and the label is easily recoverable from $M(x, \alpha)$. That is, we say that a set $S$ is

---

[30] The parenthetical condition is actually redundant, because it is implied by the following two conditions.

[31] **Advanced comment:** In most cases, when the standard reductions are not parsimonious, it is possible to find alternative reductions that are parsimonious (cf. [11, Sec. 7.3]). In some cases (e.g., for 3-Colorability), finding such alternatives is quite challenging.

markable if there exists a polynomial-time (marking) algorithm $M$ such that

1. For every $x, \alpha \in \{0, 1\}^*$ it holds that
   (a) $M(x, \alpha) \in S$ if and only if $x \in S$.
   (b) $|M(x, \alpha)| > |x|$.
2. There exists a polynomial-time (de-marking) algorithm $D$ such that, for every $x, \alpha \in \{0, 1\}^*$, it holds that $D(M(x, \alpha)) = \alpha$.

Note that all natural NP-sets (e.g., those considered in this chapter) are markable (e.g., for SAT, one may mark a formula by augmenting it with additional satisfiable clauses that use specially designated auxiliary variables). Prove that *if S' is Karp-reducible to S and S is markable, then S' is Karp-reducible to S by a length-increasing, one-to-one, and polynomial-time invertible mapping.* Infer that for any natural NP-complete problem $S$, any set in $\mathcal{NP}$ is Karp-reducible to $S$ by a length-increasing, one-to-one, and polynomial-time invertible mapping.

*Guideline:* Let $f$ be a Karp-reduction of $S'$ to $S$, and let $M$ be the guaranteed marking algorithm. Consider the reduction that maps $x$ to $M(f(x), x)$.

### Exercise 4.24 (on the isomorphism of NP-complete sets (following [2]))
Suppose that $S$ and $T$ are Karp-reducible to each other by length-increasing, one-to-one, and polynomial-time invertible mappings, denoted $f$ and $g$, respectively. Using the following guidelines, prove that $S$ and $T$ are "effectively" *isomorphic*; that is, present a polynomial-time computable and invertible one-to-one mapping $\phi$ such that $T = \phi(S) \stackrel{\text{def}}{=} \{\phi(x) : x \in S\}$.

1. Let $F \stackrel{\text{def}}{=} \{f(x) : x \in \{0, 1\}^*\}$ and $G \stackrel{\text{def}}{=} \{g(x) : x \in \{0, 1\}^*\}$. Using the length-increasing condition of $f$ (resp., $g$), prove that $F$ (resp., $G$) is a proper subset of $\{0, 1\}^*$. Prove that for every $y \in \{0, 1\}^*$ there exists a unique triple $(j, x, i) \in \{1, 2\} \times \{0, 1\}^* \times (\{0\} \cup \mathbb{N})$ that satisfies one of the following two conditions:
   (a) $j = 1, x \in \overline{G} \stackrel{\text{def}}{=} \{0, 1\}^* \setminus G$, and $y = (g \circ f)^i(x)$;
   (b) $j = 2, x \in \overline{F} \stackrel{\text{def}}{=} \{0, 1\}^* \setminus F$, and $y = (g \circ f)^i(g(x))$.
   (In both cases $h^0(z) \stackrel{\text{def}}{=} z, h^i(z) \stackrel{\text{def}}{=} h(h^{i-1}(z))$, and $(g \circ f)(z) \stackrel{\text{def}}{=} g(f(z))$.)

   Hint: consider the maximal sequence of inverse operations $g^{-1}, f^{-1}, g^{-1}, \ldots$ that can be applied to $y$, and note that each inverse shrinks the current string.)

2. Let $U_1 \stackrel{\text{def}}{=} \{(g \circ f)^i(x) : x \in \overline{G} \wedge i \geq 0\}$ and $U_2 \stackrel{\text{def}}{=} \{(g \circ f)^i(g(x)) : x \in \overline{F} \wedge i \geq 0\}$. Prove that $(U_1, U_2)$ is a partition of $\{0, 1\}^*$. Using the fact that $f$ and $g$ are length-increasing and polynomial-time invertible, present a polynomial-time procedure for deciding membership in the set $U_1$.

Prove the same for the sets $V_1 = \{(f \circ g)^i(x) : x \in \overline{F} \wedge i \geq 0\}$ and $V_2 = \{(f \circ g)^i(f(x)) : x \in \overline{G} \wedge i \geq 0\}$.

3. Note that $U_2 \subseteq G$, and define $\phi(x) \stackrel{\text{def}}{=} f(x)$ if $x \in U_1$ and $\phi(x) \stackrel{\text{def}}{=} g^{-1}(x)$ otherwise.

   (a) Prove that $\phi$ is a Karp-reduction of $S$ to $T$.

   (b) Note that $\phi$ maps $U_1$ to $f(U_1) = \{f(x) : x \in U_1\} = V_2$ and $U_2$ to $g^{-1}(U_2) = \{g^{-1}(x) : x \in U_2\} = V_1$. Prove that $\phi$ is one-to-one and onto. Observe that $\phi^{-1}(x) = f^{-1}(x)$ if $x \in f(U_1)$ and $\phi^{-1}(x) = g(x)$ otherwise. Prove that $\phi^{-1}$ is a Karp-reduction of $T$ to $S$. Infer that $\phi(S) = T$.

Using Exercise 4.23, infer that all natural NP-complete sets are isomorphic.

**Exercise 4.25** Referring to the proof of Theorem 4.12, prove that the function $f$ is unbounded (i.e., for every $i$ there exists an $n$ such that $n^3$ steps of the process defined in the proof allow for failing the $i + 1^{\text{st}}$ machine).

*Guideline:* Note that $f$ is monotonically non-decreasing (because more steps allow for failure of at least as many machines). Assume, toward the contradiction that $f$ is bounded. Let $i = \max_{n \in \mathbb{N}}\{f(n)\}$ and $n'$ be the smallest integer such that $f(n') = i$. If $i$ is odd then the set $F$ determined by $f$ is cofinite (because $F = \{x : f(|x|) \equiv 1 \pmod 2\} \supseteq \{x : |x| \geq n'\}$). In this case, the $i + 1^{\text{st}}$ machine tries to decide $S \cap F$ (which differs from $S$ on finitely many strings), and must fail on some $x$. Derive a contradiction by showing that the number of steps taken till reaching and considering this $x$ is at most $\exp(\text{poly}(|x|))$, which is smaller than $n^3$ for some sufficiently large $n$. A similar argument applies to the case that $i$ is even, where we use the fact that $F \subseteq \{x : |x| < n'\}$ is finite and so the relevant reduction of $S$ to $S \cap F$ must fail on some input $x$.

**Exercise 4.26 (universal verification procedures)** A natural notion, which arises from viewing NP-complete problems as "encoding" all problems in NP, is the notion of a "universal" NP-proof system. We say that an NP-proof system is universal if verification in any other NP-proof system can be reduced to verification in it. Specifically, following Definition 2.5, let $V$ and $V'$ be verification procedures for $S \in \mathcal{NP}$ and $S' \in \mathcal{NP}$, respectively. We say that verification with respect to $V'$ is reduced to verification with respect to $V$ if there exists two polynomial-time computable functions $f, h : \{0, 1\}^* \to \{0, 1\}^*$ such that for every $x, y \in \{0, 1\}^*$ it holds that $V'(x, y) = V(f(x), h(x, y))$. Prove the existence of universal NP-proof systems and show that the natural NP-proof system for SAT is universal.

*Guideline:* See Exercise 4.20.

# 5

# Three Relatively Advanced Topics

In this chapter we discuss three relatively advanced topics. The first topic, which was alluded to in previous chapters, is the notion of promise problems (Section 5.1). Next, we present an optimal algorithm for solving ("candid") NP-search problems (Section 5.2). Finally, in Section 5.3, we briefly discuss the class (denoted coNP) of sets that are complements of sets in NP.

## Teaching Notes

Typically, the foregoing topics are not mentioned in a basic course on complexity. Still, we believe that these topics deserve at least a mention in such a course. This holds especially with respect to the notion of promise problems. Furthermore, depending on time constraints, we recommend presenting all three topics in class (at least at an overview level).

We comment that the notion of promise problems was originally introduced in the context of decision problems, and is typically used only in that context. However, given the importance that we attach to an explicit study of search problems, we extend the formulation of promise problems to search problems as well. In that context, it is also natural to introduce the notion of a "candid search problem" (see Definition 5.2).

## 5.1 Promise Problems

Promise problems are natural generalizations of search and decision problems. These generalizations are obtained by explicitly considering a set of legitimate instances (rather than considering any string as a legitimate instance). As noted previously, this generalization provides a more adequate formulation of natural computational problems (and, indeed, this formulation is used in all informal discussions). For example, in Section 4.3.2 we presented such problems using phrases like "given a graph and an integer..." (or "given a collection of sets..."). In other words, we assumed that the input instance has a certain format (or rather we "promised the solver" that this is the case). Indeed, we claimed that in these cases, the assumption can be removed without affecting the complexity of the problem, but we avoided providing a formal treatment of this issue, which we do next.[1]

## 5.1.1 Definitions

Promise problems are defined by specifying a set of admissible instances. Candidate solvers of these problems are only required to handle these admissible instances. Intuitively, the designer of an algorithm solving such a problem is promised that the algorithm will never encounter an inadmissible instance (and so the designer need not care about how the algorithm performs on inadmissible inputs).

### 5.1.1.1 Search Problems with a Promise
In the context of search problems, a promise problem is a relaxation in which one is only required to find solutions to instances in a predetermined set, called the promise. The requirement regarding efficient checkability of solutions is adapted in an analogous manner.

**Definition 5.1** (search problems with a promise): *A* search problem with a promise *consists of a binary relation* $R \subseteq \{0, 1\}^* \times \{0, 1\}^*$ *and a* promise set *P. Such a problem is also referred to as the* search problem $R$ with promise $P$.

- *The search problem $R$ with promise $P$ is* solved by algorithm $A$ *if for every* $x \in P$ *it holds that* $(x, A(x)) \in R$ *if* $x \in S_R$ *and* $A(x) = \bot$ *otherwise, where* $S_R = \{x : R(x) \neq \emptyset\}$ *and* $R(x) = \{y : (x, y) \in R\}$.
  The time complexity of $A$ on inputs in $P$ *is defined as* $T_{A|P}(n) \stackrel{\text{def}}{=}$ $\max_{x \in P \cap \{0,1\}^n} \{t_A(x)\}$, *where* $t_A(x)$ *is the running time of $A(x)$ and* $T_{A|P}(n) = 0$ *if* $P \cap \{0, 1\}^n = \emptyset$.
- *The search problem $R$ with promise $P$ is in the* promise problem extension of $\mathcal{PF}$ *if there exists a polynomial-time algorithm that solves this problem.*[2]

---

[1] **Advanced comment:** The notion of promise problems was originally introduced in the context of decision problems, and is typically used only in that context. However, we believe that promise problems are as natural in the context of search problems.

[2] In this case, it does not matter whether the time complexity of $A$ is defined on inputs in $P$ or on all possible strings. Suppose that $A$ has (polynomial) time complexity $T$ on inputs in $P$; then we can modify $A$ to halt on any input $x$ after at most $T(|x|)$ steps. This modification may only effect the output of $A$ on inputs not in $P$ (which are inputs that do not matter anyhow). The

- *The search problem R with promise P is in the* promise problem extension of
  *$\mathcal{PC}$ if there exists a polynomial T and an algorithm A such that, for every
  $x \in P$ and $y \in \{0, 1\}^*$, algorithm A makes at most $T(|x|)$ steps and it holds
  that $A(x, y) = 1$ if and only if $(x, y) \in R$.*

We stress that nothing is required of the solver in the case that the input violates
the promise (i.e., $x \notin P$); in particular, in such a case the algorithm may halt
with a wrong output. (Indeed, the standard formulations of $\mathcal{PF}$ and $\mathcal{PC}$ are
obtained by considering the trivial promise $P = \{0, 1\}^*$.)[3]

In addition to the foregoing motivation for promise problems, we mention
one natural class of search problems with a promise. These are search problem
in which the promise is that the instance has a solution; that is, in terms of
Definition 5.1, we consider a search problem $R$ with the promise $P = S_R$. We
refer to such search problems by the name *candid search problems*.

**Definition 5.2** (candid search problems): *An algorithm A solves the* candid
search problem of the binary relation $R$ *if for every $x \in S_R$ (i.e., for every $(x, y) \in
R$) it holds that $(x, A(x)) \in R$. The time complexity of such an algorithm is
defined as $T_{A|S_R}(n) \stackrel{\text{def}}{=} \max_{x \in S_R \cap \{0,1\}^n} \{t_A(x)\}$, where $t_A(x)$ is the running time of
$A(x)$ and $T_{A|S_R}(n) = 0$ if $S_R \cap \{0, 1\}^n = \emptyset$.*

Note that nothing is required when $x \notin S_R$: In particular, algorithm $A$ may
either output a wrong solution (although no solutions exist) or run for more than
$T_{A|S_R}(|x|)$ steps. The first case can be essentially eliminated whenever $R \in \mathcal{PC}$.
Furthermore, for $R \in \mathcal{PC}$, if we "know" the time complexity of algorithm $A$
(e.g., if we can compute $T_{A|S_R}(n)$ in poly($n$)-time), then we may modify $A$ into
an algorithm $A'$ that solves the (general) search problem of $R$ (i.e., halts with
a correct output on each input) in time $T_{A'}$ such that $T_{A'}(n)$ essentially equals
$T_{A|S_R}(n) + \text{poly}(n)$; see Exercise 5.2. However, we do not necessarily know the
running time of an algorithm that we *consider* (or *analyze*). Furthermore, as
we shall see in Section 5.2, *the naive assumption by which we always know the
running time of an algorithm that we design is not valid either.*

### 5.1.1.2 Decision Problems with a Promise
In the context of decision problems, a promise problem is a relaxation in
which one is only required to determine the status of instances that belong to a
predetermined set, called the promise. The requirement of efficient verification

---

modification can be implemented in polynomial time by computing $t = T(|x|)$ and emulating
the execution of $A(x)$ for $t$ steps. A similar comment applies to the definition of $\mathcal{PC}$, $\mathcal{P}$, and
$\mathcal{NP}$.

[3] Here we refer to the alternative formulation of $\mathcal{PC}$ outlined in Section 2.5.

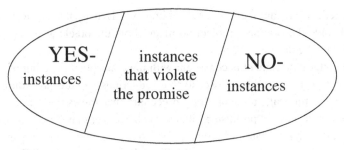

Figure 5.1. A schematic depiction of a promise problem.

is adapted in an analogous manner. In view of the standard usage of the term, we refer to *decision problems with a promise* by the name *promise problems*. Formally, promise problems refer to a three-way partition of the set of all strings into yes-instances, no-instances, and instances that violate the promise. (See schematic depiction in Figure 5.1.) Standard decision problems are obtained as a special case by insisting that all inputs are allowed (i.e., the promise is trivial).

**Definition 5.3** (promise problems): *A promise problem consists of a pair of non-intersecting sets of strings, denoted* $(S_{yes}, S_{no})$, *and* $S_{yes} \cup S_{no}$ *is called the* promise.

- *The promise problem* $(S_{yes}, S_{no})$ *is* solved by algorithm $A$ *if for every* $x \in S_{yes}$ *it holds that* $A(x) = 1$ *and for every* $x \in S_{no}$ *it holds that* $A(x) = 0$. *The promise problem is in the* promise problem extension of $\mathcal{P}$ *if there exists a polynomial-time algorithm that solves it.*
- *The promise problem* $(S_{yes}, S_{no})$ *is in the* promise problem extension of $\mathcal{NP}$ *if there exists a polynomial $p$ and a polynomial-time algorithm $V$ such that the following two conditions hold:*
  1. Completeness: *For every* $x \in S_{yes}$, *there exists $y$ of length at most* $p(|x|)$ *such that* $V(x, y) = 1$.
  2. Soundness: *For every* $x \in S_{no}$ *and every $y$, it holds that* $V(x, y) = 0$.

We stress that for algorithms of polynomial-time complexity, it does not matter whether the time complexity is defined only on inputs that satisfy the promise or on all strings (see footnote 2). Thus, the extended classes $\mathcal{P}$ and $\mathcal{NP}$ (like $\mathcal{PF}$ and $\mathcal{PC}$) are invariant under this choice.

### 5.1.1.3 Reducibility Among Promise Problems
The notion of a Cook-reduction extends naturally to promise problems, when postulating that a query that violates the promise (of the problem at the target

of the reduction) may be answered arbitrarily.[4] That is, the oracle machine should solve the original problem no matter how the oracle answers queries that violate the promise.

The latter requirement is consistent with the conceptual meaning of reductions and promise problems. Recall that reductions capture procedures that make subroutine calls to an arbitrary procedure that solves the "target" problem. But in the case of promise problems, such a solver may behave arbitrarily on instances that violate the promise. We stress that the main property of a reduction is preserved (see Exercise 5.3): *If the promise problem* $\Pi$ *is Cook-reducible to a promise problem that is solvable in polynomial time, then* $\Pi$ *is solvable in polynomial time.*

**Caveat.** The extension of a complexity class to promise problems does not necessarily inherit the "structural" properties of the standard class. For example, in contrast to Theorem 5.7, there exist promise problems in $\mathcal{NP} \cap \mathrm{co}\mathcal{NP}$ such that every set in $\mathcal{NP}$ can be Cook-reduced to them, see Exercise 5.4. Needless to say, $\mathcal{NP} = \mathrm{co}\mathcal{NP}$ does not seem to follow from Exercise 5.4. See further discussion in §5.1.2.4.

### 5.1.2 Applications and Limitations

The following discussion refers to both the decision and the search versions of promise problems. We start with two generic applications, and later consider some specific applications. (Other applications are surveyed in [12].) We also elaborate on the foregoing caveat.

#### 5.1.2.1 Formulating Natural Computational Problems

Recall that promise problems offer the most direct way of formulating natural computational problems. Indeed, this is a major application of the notion of promise problems (although this application usually goes unnoticed). Specifically, the presentation of natural computational problems refers (usually implicitly) to some natural format, and this can be explicitly formulated by defining a (promise problem with a) promise that equals all strings in that format. Thus, the notion of a promise problem allows the discarding of inputs that do not adhere

---

[4] It follows that Karp-reductions among promise problems are not allowed to make queries that violate the promise. Specifically, we say that the promise problem $\Pi = (\Pi_{\mathrm{yes}}, \Pi_{\mathrm{no}})$ is Karp-reducible to the promise problem $\Pi' = (\Pi'_{\mathrm{yes}}, \Pi'_{\mathrm{no}})$ if there exists a polynomial-time mapping $f$ such that for every $x \in \Pi_{\mathrm{yes}}$ (resp., $x \in \Pi_{\mathrm{no}}$) it holds that $f(x) \in \Pi'_{\mathrm{yes}}$ (resp., $f(x) \in \Pi'_{\mathrm{no}}$).

to this format (and a focus on inputs that do adhere to this format). For example, when referring to computational problems regarding graphs, the promise mandates that the input is a graph (or, rather, the standard representation of some graph).

We mention that, typically, the format (or rather the promise) is easily recognizable, and so the complexity of the promise problem can be captured by a corresponding problem (with a trivial promise); see Section 5.1.3 for further discussion.

### 5.1.2.2 Restricting a Computational Problem

In addition to the foregoing application of promise problems, we mention their use in formulating the natural notion of a *restriction of a computational problem to a subset of the instances*. Specifically, such a restriction means that the promise set of the restricted problem is a subset of the promise set of the unrestricted problem.

**Definition 5.4** (restriction of computational problems):

- *For any $P' \subseteq P$ and binary relation $R$, we say that the search problem $R$ with promise $P'$ is a* restriction *of the search problem $R$ with promise $P$.*
- *We say that the promise problem $(S'_{yes}, S'_{no})$ is a* restriction *of the promise problem $(S_{yes}, S_{no})$ if both $S'_{yes} \subseteq S_{yes}$ and $S'_{no} \subseteq S_{no}$ hold.*

For example, when we say that 3SAT is a restriction of SAT, we refer to the fact that the set of allowed instances is now restricted to 3CNF formulae (rather than to arbitrary CNF formulae). In both cases, the computational problem is to determine satisfiability (or to find a satisfying assignment), but the set of instances (i.e., the promise set) is further restricted in the case of 3SAT. The fact that a restricted problem is never harder than the original problem is captured by the fact that the restricted problem is Karp-reducible to the original one (via the identity mapping).

### 5.1.2.3 Non-generic Applications

In addition to the two aforementioned generic uses of the notion of a promise problem, we mention that this notion provides adequate formulations for a variety of specific Computational Complexity notions and results. One example is the notion of a candid search problem (i.e., Definition 5.2). Two other examples follow:

1. *Unique solutions*: For a binary relation $R$, we refer to the set of instances that have (at most) a single solution; that is, the promise is $P = \{x : |R(x)| \leq 1\}$, where $R(x) = \{y : (x, y) \in R\}$. Two natural problems that arise are the search

problem of $R$ with promise $P$ and the promise problem $(P \cap S_R, P \setminus S_R)$, where $S_R = \{x : R(x) \neq \emptyset\}$. One fundamental question regarding these promise problems is how their complexity relates to the complexity of the original problem (e.g., the standard search problem of $R$). For details, see [13, Sec. 6.2.3].

2. *Gap problems*: The complexity of various approximation tasks can be captured by the complexity of appropriate "gap problems"; for details, see [13, Sec. 10.1]. For example, approximating the value of an optimal solution is computationally equivalent to the promise problem of distinguishing instances having solutions of high value from instances having only solutions of low value, where the promise rules out instances that have an optimal solution of intermediate value.

In all of these cases, promise problems allow discussion of natural computational problems and making statements about their inherent complexity. Thus, the complexity of promise problems (and classes of such problems) addresses natural questions and concerns. In particular, demonstrating the efficient solvability (resp., intractability) of such a promise problem (or of a class of such problems) carries the same conceptual message as demonstrating the efficient solvability (resp., intractability) of a standard problem (or of a class of corresponding standard problems). For example, saying that some promise problem cannot be solved by a polynomial-time algorithm carries the same conceptual message as saying that some standard (search or decision) problem cannot be solved by a polynomial-time algorithm.

### 5.1.2.4 Limitations

Although the promise problem classes that correspond to $\mathcal{P}$ and $\mathcal{PF}$ preserve the intuitive meaning of the corresponding standard classes of (search or decision) problems, the situation is less clear with respect to $\mathcal{NP}$ and $\mathcal{PC}$. Things become even worse when we consider the promise problem classes that correspond to $\mathcal{NP} \cap \text{co}\mathcal{NP}$, where $\text{co}\mathcal{NP} = \{\{0, 1\}^* \setminus S : S \in \mathcal{NP}\}$. Specifically, for $S \in \mathcal{NP} \cap \text{co}\mathcal{NP}$ it holds that *every* instance $x$ has an NP-witness for membership in the corresponding set (i.e., either $S$ or $\overline{S} = \{0, 1\}^* \setminus S$); however, for a promise problem $(S_{\text{yes}}, S_{\text{no}})$ in the corresponding "extension of $\mathcal{NP} \cap \text{co}\mathcal{NP}$" it does *not* necessarily hold that *every* $x$ has an NP-witness for membership in the corresponding set (i.e., either $S_{\text{yes}}$ or $S_{\text{no}}$ or $\{0, 1\}^* \setminus (S_{\text{yes}} \cup S_{\text{no}})$). The effect of this discrepancy is demonstrated in the discrepancy between Theorem 5.7 and Exercise 5.4.

In general, structural properties of classes of promise problems do not necessarily reflect the properties of the corresponding decision problems. This follows from the fact that the answer of an oracle for a promise problem is not necessarily determined by the problem. Furthermore, the (standard) definitions of classes of promise problems do not refer to the complexity of the promise, which may vary from being trivial to being efficiently recognizable to being intractable or even undecidable.

### 5.1.3 The Standard Convention of Avoiding Promise Problems

Recall that although promise problems provide a good framework for presenting natural computational problems, we managed to avoid this framework in previous chapters. This was done by relying on the fact that for all of the (natural) problems considered in the previous chapters, it is easy to decide whether or not a given instance satisfies the promise, which in turn refers to a standard encoding of objects as strings. Details follow.

Let us first recall some natural computational problems. For example, SAT (resp., 3SAT) refers to CNF (resp., 3CNF) formulae, which means that we implicitly consider the promise that the input is in CNF (resp., in 3CNF). Indeed, this promise is efficiently recognizable (i.e., given a formula it is easy to decide whether or not it is in CNF (resp., in 3CNF)). Actually, the issue arises already when talking about formulae, because we are actually given a string that is supposed to encode a formula (under some predetermined encoding scheme). Thus, even for a problem concerning arbitrary formulae, we use a promise (i.e., that the input string is a valid encoding of some formula), which is easy to decide for natural encoding schemes. The same applies to all combinatorial problems we considered, because these problems (in their natural formulations) refer to objects like sets and graphs, which are encoded as strings (using some encoding scheme).

Thus, in all of these cases, the natural computational problem refers to objects of some type, and this natural problem is formulated by considering a promise problem in which the promise is the set of all strings that encode such objects. Furthermore, in all of these cases, the promise (i.e., the set of legal encodings) is efficiently recognizable (i.e., membership in it can be decided in polynomial time). In these cases, we may avoid mentioning the promise by using one of the following two "nasty" conventions:

1. *Fictitiously extending the set of instances to the set of all possible strings* (and allowing trivial solutions for the corresponding dummy instances). For example, in the case of a search problem, we may either define all instances that violate the promise to have no solution or define them to have a trivial solution (e.g., be a solution for themselves); that is, for a search problem $R$

with promise $P$, we may consider the (standard) search problem of $R$ where $R$ is modified such that $R(x) = \emptyset$ for every $x \notin P$ (or, say, $R(x) = \{x\}$ for every $x \notin P$). In the case of a promise (decision) problem $(S_{yes}, S_{no})$, we may consider the problem of deciding membership in $S_{yes}$, which means that instances that violate the promise are considered as no-instances.

2. *Considering every string as a valid encoding of some object* (i.e., efficiently identifying strings that violate the promise with strings that satisfy the promise).[5] For example, fixing any string $x_0$ that satisfies the promise, we consider every string that violates the promise as if it were $x_0$. In the case of a search problem $R$ with promise $P$, this means considering the (standard) search problem of $R$ where $R$ is modified such that $R(x) = R(x_0)$ for every $x \notin P$. Similarly, in the case of a promise (decision) problem $(S_{yes}, S_{no})$, we consider the problem of deciding membership in $S_{yes}$ (provided $x_0 \in S_{no}$ and otherwise we consider the problem of deciding membership in $\{0, 1\}^* \setminus S_{no}$).

We stress that *in the case that the promise is efficiently recognizable*, the aforementioned conventions (or modifications) do not affect the complexity of the relevant (search or decision) problem. That is, rather than considering the original promise problem, we consider a (search or decision) problem (without a promise) that is computational equivalent to the original one. Thus, in some sense we lose nothing by studying the latter problem rather than the original one (i.e., the original promise problem). However, to get to this situation we need the notion of a promise problem, which allows a formulation of the original natural problem.

Indeed, even in the case that the original natural (promise) problem and the problem (without a promise) that was derived from it are computationally equivalent, it is useful to have a formulation that allows for distinguishing between them (as we do distinguish between the different NP-complete problems although they are all computationally equivalent). This conceptual concern becomes of crucial importance in the case (to be discussed next) that the promise (referred to in the promise problem) is *not* efficiently recognizable.

In the case that the promise is not efficiently recognizable, the foregoing transformations of promise problems into standard (decision and search) problems do not necessarily preserve the complexity of the problem. In this case, the terminology of promise problems is unavoidable. Consider, for example, the problem of deciding whether a Hamiltonian graph is 3-colorable. On the face of it, such a problem may have fundamentally different complexity than the problem of deciding whether a given graph is both Hamiltonian and 3-colorable.

---

[5] Unlike in the first convention, this means that the dummy instances inherit the solutions to some real instances.

In spite of the foregoing issues, we have adopted the convention of focusing on standard decision and search problems. That is, by default, all computational problems and complexity classes discussed in other sections of this book refer to standard decision and search problems, and the only exception in which we refer to promise problems (outside of the current section) is explicitly stated as such (see Section 5.2). This is justified by our focus on natural computational problems, which can be stated as standard (decision and search) problems by using the foregoing conventions.

## 5.2 Optimal Search Algorithms for NP

This section refers to solving the candid search problem of any relation in $\mathcal{PC}$. Recall that $\mathcal{PC}$ is the class of search problems that allow for efficient checking of the correctness of candidate solutions (see Definition 2.3), and that the candid search problem is a search problem in which the solver is promised that the given instance has a solution (see Definition 5.2).

We claim the existence of an *optimal algorithm for solving the candid search problem of any relation in* $\mathcal{PC}$. Furthermore, we will explicitly present such an algorithm and prove that it is optimal in a very strong sense: For any algorithm solving the candid search problem of $R \in \mathcal{PC}$, our algorithm solves the same problem in time that is at most a constant factor slower (ignoring a fixed additive polynomial term, which may be disregarded in the case that the problem is not solvable in polynomial time).

Needless to say, we do not know the time complexity of the aforementioned optimal algorithm (indeed, if we knew it, then we would have resolved the P-vs-NP Question). In fact, the P-vs-NP Question boils down to determining the time complexity of a single explicitly presented algorithm (i.e., the optimal algorithm claimed in Theorem 5.5).[6]

**Theorem 5.5:** *For every binary relation $R \in \mathcal{PC}$ there exists an algorithm $A$ that satisfies the following:*

1. *Algorithm $A$ solves the candid search problem of $R$.*
2. *There exists a polynomial $p$ such that for every algorithm $A'$ that solves the candid search problem of $R$, it holds that $t_A(x) = O(t_{A'}(x) + p(|x|))$ (for any $x \in S_R$), where $t_A(x)$ (resp., $t_{A'}(x)$) denotes the number of steps taken by $A$ (resp., $A'$) on input $x$.*

Interestingly, we establish the optimality of $A$ without knowing what its (optimal) running time is. Furthermore, the optimality claim is "instance-based"

---

[6] That is, $\mathcal{P} = \mathcal{NP}$ if and only if the optimal algorithm of Theorem 5.5 has polynomial-time complexity.

(i.e., it refers to any input) rather than "global" (i.e., referring to the (worst-case) time complexity as a function of the input length).

We stress that the hidden constant in the O-notation depends only on $A'$, but in the following proof this dependence is exponential in the length of the description of algorithm $A'$ (and it is not known whether a better dependence can be achieved). Indeed, this dependence, as well as the idea underlying it, constitute one negative aspect of this otherwise amazing result. Another negative aspect is that the optimality of algorithm $A$ refers only to inputs that have a solution (i.e., inputs in $S_R$).[7] Finally, we note that the theorem as stated refers only to models of computation that have machines that can emulate a given number of steps of other machines with a constant overhead. We mention that in most natural models, the overhead of such emulation is at most poly-logarithmic in the number of steps, in which case it holds that $t_A(x) = \widetilde{O}(t_{A'}(x) + p(|x|))$, where $\widetilde{O}(t) = \text{poly}(\log t) \cdot t$.

**Proof Sketch:** Fixing $R$, we let $M$ be a polynomial-time algorithm that decides membership in $R$, and let $p$ be a polynomial bounding the running time of $M$ (as a function of the length of the first element in the input pair). Using $M$, we present an algorithm $A$ that solves the candid search problem of $R$ as follows. On input $x$, algorithm $A$ emulates ("in parallel") the executions of all possible search algorithms (on input $x$), checks the result provided by each of them (using $M$), and halts whenever it recognizes a correct solution. Indeed, most of the emulated algorithms are totally irrelevant to the search, but using $M$ we can screen the bad solutions offered by them and output a good solution once obtained.

Since there are infinitely many possible algorithms, it may not be clear what we mean by the expression "emulating all possible algorithms in parallel." What we mean is emulating them at different "rates" such that the infinite sum of these rates converges to 1 (or to any other constant). Specifically, we will emulate the $i^{\text{th}}$ possible algorithm at rate $1/(i+1)^2$, which means emulating a single step of this algorithm per $(i+1)^2$ emulation steps (performed for all algorithms).[8] Note that a straightforward implementation of this idea may create a significant overhead, which is involved in switching frequently from the emulation of one machine to the emulation of another. Instead, we present an alternative implementation that proceeds in iterations.

---

[7] We stress that Exercise 5.2 is not applicable here, because we do not know $T_{A|S_R}(\cdot)$ (let alone that we do not have a poly$(n)$-time algorithm for computing the mapping $n \mapsto T_{A|S_R}(n)$).

[8] Indeed, our choice of using the rate function $\rho(i) = 1/(i+1)^2$ is rather arbitrary and was adopted for the sake of simplicity (i.e., being the reciprocal of a small polynomial). See further discussion in Exercise 5.6.

In the $j^{\text{th}}$ iteration, for $i = 1, \ldots, 2^{j/2} - 1$, algorithm $A$ emulates $2^j/(i + 1)^2$ steps of the $i^{\text{th}}$ machine (where the machines are ordered according to the lexicographic order of their descriptions). Each of these emulations is conducted in one chunk, and thus the overhead of switching between the various emulations is insignificant (in comparison to the total number of steps being emulated).[9] In the case that one of these emulations (on input $x$) halts with output $y$, algorithm $A$ invokes $M$ on input $(x, y)$, and outputs $y$ if and only if $M(x, y) = 1$. Furthermore, the verification of a solution provided by a candidate algorithm is also emulated at the expense of its step count. (Put in other words, we augment each algorithm with a canonical procedure (i.e., $M$) that checks the validity of the solution offered by the algorithm.)

By its construction, whenever $A(x)$ outputs a string $y$ (i.e., $y \neq \perp$) it must hold that $(x, y) \in R$. To show the optimality of $A$, we consider an arbitrary algorithm $A'$ that solves the candid search problem of $R$. Our aim is to show that $A$ is not much slower than $A'$. Intuitively, this is the case because the overhead of $A$ results from emulating other algorithms (in addition to $A'$), but the total number of emulation steps wasted (due to these algorithms) is inversely proportional to the rate of algorithm $A'$, which in turn is exponentially related to the length of the description of $A'$. The punch line is that since $A'$ is fixed, the length of its description is a constant. Details follow.

For every $x$, let us denote by $t'(x)$ the number of steps taken by $A'$ on input $x$, where $t'(x)$ also accounts for the running time of $M(x, \cdot)$; that is, $t'(x) = t_{A'}(x) + p(|x|)$, where $t_{A'}(x)$ is the number of steps taken by $A'(x)$ itself. Then, the emulation of $t'(x)$ steps of $A'$ on input $x$ is "covered" by the $j^{\text{th}}$ iteration of $A$, provided that $2^j/(2^{|A'|+1})^2 \geq t'(x)$ where $|A'|$ denotes the length of the description of $A'$. (Indeed, we use the fact that the algorithms are emulated in lexicographic order, and note that there are at most $2^{|A'|+1} - 2$ algorithms that precede $A'$ in lexicographic order.) Thus, on input $x$, algorithm $A$ halts after at most $j_{A'}(x)$ iterations, where $j_{A'}(x) = 2(|A'| + 1) + \log_2(t_{A'}(x) + p(|x|))$, after emulating a total number of steps that is at most

$$t(x) \stackrel{\text{def}}{=} \sum_{j=1}^{j_{A'}(x)} \sum_{i=1}^{2^{j/2}-1} \frac{2^j}{(i + 1)^2} \tag{5.1}$$

$$< 2^{j_{A'}(x)+1} = 2^{2|A'|+3} \cdot (t_{A'}(x) + p(|x|)), \tag{5.2}$$

---

[9] For simplicity, we start each emulation from scratch; that is, in the $j^{\text{th}}$ iteration, algorithm $A$ emulates the first $2^j/(i + 1)^2$ steps of the $i^{\text{th}}$ machine. Alternatively, we may maintain a record of the configuration in which we stopped in the $j - 1^{\text{st}}$ iteration and resume the computation from that configuration for another $2^j/(i + 1)^2$ steps, but this saving (of $\sum_{k<j} 2^k/(i + 1)^2$ steps) is clearly insignificant.

where the inequality uses $\sum_{i=1}^{2^{j/2}-1} \frac{1}{(i+1)^2} < \sum_{i\geq 1} \frac{1}{(i+1)\cdot i} = \sum_{i\geq 1} \left(\frac{1}{i} - \frac{1}{i+1}\right) = 1$ and $\sum_{j=1}^{j_{A'}(x)} 2^j < 2^{j_{A'}(x)+1}$. The question of how much time is required for emulating these many steps depends on the specific model of computation. In many models of computation (e.g., a two-tape Turing machine), emulation is possible within poly-logarithmic overhead (i.e., $t$ steps of an arbitrary machine can be emulated by $\widetilde{O}(t)$ steps of the emulating machine), and in some models this emulation can even be performed with constant overhead. The theorem follows. ◻

**Comment.** By construction, the foregoing algorithm $A$ does not halt on input $x \notin S_R$. This can be easily rectified by letting $A$ emulate a straightforward exhaustive search for a solution, and halt with output $\bot$ if and only if this exhaustive search indicates that there is no solution to the current input. This extra emulation can be performed in parallel to all other emulations (e.g., at a rate of one step for the extra emulation per each step of everything else).

## 5.3 The Class coNP and Its Intersection with NP

By prepending the name of a complexity class (of decision problems) with the prefix "co" we mean the class of complement sets; that is,

$$\text{co}\mathcal{C} \stackrel{\text{def}}{=} \{\{0, 1\}^* \setminus S : S \in \mathcal{C}\}. \tag{5.3}$$

Specifically, $\text{co}\mathcal{NP} = \{\{0, 1\}^* \setminus S : S \in \mathcal{NP}\}$ is the class of sets that are complements of sets in $\mathcal{NP}$.

Recalling that each set in $\mathcal{NP}$ is characterized by its witness relation such that $x \in S$ if and only if there exists an adequate NP-witness, it follows that this set's complement consists of all instances for which there are no NP-witnesses (i.e., $x \in \{0, 1\}^* \setminus S$ if there is no NP-witness for $x$ being in $S$). For example, SAT $\in \mathcal{NP}$ implies that the set of unsatisfiable CNF formulae is in $\text{co}\mathcal{NP}$. Likewise, the set of graphs that are not 3-colorable is in $\text{co}\mathcal{NP}$. (Jumping ahead, we mention that it is widely believed that these sets are not in $\mathcal{NP}$.)

Another perspective on $\text{co}\mathcal{NP}$ is obtained by considering the search problems in $\mathcal{PC}$. Recall that for such $R \in \mathcal{PC}$, the set of instances having a solution (i.e., $S_R = \{x : \exists y \text{ s.t. } (x, y) \in R\}$) is in $\mathcal{NP}$. It follows that the set of instances having no solution (i.e., $\{0, 1\}^* \setminus S_R = \{x : \forall y \ (x, y) \notin R\}$) is in $\text{co}\mathcal{NP}$.

It is widely believed that $\mathcal{NP} \neq \text{co}\mathcal{NP}$ (which means that $\mathcal{NP}$ is not closed under complementation). Indeed, this conjecture implies $\mathcal{P} \neq \mathcal{NP}$ (because $\mathcal{P}$ is closed under complementation). The conjecture $\mathcal{NP} \neq \text{co}\mathcal{NP}$ means that some sets in co$\mathcal{NP}$ do not have NP-proof systems (because $\mathcal{NP}$ is the class of sets having NP-proof systems). As we will show next, under this conjecture, the complements of NP-complete sets do not have NP-proof systems; for example, there exists no NP-proof system for proving that a given CNF formula is not satisfiable. We first establish this fact for NP-completeness in the standard sense (i.e., under Karp-reductions, as in Definition 4.1).

**Proposition 5.6:** *Suppose that* $\mathcal{NP} \neq$ co$\mathcal{NP}$ *and let* $S \in \mathcal{NP}$ *such that every set in* $\mathcal{NP}$ *is Karp-reducible to* $S$. *Then* $\overline{S} \stackrel{\text{def}}{=} \{0, 1\}^* \setminus S$ *is not in* $\mathcal{NP}$.

In other words, *if* $S$ *is* $\mathcal{NP}$-*complete* (under Karp-reductions) *and* $\overline{S} \in \mathcal{NP}$, *then* $\mathcal{NP} =$ co$\mathcal{NP}$.

**Proof Sketch:** We first observe that the fact that every set in $\mathcal{NP}$ is Karp-reducible to $S$ implies that every set in co$\mathcal{NP}$ is Karp-reducible to $\overline{S}$ (see Exercise 5.8). We next claim (and prove later) that *if* $S'$ *is in* $\mathcal{NP}$, *then every set that is Karp-reducible to* $S'$ *is also in* $\mathcal{NP}$. Applying the claim to $S' = \overline{S}$, we conclude that $\overline{S} \in \mathcal{NP}$ implies co$\mathcal{NP} \subseteq \mathcal{NP}$, which in turn implies $\mathcal{NP} =$ co$\mathcal{NP}$ (see Exercise 5.7) in contradiction to the main hypothesis.

We now turn to prove the foregoing claim; that is, we prove that *if* $S'$ *has an NP-proof system and* $S''$ *is Karp-reducible to* $S'$, *then* $S''$ *has an NP-proof system*. Let $V'$ be the verification procedure associated with $S'$, and let $f$ be a Karp-reduction of $S''$ to $S'$. Then, we define the verification procedure $V''$ (for membership in $S''$) by $V''(x, y) = V'(f(x), y)$. That is, any NP-witness for $f(x) \in S'$ serves as an NP-witness for $x \in S''$ (and these are the only NP-witnesses for $x \in S''$). This may not be a "natural" proof system (for $S''$), but it is definitely an NP-proof system for $S''$. $\square$

Assuming that $\mathcal{NP} \neq$ co$\mathcal{NP}$, Proposition 5.6 implies that sets in $\mathcal{NP} \cap$ co$\mathcal{NP}$ cannot be NP-complete with respect to Karp-reductions. In light of other limitations of Karp-reductions (see, e.g., Exercise 3.4), one may wonder whether or not the exclusion of NP-complete sets from the class $\mathcal{NP} \cap$ co$\mathcal{NP}$ is due to the use of a restricted notion of reductions (i.e., Karp-reductions). The following theorem asserts that this is not the case: *Some sets in* $\mathcal{NP}$ *cannot be reduced to sets in the intersection* $\mathcal{NP} \cap$ co$\mathcal{NP}$ *even under general reductions* (i.e., Cook-reductions).

**Theorem 5.7:** *If every set in* $\mathcal{NP}$ *can be Cook-reduced to some set in* $\mathcal{NP} \cap$ co$\mathcal{NP}$, *then* $\mathcal{NP} =$ co$\mathcal{NP}$.

In particular, assuming $\mathcal{NP} \neq \text{co}\mathcal{NP}$, no set in $\mathcal{NP} \cap \text{co}\mathcal{NP}$ can be NP-complete, even when NP-completeness is defined with respect to Cook-reductions. Since $\mathcal{NP} \cap \text{co}\mathcal{NP}$ is conjectured to be a proper superset of $\mathcal{P}$, it follows (assuming $\mathcal{NP} \neq \text{co}\mathcal{NP}$) that there are decision problems in $\mathcal{NP}$ that are neither in $\mathcal{P}$ nor NP-hard (i.e., specifically, the decision problems in $(\mathcal{NP} \cap \text{co}\mathcal{NP}) \setminus \mathcal{P}$). We stress that Theorem 5.7 refers to standard decision problems and not to promise problems (see Section 5.1 and Exercise 5.4).

**Proof:** Analogously to the proof of Proposition 5.6, the current proof boils down to proving that *if $S$ is Cook-reducible to a set in $\mathcal{NP} \cap \text{co}\mathcal{NP}$, then $S \in \mathcal{NP} \cap \text{co}\mathcal{NP}$*. Using this claim, the theorem's hypothesis implies that $\mathcal{NP} \subseteq \mathcal{NP} \cap \text{co}\mathcal{NP}$, which in turn implies $\mathcal{NP} \subseteq \text{co}\mathcal{NP}$ and $\mathcal{NP} = \text{co}\mathcal{NP}$ (see Exercise 5.7).

Fixing any $S$ and $S' \in \mathcal{NP} \cap \text{co}\mathcal{NP}$ such that $S$ is Cook-reducible to $S'$, we prove that $S \in \mathcal{NP}$ (and the proof that $S \in \text{co}\mathcal{NP}$ is similar).[10] Let us denote by $M$ the oracle machine reducing $S$ to $S'$. That is, on input $x$, machine $M$ makes queries and decides whether or not to accept $x$, and its decision is correct provided that all queries are answered according to $S'$. To show that $S \in \mathcal{NP}$, we will present an NP-proof system for $S$. This proof system, denoted $V$, accepts an alleged (instance-witness) pair of the form $(x, \langle (z_1, \sigma_1, w_1), \ldots, (z_t, \sigma_t, w_t) \rangle)$ if the following two conditions hold:

1. On input $x$, machine $M$ accepts after making the queries $z_1, \ldots, z_t$, and obtaining the corresponding answers $\sigma_1, \ldots, \sigma_t$.

   That is, $V$ checks that, on input $x$, after obtaining the answers $\sigma_1, \ldots, \sigma_{i-1}$ to the first $i - 1$ queries, the $i^{\text{th}}$ query made by $M$ equals $z_i$. In addition, $V$ checks that, on input $x$ and after receiving the answers $\sigma_1, \ldots, \sigma_t$, machine $M$ halts with output 1 (indicating acceptance).

   Note that $V$ does not have oracle access to $S'$. The procedure $V$, rather, emulates the computation of $M(x)$ by answering, for each $i$, the $i^{\text{th}}$ query of $M(x)$ by using the bit $\sigma_i$ (provided to $V$ as part of its input). The correctness of these answers will be verified (by $V$) separately (i.e., see the next item).

2. For every $i$, it holds that if $\sigma_i = 1$ then $w_i$ is an NP-witness for $z_i \in S'$, whereas if $\sigma_i = 0$ then $w_i$ is an NP-witness for $z_i \in \{0, 1\}^* \setminus S'$.

   Thus, if this condition holds, then it is the case that each $\sigma_i$ indicates the correct status of $z_i$ with respect to $S'$ (i.e., $\sigma_i = 1$ if and only if $z_i \in S'$).

---

[10] Alternatively, we show that $S \in \text{co}\mathcal{NP}$ by applying the following argument to $\overline{S} \stackrel{\text{def}}{=} \{0, 1\}^* \setminus S$ and noting that $\overline{S}$ is Cook-reducible to $S'$ (via $S$, or alternatively that $\overline{S}$ is Cook-reducible to $\{0, 1\}^* \setminus S' \in \mathcal{NP} \cap \text{co}\mathcal{NP}$).

We stress that we have used the fact that both $S'$ and $\overline{S}' \stackrel{\text{def}}{=} \{0, 1\}^* \setminus S$ have NP-proof systems, and we have referred to the corresponding NP-witnesses.

Note that $V$ is indeed an NP-proof system for $S$. Firstly, the length of the corresponding witnesses is bounded by the running time of the reduction (and the length of the NP-witnesses supplied for the various queries). Next note that $V$ runs in polynomial time (i.e., verifying the first condition requires an emulation of the polynomial-time execution of $M$ on input $x$ when using the $\sigma_i$'s to emulate the oracle, whereas verifying the second condition is done by invoking the relevant NP-proof systems). Finally, observe that $x \in S$ if and only if there exists a sequence $y \stackrel{\text{def}}{=} ((z_1, \sigma_1, w_1), \ldots, (z_t, \sigma_t, w_t))$ such that $V(x, y) = 1$. In particular, $V(x, y) = 1$ holds only if $y$ contains a valid sequence of queries and answers as made in a computation of $M$ on input $x$ and oracle access to $S'$, and $M$ accepts based on that sequence. ∎

**The World View – a Digest.** Recall that on top of the $\mathcal{P} \neq \mathcal{NP}$ conjecture, we mentioned two other conjectures (which clearly imply $\mathcal{P} \neq \mathcal{NP}$):

1. The conjecture that $\mathcal{NP} \neq \text{co}\mathcal{NP}$ (equivalently, $\mathcal{NP} \cap \text{co}\mathcal{NP} \neq \mathcal{NP}$).
   This conjecture is equivalent to the conjecture that CNF formulae have no short proofs of unsatisfiability (i.e., the set $\{0, 1\}^* \setminus \text{SAT}$ has no NP-proof system).
2. The conjecture that $\mathcal{NP} \cap \text{co}\mathcal{NP} \neq \mathcal{P}$.
   Notable candidates for the class $(\mathcal{NP} \cap \text{co}\mathcal{NP}) \setminus \mathcal{P}$ include decision problems that are computationally equivalent to the integer factorization problem (i.e., the search problem (in $\mathcal{PC}$) in which, given a composite number, the task is to find its prime factors).

Combining these conjectures, we get the world view depicted in Figure 5.2, which also shows the class of $\text{co}\mathcal{NP}$-complete sets (defined next).

**Definition 5.8:** *A set $S$ is called $\text{co}\mathcal{NP}$-hard if every set in $\text{co}\mathcal{NP}$ is Karp-reducible to $S$. A set is called $\text{co}\mathcal{NP}$-complete if it is both in $\text{co}\mathcal{NP}$ and $\text{co}\mathcal{NP}$-hard.*

Indeed, insisting on Karp-reductions is essential for a distinction between $\mathcal{NP}$-hardness and $\text{co}\mathcal{NP}$-hardness. Furthermore, the class of problems that are Karp-reducible to $\mathcal{NP}$ equals $\mathcal{NP}$ (see Exercise 5.9), whereas the class of problems that are Karp-reducible to $\text{co}\mathcal{NP}$ equals $\text{co}\mathcal{NP}$ (because $S$ is Karp-reducible to $S'$ if and only if $\{0, 1\}^* \setminus S$ is Karp-reducible to $\{0, 1\}^* \setminus S'$). In contrast, recall that the class of problems that are Cook-reducible to $\mathcal{NP}$

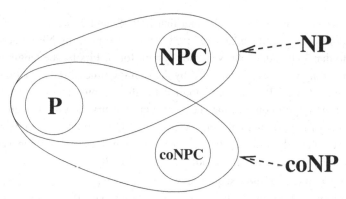

Figure 5.2. The world view under $\mathcal{P} \neq \mathrm{co}\mathcal{NP} \cap \mathcal{NP} \neq \mathcal{NP}$.

(resp., to $\mathrm{co}\mathcal{NP}$) contains $\mathcal{NP} \cup \mathrm{co}\mathcal{NP}$. This class, commonly denoted $\mathcal{P}^{\mathcal{NP}}$, is further discussed in Exercise 5.13.

## Exercises

### Exercise 5.1 (a quiz)

1. What are promise problems?
2. What is the justification for ignoring the promise (in a promise problem) whenever it is polynomial-time recognizable?
3. What is a candid search problem?
4. Could the P-vs-NP Question boil down to determining the time complexity of a single (known) algorithm?
5. What is the class $\mathrm{co}\mathcal{NP}$?
6. How does $\mathcal{NP}$ relate to the class of decision problems that are Cook-reducible to $\mathcal{NP}$?
7. How does $\mathcal{NP}$ relate to the class of decision problems that are Karp-reducible to $\mathcal{NP}$?

### Exercise 5.2
Let $R \in \mathcal{PC}$ and suppose that $A$ solves the candid search problem of $R$ in time complexity $T_{A|S_R}$. Prove that if the mapping $n \mapsto T_{A|S_R}(n)$ can be computed in $\mathrm{poly}(n)$-time, then the standard search problem of $R$ (as well as the decision problem $S_R$) can be solved in time $T_{A'}(n) = \widetilde{O}(T_{A|S_R}(n)) + \mathrm{poly}(n)$, where $\widetilde{O}(t) = \mathrm{poly}(\log t) \cdot t$.

*Guideline:* Consider an algorithm $A'$ that on input $x$ first computes $t \leftarrow T_{A|S_R}(|x|)$, and then emulates the execution of $A(x)$ for at most $t$ steps. (The poly-logarithmic factor is due to the overhead of this emulation.) If $A(x)$ halts with output $y$, then $A'$ checks whether $(x, y) \in R$, and outputs $y$ if the answer is positive (and $\perp$ otherwise).

**Exercise 5.3 (Cook-reductions preserve efficient solvability of promise problems)** Prove that if the promise problem $\Pi$ is Cook-reducible to a promise problem that is solvable in polynomial time, then $\Pi$ is solvable in polynomial time. Note that the solver may not halt on inputs that violate the promise.

*Guideline:* Use the fact that any polynomial-time algorithm that solves any promise problem can be modified such that it halts on all inputs (in polynomial time).

**Exercise 5.4 (NP-complete promise problems in coNP (following [9]))** Consider the promise problem xSAT, having instances that are pairs of CNF formulae. The yes-instances consist of pairs $(\phi_1, \phi_2)$ such that $\phi_1$ is satisfiable and $\phi_2$ is unsatisfiable, whereas the no-instances consist of pairs such that $\phi_1$ is unsatisfiable and $\phi_2$ is satisfiable.

1. Show that xSAT is in the intersection of (the promise problem classes that are analogous to) $\mathcal{NP}$ and co$\mathcal{NP}$.
2. Prove that any promise problem in $\mathcal{NP}$ is Cook-reducible to xSAT. In designing the reduction, recall that queries that violate the promise may be answered arbitrarily.

   *Guideline:* Note that the promise problem version of $\mathcal{NP}$ is reducible to SAT, and show a reduction of SAT to xSAT. Specifically, show that the search problem associated with SAT is Cook-reducible to xSAT, by adapting the ideas of the proof of Proposition 3.7. That is, suppose that we know (or assume) that $\tau$ is a prefix of a satisfying assignment to $\phi$, and we wish to extend $\tau$ by one bit. Then, for each $\sigma \in \{0, 1\}$, we construct a formula, denoted $\phi'_\sigma$, by setting the first $|\tau| + 1$ variables of $\phi$ according to the values $\tau\sigma$. We query the oracle about the pair $(\phi'_1, \phi'_0)$ and extend $\tau$ accordingly (i.e., we extend $\tau$ by the value 1 if and only if the answer is positive). Note that if both $\phi'_1$ and $\phi'_0$ are satisfiable then it does not matter which bit we use in the extension, whereas if exactly one formula is satisfiable then the oracle answer is reliable.
3. Pinpoint the source of failure of the proof of Theorem 5.7 when applied to the reduction provided in the previous item.

**Exercise 5.5** Note that Theorem 5.5 holds for any search problem in NP, and not only for NP-complete search problems. Compare the result of Theorem 5.5 to what would have followed from a corresponding result that only asserts optimal algorithms for all NP-complete search problems. Ditto with respect to a corresponding result that only asserts optimal algorithm for some NP-complete search problem.

*Guideline:* Note that we refer to a strong notion of optimality, which may not be preserved by Levin-reductions.

**Exercise 5.6** Generalizing the proof of Theorem 5.5, consider the possibility of running the $i^{\text{th}}$ machine at rate $\rho(i)$ rather than at rate $1/(i+1)^2$, where $\rho$ satisfies $\sum_{i \geq 1} \rho(i) \leq 1$. Prove that, for any "reasonable" choice of $\rho$ (e.g., $\rho(i) = 1/O(i \cdot (\log^2(i+1))$ or $\rho(i) = 2^{-i})$, the result of Theorem 5.5 remains intact, although the constant hidden in the O-notation is effected. What should be required of a "reasonable" choice of $\rho$?

*Guideline:* Note that our choice of $\rho(i) = 1/(i+1)^2$ was quite good, although $\rho(i) = 1/O(i \cdot (\log^2(i+1))$ is better.

**Exercise 5.7** For any class $\mathcal{C}$, prove that $\mathcal{C} \subseteq \text{co}\mathcal{C}$ if and only if $\mathcal{C} = \text{co}\mathcal{C}$.

**Exercise 5.8** Prove that $S_1$ is Karp-reducible to $S_2$ if and only if $\{0, 1\}^* \setminus S_1$ is Karp-reducible to $\{0, 1\}^* \setminus S_2$.

**Exercise 5.9** Prove that a set $S$ is Karp-reducible to some set in $\mathcal{NP}$ if and only if $S$ is in $\mathcal{NP}$.

*Guideline:* For the non-trivial direction, see the proof of Proposition 5.6.

**Exercise 5.10** Recall that the empty set is not Karp-reducible to $\{0, 1\}^*$, whereas any set is Cook-reducible to its complement. Thus, our focus here is on the *Karp-reducibility of non-trivial sets to their complements*, where a set is non-trivial if it is neither empty nor contains all strings. Furthermore, since any non-trivial set in $\mathcal{P}$ is Karp-reducible to its complement (see Exercise 3.4), we assume that $\mathcal{P} \neq \mathcal{NP}$ and focus on sets in $\mathcal{NP} \setminus \mathcal{P}$.

1. Prove that $\mathcal{NP} = \text{co}\mathcal{NP}$ implies that some sets in $\mathcal{NP} \setminus \mathcal{P}$ are Karp-reducible to their complements.
2. Prove that $\mathcal{NP} \neq \text{co}\mathcal{NP}$ implies that some sets in $\mathcal{NP} \setminus \mathcal{P}$ are not Karp-reducible to their complements.

*Guideline:* Use NP-complete sets in both parts, and Exercise 5.9 in the second part.

**Exercise 5.11** (TAUT *is coNP-complete*) Prove that the following problem, denoted TAUT, is co$\mathcal{NP}$-complete (even when the formulae are restricted to 3DNF). An instance of the problem consists of a DNF formula, and the problem is to determine whether this formula is a tautology (i.e., a formula that evaluates to `true` under every possible truth assignment).

*Guideline:* Reduce from $\overline{\text{SAT}}$ (i.e., the complement of SAT), using the fact that $\phi$ is unsatisfiable if and only if $\neg\phi$ is a tautology.[11]

**Exercise 5.12 (the class $\mathcal{NP} \cap \text{co}\mathcal{NP}$)** Prove that a set $S$ is in $\mathcal{NP} \cap \text{co}\mathcal{NP}$ if and only if the set $S' \stackrel{\text{def}}{=} \{(x, \chi_S(x)) : x \in \{0, 1\}^*\}$ is in $\mathcal{NP}$, where $\chi_S : \{0, 1\}^* \to \{0, 1\}$ is the characteristic function of $S$ (i.e., $\chi_S(x) = 1$ if and only if $x \in S$).

*Guideline:* An NP-proof systems for $S'$ can be obtained by combining NP-proof systems for $S$ and $\overline{S}$, whereas NP-proof systems for $S$ and $\overline{S}$ can be derived from any NP-proof system for $S'$.

**Exercise 5.13 (the class $\mathcal{P}^{\mathcal{NP}}$)** Recall that $\mathcal{P}^{\mathcal{NP}}$ denotes the class of problems that are Cook-reducible to $\mathcal{NP}$. Prove the following (simple) facts.

1. For every class $\mathcal{C}$, the class of problems that are Cook-reducible to $\mathcal{C}$ equals the class of problems that are Cook-reducible to co$\mathcal{C}$. In particular, $\mathcal{P}^{\mathcal{NP}}$ equals the class of problems that are Cook-reducible to co$\mathcal{NP}$.
2. The class $\mathcal{P}^{\mathcal{NP}}$ is closed under complementation (i.e., $\mathcal{P}^{\mathcal{NP}} = \text{co}\mathcal{P}^{\mathcal{NP}}$).

Note that each of the foregoing items implies that $\mathcal{P}^{\mathcal{NP}}$ contains $\mathcal{NP} \cup \text{co}\mathcal{NP}$.

**Exercise 5.14** Assuming that $\mathcal{NP} \neq \text{co}\mathcal{NP}$, prove that the problem of finding a maximum clique (resp., independent set) in a given graph is not in $\mathcal{PC}$. Prove the same for the following problems:

- Finding a minimum vertex cover in a given graph.
- Finding an assignment that satisfies the maximum number of equations in a given system of linear equations over GF(2) (cf. Exercise 4.9.)

We stress that maximum and minimum refer to the optimum taken over all legitimate solutions, whereas the terms maximal and minimal refer to a "local optimum" (i.e., optimal with respect to augmenting the current solution or omitting elements from it, respectively).

*Guideline:* Note that the set of pairs $(G, K)$ such that the graph $G$ contains no clique of size $K$ is co$\mathcal{NP}$-complete.

---

[11] Note that, given a CNF formula $\phi$, we can easily obtain a DNF formula for $\neg\phi$ (by applying de-Morgan's Law).

***Exercise 5.15 (the class*** $\mathcal{P}$/poly, ***revisited)*** In continuation of Exercise 1.16, prove that $\mathcal{P}$/poly equals the class of sets that are Cook-reducible to a sparse set, where a set $S$ is called sparse if there exists a polynomial $p$ such that for every $n$ it holds that $|S \cap \{0, 1\}^n| \le p(n)$.

*Guideline:* For any set in $\mathcal{P}$/poly, encode the advice sequence $(a_n)_{n \in \mathbb{N}}$ as a sparse set $\{(1^n, i, \sigma_{n,i}) : n \in \mathbb{N}, \ i \le |a_n|\}$, where $\sigma_{n,i}$ is the $i^{\text{th}}$ bit of $a_n$. For the opposite direction, note that the emulation of a Cook-reduction to a set $S$, on input $x$, only requires knowledge of $S \cap \bigcup_{i=1}^{\text{poly}(|x|)} \{0, 1\}^i$.

***Exercise 5.16*** In continuation of Exercise 5.15, we consider the class of sets that are *Karp-reducible* to a sparse set. It can be proved that this class contains SAT if and only if $\mathcal{P} = \mathcal{NP}$ (see [23]).[12] Here, we only consider the special case in which the sparse set is contained in a polynomial-time decidable set that is itself sparse (e.g., the latter set may be $\{1\}^*$, in which case the former set may be an arbitrary unary set). Actually, the aim of this exercise is to establish the following (seemingly stronger) claim:[13]

> *If* SAT *is Karp-reducible to a set* $S \subseteq G$ *such that* $G \in \mathcal{P}$ *and* $G \setminus S$ *is sparse, then* SAT $\in \mathcal{P}$.

Using the hypothesis, we outline a polynomial-time procedure for solving the search problem of SAT and leave the task of providing the details as an exercise. The procedure (looking for a satisfying assignment) conducts a DFS on the tree of all possible partial truth assignments to the input formula,[14] while truncating the search at nodes that correspond to partial truth assignments that were already demonstrated to be useless (i.e., correspond to a partial truth assignment that cannot be completed to a satisfying assignment).

*Guideline:* The key observation is that each internal node (which yields a formula derived from the initial formula by instantiating the corresponding partial truth assignment) is mapped by the Karp-reduction either to a string not in $G$ (in which case we conclude that the sub-tree contains no satisfying assignments and backtrack from this node) or to a string in $G$. In the latter case, unless we already know that this string is not in $S$, we *start a scan of the sub-tree rooted at this node*. However, once we backtrack from this internal node, we know that the corresponding member of $G$ is not in $S$, and we will never

---

[12] An alternative presentation is available from the book's Web site.

[13] This claim is seemingly stronger because $G$ itself is not assumed to be sparse.

[14] For an $n$-variable formula, the leaves of the tree correspond to all possible $n$-bit long strings, and an internal node corresponding to $\tau$ is the parent of the nodes corresponding to $\tau 0$ and $\tau 1$.

scan again a sub-tree rooted at a node that is mapped to this string (which was detected to be in $G \setminus S$). Also note that once we reach a leaf, we can check by ourselves whether or not it corresponds to a satisfying assignment to the initial formula. When analyzing the foregoing procedure, prove that when given an $n$-variable formula $\phi$ as input, the number of times we start to scan a sub-tree is at most $n \cdot |\bigcup_{i=1}^{\text{poly}(|\phi|)} \{0, 1\}^i \cap (G \setminus S)|$.

# Historical Notes

The following brief account decouples the development of the theory of computation (which was the focus of Chapter 1) from the emergence of the P-vs-NP Question and the theory of NP-completeness (studied in Chapters 2–5).

## On Computation and Efficient Computation

The interested reader may find numerous historical accounts of the developments that led to the emergence of the theory of computation. The following brief account is different from most of these historical accounts in that its perspective is the one of the current research in computer science.

The theory of uniform computational devices emerged in the work of Turing [32]. This work put forward a natural model of computation, based on concrete machines (indeed Turing machines), which has been instrumental for subsequent studies. In particular, this model provides a convenient stage for the introduction of natural complexity measures referring to computational tasks.

The notion of a Turing machine was put forward by Turing with the explicit intention of providing a general formulation of the notion of computability [32]. The original motivation was to provide a formalization of Hilbert's challenge (posed in 1900 and known as Hilbert's Tenth Problem), which called for designing a method for determining the solvability of Diophantine equations. Indeed, this challenge referred to a specific decision problem (later called the *Entscheidungsproblem* (German for the *Decision Problem*)), but Hilbert did not provide a formulation of the notion of "(a method for) solving a decision problem." (We mention that in 1970, the *Entscheidungsproblem* was proved to be undecidable (see [24]).)

In addition to introducing the Turing machine model and arguing that it corresponds to the intuitive notion of computability, Turing's paper [32] introduces universal machines, and contains proofs of undecidability (e.g., of the Halting Problem). (Rice's Theorem (Theorem 1.6) is proven in [27], and the undecidability of the Post Correspondence Problem (Theorem 1.7) is proven in [26].)

The Church-Turing Thesis is attributed to the works of Church [4] and Turing [32]. In both works, this thesis is invoked for claiming that the fact that some problem cannot be solved in a specific model of computation implies that this problem cannot be solved in any "reasonable" model of computation. The RAM model is attributed to von Neumann's report [33].

The association of efficient computation with polynomial-time algorithms is attributed to the papers of Cobham [5] and Edmonds [7]. It is interesting to note that Cobham's starting point was his desire to present a philosophically sound concept of efficient algorithms, whereas Edmonds's starting point was his desire to articulate why certain algorithms are "good" in practice.

The theory of non-uniform computational devices emerged in the work of Shannon [29], which introduced and initiated the study of Boolean circuits. The formulation of machines that take advice (as well as the equivalence to the circuit model) originates in [18].

## On NP and NP-Completeness

Many sources provide historical accounts of the developments that led to the formulation of the *P-vs-NP Problem* and to the discovery of the theory of NP-completeness (see, e.g., [11, Sec. 1.5] and [31]). Still, we feel that we should not refrain from offering our own impressions, which are *based on the texts of the original papers.*

Nowadays, the theory of NP-completeness is commonly attributed to Cook [6], Karp [17], and Levin [21]. It seems that Cook's starting point was his interest in theorem-proving procedures for propositional calculus [6, p. 151]. Trying to provide evidence for the difficulty of deciding whether or not a given formula is a tautology, he identified $\mathcal{NP}$ as a class containing "many apparently difficult problems" (cf, e.g., [6, p. 151]), and showed that any problem in $\mathcal{NP}$ is reducible to deciding membership in the set of 3DNF tautologies. In particular, Cook emphasized the importance of the concept of polynomial-time reductions and the complexity class $\mathcal{NP}$ (both explicitly defined for the first time in his paper). He also showed that CLIQUE is computationally equivalent to SAT, and envisioned a class of problems of the same nature.

Karp's paper [17] can be viewed as fulfilling Cook's prophecy: Stimulated by Cook's work, Karp demonstrated that a "large number of classic difficult computational problems, arising in fields such as mathematical programming, graph theory, combinatorics, computational logic and switching theory, are [NP-]complete (and thus equivalent)" [17, p. 86]. Specifically, his list of twenty-one NP-complete problems includes Integer Linear Programming, Hamilton Circuit, Chromatic Number, Exact Set Cover, Steiner Tree, Knapsack, Job Scheduling, and Max Cut. Interestingly, Karp defined $\mathcal{NP}$ in terms of verification procedures (i.e., Definition 2.5), pointed to its relation to "backtrack search of polynomial bounded depth" [17, p. 86], and viewed $\mathcal{NP}$ as the residence of a "wide range of important computational problems" (which seem not to be in $\mathcal{P}$).

Independently of these developments, while being in the USSR, Levin proved the existence of "universal search problems" (where universality meant NP-completeness). The starting point of Levin's work [21] was his interest in the *"perebor"* conjecture asserting the inherent need for brute force in some search problems that have efficiently checkable solutions (i.e., problems in $\mathcal{PC}$). Levin emphasized the implication of polynomial-time reductions on the relation between the time complexity of the related problems (for any growth rate of the time-complexity), asserted the NP-completeness of six "classical search problems," and claimed that the underlying method "provides a means for readily obtaining" similar results for "many other important search problems."

It is interesting to note that although the works of Cook [6], Karp [17], and Levin [21] were received with different levels of enthusiasm, *none of their contemporaries realized the depth of the discovery and the difficulty of the question posed* (i.e., the P-vs-NP Question). This fact is evident in every account from the early 1970s, and may explain the frustration of the corresponding generation of researchers over the failure to resolve the P-vs-NP Question, which they expected to be resolved in their lifetime (if not in a matter of a few years). Needless to say, the author's opinion is that there was absolutely no justification for these expectations, and that one should have actually expected quite the opposite.

We mention that the three "founding papers" of the theory of NP-completeness (i.e., Cook [6], Karp [17], and Levin [21]) use the three different types of reductions used in this book. Specifically, Cook uses the general notion of polynomial-time reduction [6], often referred to as Cook-reductions (Definition 3.1). The notion of Karp-reductions (Definition 3.3) originates from Karp's paper [17], whereas its augmentation to search problems (i.e., Definition 3.4) originates from Levin's paper [21]. It is worth stressing that Levin's work is stated in terms of search problems, unlike Cook's and Karp's works, which treat decision problems.

The reductions presented in Section 4.3.2 are not necessarily the original ones. Most notably, the reduction establishing the NP-hardness of the Independent Set problem (i.e., Proposition 4.10) is adapted from [10]. In contrast, the reductions presented in Section 4.3.1 are merely a reinterpretation of the original reduction as presented in [6]. The equivalence of the two definitions of $\mathcal{NP}$ (i.e., Theorem 2.8) was proven in [17].

The existence of NP-sets that are neither in P nor NP-complete (i.e., Theorem 4.12) was proven by Ladner [20], Theorem 5.7 was proven by Selman [28], and the existence of optimal search algorithms for NP-relations (i.e., Theorem 5.5) was proven by Levin [21]. (Interestingly, the latter result was proven in the same paper in which Levin presented the discovery of NP-completeness, independently of Cook and Karp.) Promise problems were explicitly introduced by Even, Selman, and Yacobi [9]; see [12] for a survey of their numerous applications. A more detailed description of probabilistic proof systems, including proper credits for the results mentioned in Section 4.3.5, can be found in [13, Chap. 9].

# Epilogue: A Brief Overview
# of Complexity Theory

Out of the tough came forth sweetness.[1]
*Judges, 14:14*

The following brief overview is intended to give a flavor of the questions
addressed by Complexity Theory. It includes a brief review of the contents of
the current book, as well as a brief overview of several more advanced topics.
The latter overview is quite vague, and is merely meant as a teaser toward
further study (cf., e.g., [13]).

## Absolute Goals and Relative Results

Complexity Theory is concerned with the study of the *intrinsic complexity* of
computational tasks. Its "final" goals include the determination of the complexity of any well-defined task. Additional goals include obtaining an understanding of the relations between various computational phenomena (e.g., relating
one fact regarding Computational Complexity to another). Indeed, we may say
that the former type of goals is concerned with *absolute* answers regarding
specific computational phenomena, whereas the latter type is concerned with
questions regarding the *relation* between computational phenomena.

Interestingly, so far Complexity Theory has been more successful in coping
with goals of the latter ("relative") type. In fact, the failure to resolve questions
of the "absolute" type led to the flourishing of methods for coping with questions of the "relative" type. Musing for a moment, let us say that, in general,
the difficulty of obtaining absolute answers may naturally lead to a search for
conditional answers, which may in turn reveal interesting relations between

---

[1] The quotation is commonly interpreted as meaning that benefit arose out of misfortune.

169

phenomena. Furthermore, the lack of absolute understanding of individual phenomena seems to facilitate the development of methods for relating different phenomena. Anyhow, this is what happened in Complexity Theory.

Putting aside for a moment the frustration caused by the failure to obtain absolute answers, we must admit that there is something fascinating in the success of relating different phenomena: In some sense, relations between phenomena are more revealing than absolute statements about individual phenomena. Indeed, the first example that comes to mind is the theory of NP-completeness. Let us consider this theory for a moment, from the perspective of these two types of goals.

## P, NP, and NP-completeness

Complexity Theory has failed to determine the intrinsic complexity of tasks such as finding a satisfying assignment to a given (satisfiable) propositional formula or finding a 3-coloring of a given (3-colorable) graph. But it has succeeded in establishing that these two seemingly different computational tasks are in some sense the same (or, more precisely, are computationally equivalent). We find this success amazing and exciting, and hope that the reader shares these feelings. The same feeling of wonder and excitement is generated by many of the other discoveries of Complexity Theory. Indeed, the reader is invited to join a fast tour of some of the other questions and answers that make up the field of Complexity Theory.

We will start with the *P versus NP Question* (and, indeed, briefly review the contents of Chapter 2). Our daily experience is that it is harder to solve a problem than it is to check the correctness of a solution (e.g., think of either a puzzle or a research problem). Is this experience merely a coincidence or does it represent a fundamental fact of life (i.e., a property of the world)? Could you imagine a world in which solving any problem is not significantly harder than checking a solution to it? Would the term "solving a problem" not lose its meaning in such a hypothetical (and impossible, in our opinion) world? The denial of the plausibility of such a hypothetical world (in which "solving" is not harder than "checking") is what "P different from NP" actually means, where P represents tasks that are efficiently solvable and NP represents tasks for which solutions can be efficiently checked.

The mathematically (or theoretically) inclined reader may also consider the task of proving theorems versus the task of verifying the validity of proofs. Indeed, finding proofs is a special type of the aforementioned task of "solving a problem" (and verifying the validity of proofs is a corresponding case of checking correctness). Again, "P different from NP" means that there are theorems that are harder to prove than to be convinced of their correctness when presented with a proof. This means that the notion of a "proof" is meaningful; that is, proofs do help when seeking to be convinced of the correctness of assertions. Here, NP represents sets of assertions that can be efficiently verified with the help of adequate proofs, and P represents sets of assertions that can be efficiently verified from scratch (i.e., without proofs).

In light of the foregoing discussion, it is clear that the P versus NP Question is a fundamental scientific question of far-reaching consequences. The fact that this question seems beyond our current reach led to the development of the theory of *NP-completeness*. Loosely speaking, this theory (presented in Chapter 4) identifies a set of computational problems that are as hard as NP. That is, the fate of the P versus NP Question lies with each of these problems: If any of these problems is easy to solve, then so are all problems in NP. Thus, showing that a problem is NP-complete provides evidence of its intractability (assuming, of course, "P different than NP"). Indeed, demonstrating the NP-completeness of computational tasks is a central tool in indicating hardness of natural computational problems, and it has been used extensively both in computer science and in other disciplines. We note that NP-completeness indicates not only the conjectured intractability of a problem but also its "richness," in the sense that the problem is rich enough to "encode" any other problem in NP. The use of the term "encoding" is justified by the exact meaning of NP-completeness, which in turn establishes relations between different computational problems (without referring to their "absolute" complexity).

## Some Advanced Topics

The foregoing discussion of NP-completeness hints at *the importance of representation*, since it referred to different problems that encode one another. Indeed, the importance of representation is a central aspect of Complexity Theory. In general, Complexity Theory is concerned with problems for which the solutions are implicit in the problem's statement (or rather in the instance). That is, the problem (or rather its instance) contains all necessary information, and one merely needs to process this information in order to supply the answer.[2] Thus, Complexity Theory is concerned with manipulation of information, and

---

[2] In contrast, in other disciplines, solving a problem may require gathering information that is not available in the problem's statement. This information may either be available from auxiliary (past) records or be obtained by conducting new experiments.

with its transformation from one representation (in which the information is given) to another representation (which is the one desired). Indeed, a solution to a computational problem is merely a different representation of the information given, that is, a representation in which the answer is explicit rather than implicit. For example, the answer to the question of whether or not a given Boolean formula is satisfiable is implicit in the formula itself (but the task is to make the answer explicit). Thus, Complexity Theory clarifies a central issue regarding representation, that is, the distinction between what is explicit and what is implicit in a representation. Furthermore, it even suggests a quantification of the level of non-explicitness.

In general, Complexity Theory provides new viewpoints on various phenomena that were also considered by past thinkers. Examples include the aforementioned concepts of solutions, proofs, and representation, as well as concepts like randomness, knowledge, interaction, secrecy, and learning. We next discuss the latter concepts and the perspective offered by Complexity Theory.

The concept of *randomness* has puzzled thinkers for ages. Their perspective can be described as ontological: They asked "what is randomness" and wondered whether it exists at all (or whether the world is deterministic). The perspective of Complexity Theory is behavioristic: It is based on defining objects as equivalent if they cannot be told apart by any efficient procedure. That is, a coin toss is (defined to be) "random" (even if one believes that the universe is deterministic) if it is infeasible to predict the coin's outcome. Likewise, a string (or a distribution on strings) is "random" if it is infeasible to distinguish it from the uniform distribution (regardless of whether or not one can generate the latter). Interestingly, randomness (or rather, pseudorandomness) defined this way is efficiently expandable; that is, under a reasonable complexity assumption (to be discussed next), short pseudorandom strings can be deterministically expanded into long pseudorandom strings. Indeed, it turns out that randomness is intimately related to intractability. Firstly, note that the very definition of pseudorandomness refers to intractability (i.e., the infeasibility of distinguishing a pseudorandomness object from a uniformly distributed object). Secondly, as stated, a complexity assumption, which refers to the existence of functions that are easy to evaluate but hard to invert (called *one-way functions*), implies the existence of deterministic programs (called *pseudorandom generators*) that stretch short random seeds into long pseudorandom sequences. In fact, it turns out that the existence of pseudorandom generators is equivalent to the existence of one-way functions.

Complexity Theory offers its own perspective on the concept of *knowledge* (and distinguishes it from information). Specifically, Complexity Theory views knowledge as the result of a hard computation. Thus, whatever can be efficiently done by anyone is not considered knowledge. In particular, the result of an easy computation applied to publicly available information is not considered knowledge. In contrast, the value of a hard-to-compute function applied to publicly available information is knowledge, and if somebody provides you with such a value, then that person has provided you with knowledge. This discussion is related to the notion of *zero-knowledge* interactions, which are interactions in which no knowledge is gained. Such interactions may still be useful, because they may convince a party of the *correctness* of specific data that was provided beforehand. For example, a zero-knowledge interactive proof may convince a party that a given graph is 3-colorable without yielding any 3-coloring.

The foregoing paragraph has explicitly referred to *interaction*, viewing it as a vehicle for gaining knowledge and/or gaining confidence. Let us highlight the latter application by noting that it may be easier to verify an assertion when one is allowed to interact with a prover rather than when reading a proof. Put differently, interaction with a good teacher may be more beneficial than reading any book. We comment that the added power of such *interactive proofs* is rooted in their being randomized (i.e., the verification procedure is randomized), because if the verifier's questions can be determined beforehand, then the prover may just provide the transcript of the interaction as a traditional written proof.

Another concept related to knowledge is that of *secrecy*: Knowledge is something that one party may have but another party does not have (and cannot feasibly obtain by itself) – thus, in some sense knowledge is a secret. In general, Complexity Theory is related to *cryptography*, where the latter is broadly defined as the study of systems that are easy to use but hard to abuse. Typically, such systems involve secrets, randomness, and interaction, as well as a complexity gap between the ease of proper usage and the infeasibility of causing the system to deviate from its prescribed behavior. Thus, much of cryptography is based on Complexity theoretic assumptions, and its results are typically transformations of relatively simple computational primitives (e.g., one-way functions) into more complex cryptographic applications (e.g., secure encryption schemes).

We have already mentioned the concept of *learning* when referring to learning from a teacher versus learning from a book. Recall that Complexity Theory provides evidence to the advantage of the former. This is in the context of gaining knowledge about publicly available information. In contrast, computational learning theory is concerned with learning objects that are only partially available to the learner (i.e., reconstructing a function based on its value at a few random locations or even at locations chosen by the learner). Still, Complexity Theory sheds light on the intrinsic limitations of learning (in this sense).

Complexity Theory deals with a variety of computational tasks. We have already mentioned two fundamental types of tasks: *searching for solutions* (or, rather, "finding solutions") and *making decisions* (e.g., regarding the validity of assertions). We have also hinted that in some cases these two types of tasks can be related. Now we consider two additional types of tasks: *counting the number of solutions* and *generating random solutions*. Clearly, both the latter tasks are at least as hard as finding arbitrary solutions to the corresponding problem, but it turns out that for some natural problems they are not significantly harder. Specifically, under some natural conditions on the problem, approximately counting the number of solutions and generating an approximately random solution is not significantly harder than finding an arbitrary solution.

Having mentioned the notion of *approximation*, we note that the study of the complexity of finding "approximate solutions" is also of natural importance. One type of approximation problems refers to an objective function defined on the set of potential solutions: Rather than finding a solution that attains the optimal value, the approximation task consists of finding a solution that attains an "almost optimal" value, where the notion of "almost optimal" may be understood in different ways, giving rise to different levels of approximation. Interestingly, in many cases, even a very relaxed level of approximation is as difficult to obtain as solving the original (exact) search problem (i.e., finding an approximate solution is as hard as finding an optimal solution). Surprisingly, these hardness-of-approximation results are related to the study of *probabilistically checkable proofs*, which are proofs that allow for ultra-fast probabilistic verification. Amazingly, every proof can be efficiently transformed into one that allows for probabilistic verification based on probing a *constant* number of bits (in the alleged proof). Turning back to approximation problems, we mention that in other cases, a reasonable level of approximation is easier to achieve than solving the original (exact) search problem.

Approximation is a natural relaxation of various computational problems. Another natural relaxation is the study of *average-case complexity*, where the "average" is taken over some "simple" distributions (representing a model of the problem's instances that may occur in practice). We stress that although it was not stated explicitly, the entire discussion so far has referred to "worst-case" analysis of algorithms. We mention that worst-case complexity is a more robust notion than average-case complexity. For starters, one avoids the controversial question of characterizing the instances that are "important in practice" and, correspondingly, the selection of the class of distributions for which average-case analysis is to be conducted. Nevertheless, a relatively robust theory of average-case complexity has been suggested, albeit it is less developed than the theory of worst-case complexity.

In view of the central role of randomness in Complexity Theory (as evident, say, in the study of pseudorandomness, probabilistic proof systems, and cryptography), one may wonder as to whether the randomness needed for the various applications can be obtained in real life. One specific question, which received a lot of attention, is the possibility of "purifying" randomness (or "extracting good randomness from bad sources"). That is, can we use "defective" sources of randomness in order to implement almost perfect sources of randomness? The answer depends, of course, on the model of such defective sources. This study turned out to be related to Complexity Theory, where the most tight connection is between some type of *randomness extractors* and some type of pseudorandom generators.

So far we have focused on the time complexity of computational tasks, while relying on the natural association of efficiency with time. However, time is not the only resource one should care about. Another important resource is *space*: the amount of (temporary) memory consumed by the computation. The study of space complexity has uncovered several fascinating phenomena, which seem to indicate a fundamental difference between space complexity and time complexity. For example, in the context of space complexity, verifying proofs of validity of assertions (of any specific type) has the same complexity as verifying proofs of invalidity for the same type of assertions.

In case the reader feels dizzy, it is no wonder. We took an ultra-fast air tour of some mountaintops, and dizziness is to be expected. For a totally different touring experience, we refer the interested reader to the author's book [13], which offers climbing the aforementioned mountains by foot, while stopping often for appreciation of the view and reflection.

**Absolute Results (also Known as Lower Bounds).** As stated in the beginning of this epilogue, absolute results are not known for many of the "big questions" of Complexity Theory (most notably the P versus NP Question). However, several highly non-trivial absolute results have been proved. For example, it was shown that using negation can speed up the computation of monotone functions (which do not require negation for their mere computation). In addition, many promising techniques were introduced and employed with the aim of providing a low-level analysis of the progress of computation. However, as stated up front, the focus of this epilogue was elsewhere.

# Appendix: Some Computational Problems

Although we view specific (natural) computational problems as secondary to (natural) complexity classes, we do use the former for clarification and illustration of the latter. This appendix provides definitions of such computational problems, grouped according to the type of objects to which they refer (i.e., graphs and Boolean formula).

We start by addressing the central issue of the representation of the various objects that are referred to in the aforementioned computational problems. The general principle is that elements of all sets are "compactly" represented as binary strings (without much redundancy). For example, the elements of a finite set $S$ (e.g., the set of vertices in a graph or the set of variables appearing in a Boolean formula) will be represented as binary strings of length $\log_2 |S|$.

## A.1 Graphs

Graph theory has long become recognized as one of the more useful mathematical subjects for the computer science student to master. The approach which is natural in computer science is the algorithmic one; our interest is not so much in existence proofs or enumeration techniques, as it is in finding efficient algorithms for solving relevant problems, or alternatively showing evidence that no such algorithms exist. Although algorithmic graph theory was started by Euler, if not earlier, its development in the last ten years has been dramatic and revolutionary.

*Shimon Even, Graph Algorithms [8]*

A simple graph $G = (V, E)$ consists of a *finite* set of vertices $V$ and a finite set of edges $E$, where each edge is an *unordered pair* of vertices; that is, $E \subseteq \{\{u, v\} : u, v \in V \wedge u \neq v\}$. This formalism does not allow self-loops and parallel edges, which are allowed in general (i.e., non-simple) graphs, where $E$ is a multi-set that may contain (in addition to two-element subsets of $V$ also) singletons (i.e., self-loops). The vertex $u$ is called an end point of the edge $\{u, v\}$, and the edge $\{u, v\}$ is said to be incident at $v$. In such a case, we say that $u$ and $v$ are adjacent in the graph, and that $u$ is a neighbor of $v$. The degree of a vertex in $G$ is defined as the number of edges that are incident at this vertex.

177

We will consider various sub-structures of graphs, the simplest one being paths. A path in a graph $G = (V, E)$ is a sequence of vertices $(v_0, \ldots, v_\ell)$ such that for every $i \in [\ell] \overset{\text{def}}{=} \{1, \ldots, \ell\}$ it holds that $v_{i-1}$ and $v_i$ are adjacent in $G$. Such a path is said to have length $\ell$. A simple path is a path in which each vertex appears at most once, which implies that the longest possible simple path in $G$ has length $|V| - 1$. The graph is called connected if there exists a path between each pair of vertices in it.

A cycle is a path in which the last vertex equals the first one (i.e., $v_\ell = v_0$). The cycle $(v_0, \ldots, v_\ell)$ is called simple if $\ell > 2$ and $|\{v_0, \ldots, v_\ell\}| = \ell$ (i.e., if $v_i = v_j$ then $i \equiv j$ (mod $\ell$), and the cycle $(u, v, u)$ is not considered simple). A graph is called acyclic (or a forest) if it has no simple cycles, and if it is also connected, then it is called a tree. Note that $G = (V, E)$ is a tree if and only if it is connected and $|E| = |V| - 1$, and that there is a unique simple path between each pair of vertices in a tree.

A subgraph of the graph $G = (V, E)$ is any graph $G' = (V', E')$ satisfying $V' \subseteq V$ and $E' \subseteq E$. Note that a simple cycle in $G$ is a connected subgraph of $G$ in which each vertex has degree exactly two. An induced subgraph of the graph $G = (V, E)$ is any subgraph $G' = (V', E')$ that contains all edges of $E$ that are contained in $V'$ (i.e., $E' = \{\{u, v\} \in E : u, v \in V'\}$). In such a case, we say that $G'$ is the subgraph induced by $V'$.

**Directed Graphs.** We will also consider (simple) directed graphs (also known as digraphs), where edges are *ordered pairs* of vertices.[1] In this case, the set of edges is a subset of $V \times V \setminus \{(v, v) : v \in V\}$, and the edges $(u, v)$ and $(v, u)$ are called anti-parallel. General (i.e., non-simple) directed graphs are defined analogously. The edge $(u, v)$ is viewed as going from $u$ to $v$, and thus is called an outgoing edge of $u$ (resp., incoming edge of $v$). The out-degree (resp., in-degree) of a vertex is the number of its outgoing edges (resp., incoming edges). Directed paths and the related objects are defined analogously; for example, $v_0, \ldots, v_\ell$ is a directed path if for every $i \in [\ell]$ it holds that $(v_{i-1}, v_i)$ is a directed edge (which is directed from $v_{i-1}$ to $v_i$). It is common to consider also a pair of anti-parallel edges as a simple directed cycle.

A directed acyclic graph (DAG) is a digraph that has no directed cycles. Every DAG has at least one vertex having out-degree (resp., in-degree) zero, called a sink (resp., a source). A simple directed acyclic graph $G = (V, E)$ is called an inward (resp., outward) directed tree if $|E| = |V| - 1$ and there exists a unique vertex, called the root, having out-degree (resp., in-degree) zero. Note that each vertex in an inward (resp., outward) directed tree can reach the root (resp., is reachable from the root) by a unique directed path.[2]

**Representation.** Graphs are commonly represented by their adjacency matrix and/or their incidence lists. The adjacency matrix of a simple graph $G = (V, E)$ is a $|V|$-by-$|V|$

---

[1] Again, the term "simple" means that self-loops and parallel (directed) edges are not allowed. In contrast, anti-parallel edges are allowed.

[2] Note that in any DAG, there is a directed path from each vertex $v$ to some sink (resp., from some source to each vertex $v$). In an inward (resp., outward) directed tree this sink (resp., source) must be unique. The condition $|E| = |V| - 1$ enforces the uniqueness of these paths, because (combined with the reachability condition) it implies that the underlying graph (obtained by disregarding the orientation of the edges) is a tree.

Boolean matrix in which the $(i, j)$-th entry equals 1 if and only if $i$ and $j$ are adjacent in $G$. The incidence list representation of $G$ consists of $|V|$ sequences such that the $i^{th}$ sequence is an ordered list of the set of edges incident at vertex $i$. (Needless to say, it is easy to transform one of these representations to the other.)

**Computational Problems.** Simple computational problems regarding graphs include determining whether a given graph is connected (and/or acyclic) and finding shortest paths in a given graph. Another simple problem is determining whether a given graph is bipartite, where a graph $G = (V, E)$ is bipartite (or 2-colorable) if there exists a 2-coloring of its vertices that does not assign neighboring vertices the same color. All of these problems are easily solvable by BFS.

Moving to more complicated tasks that are still solvable in polynomial time, we mention the problem of finding a perfect matching (or a maximum matching) in a given graph, where a matching is a subgraph in which all vertices have degree 1, a perfect matching is a matching that contains all of the graph's vertices, and a maximum matching is a matching of maximum cardinality (among all matching of the said graph).

Turning to seemingly hard problems, we mention that the problem of determining whether a given graph is 3-colorable[3] (i.e., G3C) is NP-complete. A few additional NP-complete problems follow.

- A Hamiltonian path (resp., Hamiltonian cycle) in the graph $G = (V, E)$ is a *simple* path (resp., cycle) that passes through all of the vertices of $G$. Such a path (resp., cycle) has length $|V| - 1$ (resp., $|V|$). The problem is to determine whether a given graph contains a Hamiltonian path (resp., cycle).
- An independent set (resp., clique) of the graph $G = (V, E)$ is a set of vertices $V' \subseteq V$ such that the subgraph induced by $V'$ contains no edges (resp., contains all possible edges). The problem is to determine whether a given graph has an independent set (resp., a clique) of a given size.
  A vertex cover of the graph $G = (V, E)$ is a set of vertices $V' \subseteq V$ such that each edge in $E$ has at least one end point in $V'$. Note that $V'$ is a vertex cover of $G$ if and only if $V \setminus V'$ is an independent set of $V$.

A natural computational problem, which is believed to be neither in $\mathcal{P}$ nor NP-complete, is the Graph Isomorphism problem. The input consists of two graphs, $G_1 = (V_1, E_1)$ and $G_2 = (V_2, E_2)$, and the question is whether there exist a 1-1 and onto mapping $\phi : V_1 \rightarrow V_2$ such that $\{u, v\}$ is in $E_1$ if and only if $\{\phi(u), \phi(v)\}$ is in $E_2$. (Such a mapping is called an isomorphism.)

## A.2  Boolean Formulae

In §1.4.3.1, Boolean formulae are defined as a special case of Boolean circuits (cf. §1.4.1.1). Here, we take the more traditional approach and define Boolean formulae (also

---

[3] We say that a a graph $G = (V, E)$ is 3-colorable if its vertices can be colored using three colors such that neighboring vertices are not assigned the same color.

known as propositional formulae) as structured sequences over an alphabet consisting of variable names and various connectives. It is most convenient to define Boolean formulae recursively as follows:

- A Boolean variable is a Boolean formula.
- If $\phi_1, \ldots, \phi_t$ are Boolean formulae and $\psi$ is a $t$-ary Boolean operation, then $\psi(\phi_1, \ldots, \phi_t)$ is a Boolean formula.

Typically, we consider three Boolean operations: the unary operation of negation (denoted neg or $\neg$), and the (bounded or unbounded) conjunction and disjunction (denoted $\wedge$ and $\vee$, respectively). Furthermore, the convention is to shorthand $\neg(\phi)$ by $\neg\phi$, and to write $(\wedge_{i=1}^t \phi_i)$ or $(\phi_1 \wedge \cdots \wedge \phi_t)$ instead of $\wedge(\phi_1, \ldots, \phi_t)$, and similarly for $\vee$.

Two important special cases of Boolean formulae are CNF and DNF formulae. A CNF formula is a conjunction of disjunctions of variables and/or their negation; that is, $\wedge_{i=1}^t \phi_i$ is a CNF if each $\phi_i$ has the form $(\vee_{j=1}^{t_i} \phi_{i,j})$, where each $\phi_{i,j}$ is either a variable or a negation of a variable (and is called a literal). If for every $i$ it holds that $t_i \leq k$ (e.g., $k = 2, 3$), then we say that the formula is a $k$CNF. Similarly, DNF formulae are defined as disjunctions of conjunctions of literals.

The value of a Boolean formula under a truth assignment to its variables is defined recursively along its structure. For example, $\wedge_{i=1}^t \phi_i$ has the value true under an assignment $\tau$ if and only if every $\phi_i$ has the value true under $\tau$. We say that a formula $\phi$ is satisfiable if there exists a truth assignment $\tau$ to its variables such that the value of $\phi$ under $\tau$ is true.

The set of satisfiable CNF (resp., 3CNF) formulae is denoted SAT (resp., 3SAT), and the problem of deciding membership in it is NP-complete. The set of tautologies (i.e., formula that have the value true under any assignment) is coNP-complete, even when restricted to 3DNF formulae.

# Bibliography

[1]  S. Arora and B. Barak. *Complexity Theory: A Modern Approach.* Cambridge University Press, 2009.

[2]  L. Berman and J. Hartmanis. On Isomorphisms and Density of NP and Other Complete Sets. *SIAM Journal on Computing*, Vol. 6 (2), pages 305–322, 1977.

[3]  G. Boolos, J. P. Burgess, and R. C. Jeffrey. *Computability and Logic*, 5th edition. Cambridge University Press, 2007.

[4]  A. Church. An Unsolvable Problem of Elementary Number Theory. *Amer. J. of Math.*, Vol. 58, pages 345–363, 1936.

[5]  A. Cobham. The Intristic Computational Difficulty of Functions. In *Proc. 1964 Iternational Congress for Logic Methodology and Philosophy of Science*, pages 24–30, 1964.

[6]  S. A. Cook. The Complexity of Theorem Proving Procedures. In *3rd ACM Symposium on the Theory of Computing*, pages 151–158, 1971.

[7]  J. Edmonds. Paths, Trees, and Flowers. *Canad. J. Math.*, Vol. 17, pages 449–467, 1965.

[8]  S. Even. *Graph Algorithms.* Computer Science Press, 1979.

[9]  S. Even, A. L. Selman, and Y. Yacobi. The Complexity of Promise Problems with Applications to Public-Key Cryptography. *Information and Control*, Vol. 61, pages 159–173, 1984.

[10]  U. Feige, S. Goldwasser, L. Lovász, S. Safra, and M. Szegedy. Approximating Clique is Almost NP-Complete. *Journal of the ACM*, Vol. 43, pages 268–292, 1996. Preliminary version in *32nd FOCS*, 1991.

[11]  M. R. Garey and D. S. Johnson. *Computers and Intractability: A Guide to the Theory of NP-Completeness.* W. H. Freeman and Company, New York, 1979.

[12]  O. Goldreich. On Promise Problems: A Survey. In [14]. An earlier version is available from *ECCC*, TR05-018, 2005.

[13]  O. Goldreich. *Computational Complexity: A Conceptual Perspective.* Cambridge University Press, 2008.

[14]  O. Goldreich, A. L. Rosenberg, and A. L. Selman (eds.). *Essays in Theoretical Computer Science in Memory of Shimon Even.* Springer Verlag, LNCS Festschrift, Vol. 3895, March 2006.

[15]  D. Hochbaum (ed.). *Approximation Algorithms for NP-Hard Problems.* PWS, 1996.

[16]  J. E. Hopcroft and J. D. Ullman. *Introduction to Automata Theory, Languages and Computation.* Addison-Wesley, 1979.

[17]  R. M. Karp. Reducibility among Combinatorial Problems. In *Complexity of Computer Computations*, R. E. Miller and J. W. Thatcher (eds.), Plenum Press, pages 85–103, 1972.

[18]  R. M. Karp and R. J. Lipton. Some Connections Between Nonuniform and Uniform Complexity Classes. In *12th ACM Symposium on the Theory of Computing*, pages 302–309, 1980.

[19]  E. Kushilevitz and N. Nisan. *Communication Complexity.* Cambridge University Press, 1996.

[20]  R. E. Ladner. On the Structure of Polynomial Time Reducibility. *Journal of the ACM*, Vol. 22, pages 155–171, 1975.

[21]  L. A. Levin. Universal Search Problems. *Problemy Peredaci Informacii 9*, pages 115–116, 1973 (in Russian). English translation in *Problems of Information Transmission 9*, pages 265–266.

[22]  M. Li and P. Vitanyi. *An Introduction to Kolmogorov Complexity and Its Applications.* Springer Verlag, August 1993.

[23]  S. Mahaney. Sparse Complete Sets for NP: Solution of a Conjecture of Berman and Hartmanis. *Journal of Computer and System Science*, Vol. 25, pages 130–143, 1982.

[24]  Y. Matiyasevich. *Hilbert's Tenth Problem.* MIT Press, 1993.

[25]  R. Motwani and P. Raghavan. *Randomized Algorithms.* Cambridge University Press, 1995.

[26]  E. Post. A Variant of a Recursively Unsolvable Problem. *Bull. AMS*, Vol. 52, pages 264–268, 1946.

[27]  H. G. Rice. Classes of Recursively Enumerable Sets and Their Decision Problems. *Trans. AMS*, Vol. 89, pages 25–59, 1953.

[28]  A. Selman. On the Structure of NP. *Notices Amer. Math. Soc.*, Vol. 21 (6), page 310, 1974.

[29]  C. E. Shannon. A Symbolic Analysis of Relay and Switching Circuits. *Trans. American Institute of Electrical Engineers*, Vol. 57, pages 713–723, 1938.

[30]  M. Sipser. *Introduction to the Theory of Computation.* PWS Publishing Company, 1997.

[31]  B. A. Trakhtenbrot. A Survey of Russian Approaches to Perebor (Brute Force Search) Algorithms. *Annals of the History of Computing*, Vol. 6 (4), pages 384–398, 1984.

[32]  C. E. Turing. On Computable Numbers, with an Application to the Entscheidungsproblem. *Proc. Londom Mathematical Soceity*, Ser. 2, Vol. 42, pages 230–265, 1936. A Correction, *ibid.*, Vol. 43, pages 544–546.

[33]  J. von Neumann, First Draft of a Report on the EDVAC, 1945. Contract No. W-670-ORD-492, Moore School of Electrical Engineering, University of Pennsylvania, Philadelphia. Reprinted (in part) in *Origins of Digital Computers: Selected Papers.* Springer-Verlag, Berlin and Heidelberg, pages 383–392, 1982.

# Index

## Author Index

Church, A., 165
Cobham, A., 165
Cook, S. A., 165–167
Edmonds, J., 165
Even, S., 167
Karp, R. M., 165–167
Ladner, R. E., 167
Levin, L. A., 165–167
Selman, A. L., 167
Shannon, C. E., 165
Turing, A. M., 164, 165
Yacobi, Y., 167


## Subject Index

Algorithms, *see* Computability theory
Approximation, 173
Average-case complexity, 173

Boolean circuits, 32–40, 104–113
    bounded fan-in, 35
    constant-depth, 40
    depth, 39
    monotone, 40
    size, 35–36
    unbounded fan-in, 35, 38, 40
    uniform, 36
Boolean formulae, 33, 38–39, 177–178
    clauses, 38
    CNF, 38, 104–113, 178
    DNF, 39, 178
    literals, 38

Church-Turing Thesis, 16, 17, 27
Circuits, *see* Boolean circuits
CNF, *see* Boolean formulae
Cobham-Edmonds Thesis, 27, 28, 50, 52, 108
Complexity classes
    coNP, 94, 126, 154–158
    EXP, 66, 123
    generic, 40
    IP, *see* Interactive proofs
    NP, *see* NP
    NPC, *see* NP-completeness
    NPI, 126
    P, *see* P
    PC, 55–58, 63–66, 69, 77, 80–88, 98–102,
        105, 109, 144, 151–154
    PCP, *see* Probabilistically checkable proofs
    PF, 54–55, 57–58, 63–65
    ZK, *see* Zero-knowledge
Computability theory, 1–31
Computational problems
    2SAT, 113
    3SAT, 112, 113, 123, 124, 126, 178
    3XC, 115
    Bipartiteness, 177
    Bounded Halting, 102
    Bounded Non-Halting, 102–103
    Clique, 117, 177
    Connectivity, 177
    CSAT, 104–112
    *Entscheidungsproblem*, 164
    Exact Cover, 115
    Factoring integers, 53, 72, 94, 157
    Graph 2-Colorability, 113, 177
    Graph 3-Colorability, 91, 113, 118, 123,
        125, 177

183

Computational problems (*cont.*)
  Graph Isomorphism, 91, 177
  Halting Problem, 19–21, 102, 103
  Hamiltonian path, 53, 56, 58, 60, 61, 177
  Independent Set, 117, 177
  PCP, *see* Post Correspondence Problem
  Perfect matching, 177
  Primality testing, 72
  SAT, 53, 57, 61, 85–86, 104–113, 154, 178
  Set Cover, 114
  Solving systems of equations, 53
  Spanning trees, 53
  TSP, 53, 57
  Vertex Cover, 117, 177
Computational tasks and models, 1–47
Constant-depth circuits, *see* Boolean circuits
Cook-reductions, *see* Reductions
Cryptography, 125, 172

Decision problems, 6–8, 58–65
DNF, *see* Boolean formulae

Exhaustive search, 50, 51, 66, 70

Finite automata, 31
Formulae, *see* Boolean formulae

Graph theory, 175–177

Halting Problem, *see* Computational problems
Hilbert's Tenth Problem, 164

Interactive proofs, 124, 172

Karp-reductions, *see* Reductions
Kolmogorov Complexity, 24–26, 35

Levin-reductions, *see* Reductions

Monotone circuits, *see* Boolean circuits

NP, 48–158
  as proof system, 59–62, 123, 125
  as search problem, 55–58
  Optimal search, 151–154
  traditional definition, 66–69
NP-completeness, 89–133, 155–158

O-notation, 26
One-way functions, 171
Optimal search for NP, 151–154
Oracle machines, 29–31

P, 48–158
  as search problem, 54–55, 57–58
P versus NP Question, 48–70
Polynomial-time reductions, *see* Reductions
Post Correspondence Problem, 22, 24, 43
Probabilistic proof systems, 123–126
Probabilistically checkable proofs, 125–126
Promise problems, 8, 52, 142–151, 156
Proof systems
  Interactive, *see* Interactive proofs
  NP, *see* NP
  PCP, *see* Probabilistically checkable proofs
  Probabilistic, *see* Probabilistic proof
    systems
  Zero-knowledge, *see* Zero-knowledge
Pseudorandom generators, 171
Pseudorandomness, 171

Randomness extractors, 174
Reductions
  Cook-reductions, 76–99, 120–129, 155–157
  Downward self-reducibility, 92
  Karp-reductions, 77–81, 98–120, 155
  Levin-reductions, 79–81, 83, 99–113
  parsimonious, 139
  Polynomial-time reductions, 74–129
  Self-reducibility, 83–88
  to sparse sets, 162–163
  Turing-reductions, 21, 29–31
Rice's Theorem, 21

Search problems, 5–6, 52–58, 63–65
  versus decision, 63–65, 77, 80, 83–88
Self-reducibility, *see* Reductions
Space complexity, 29

Time complexity, 10, 26–29
Turing machines, 11–18
  multi-tape, 16
  non-deterministic, 66–69
  single-tape, 15
  with advice, 36–37
Turing-reductions, *see* Reductions

Uncomputable functions, 18–22
Undecidability, 19, 22
Universal algorithms, 22–26, 28
Universal machines, 22–26

Worst-case complexity, 173

Zero-knowledge, 124–125, 172